Intersectionality and "Race" in Education

D0420824

Routledge Research in Education

For a full list of titles in this series please visit www.routledge.com

Intersectionality and "Race" in Education

Edited by Kalwant Bhopal
and John Preston

Routledge
Taylor & Francis Group
NEW YORK   LONDON

First published 2012
by Routledge
711 Third Avenue, New York, NY 10017

Simultaneously published in the UK
by Routledge
2 Park Square, Milton Park, Abingdon, Oxon OX14 4RN

*Routledge is an imprint of the Taylor & Francis Group,
an informa business*

© 2012 Taylor & Francis

First issued in paperback 2014

The right of Kalwant Bhopal and John Preston to be identified as the
authors of the editorial material, and of the authors for their individual
chapters, has been asserted in accordance with sections 77 and 78 of the
Copyright, Designs and Patents Act 1988.

Typeset in Sabon by IBT Global.

All rights reserved. No part of this book may be reprinted or reproduced or
utilised in any form or by any electronic, mechanical, or other means, now
known or hereafter invented, including photocopying and recording, or in
any information storage or retrieval system, without permission in writing
from the publishers.

Trademark Notice: Product or corporate names may be trademarks or
registered trademarks, and are used only for identification and explanation
without intent to infringe.

Library of Congress Cataloging-in-Publication Data
Intersectionality and "race" in education / edited by Kalwant Bhopal and
John Preston.
    p. cm. — (Routledge research in education)
  Includes bibliographical references and index.
  1. Discrimination in education—United States.   2. Youth, Black—
Education—United States.   3. Youth, Black—United States.—Social
conditions.   4. Success—United States.   I. Bhopal, Kalwant.
II. Preston, John.
  LC212.3.U6I68 2012
  379.2'6—dc22
  2011015560

ISBN: 978-0-415-88877-6 (hbk)
ISBN: 978-1-138-02151-8 (pbk)

Contents

Permissions

Permission to use 'Subjectivation and Performative Politics—Butler Thinking Althusser and Foucault: Intelligibility, Agency and the Raced-Nationed-Religioned Subjects of Education' by Deborah Youdell *British Journal of Sociology of Education* 27 (4): 511–528 is acknowledged with thanks to Taylor and Francis.

Permission to use, 'The White Working Class, Racism and Respectability: Victims, Degenerates and Interest-Convergence' by David Gillborn *British Journal of Educational Studies* 58 (1): 3–25 is acknowledged with thanks to James Arthur, editor of the journal, and to the Society for Educational Studies (SES).

Permission to use 'The Unhappy Marriage between Marxism and Race Critique: Political Economy and the Production of Racialized Knowledge' by Zeus Leonardo *Policy Futures in Education* 2 (3&4): 493–493 is acknowledged with thanks to Routledge.

Introduction

Intersectionality and 'Race' in Education: Theorising Difference

Kalwant Bhopal and John Preston

This book is about intersectionality and is particularly concerned with examining *theorising* intersectionalites and difference. In recent years, the concept of intersectionality has taken centre stage and become a dominant model with which to engage in how differences such as 'race', gender, class, sexuality, age, disability and religion interweave and intersect upon individual lives in a modern 'risk' society (Beck 1992). Intersectionality has become a model upon which to understand, analyse and engage with difference in which difference itself becomes a defining feature of 'otherness'. Otherness is related to the notion that identity itself is fragmented, fragile even, yet constantly evolving through multiple engagements and relationships in society; and through this complexity, intersectionality helps us to engage with understanding outsiders and what it means to be a 'stranger' in modern society. This book engages with the premise that intersectionality is to be understood as a dynamic rather than a static process. It is based on the premise that understanding *identities* is a journey, one that changes through different times in history and transforms through different spaces. Current discourses around threats to identity and the categorisation of individuals are related to macro forces, even the 'war on terror', particularly when such identities are seen as a threat to the British way of life and notions of British identity. This book is en edited collection of papers which emerged from a conference which aimed to explore how intersectionality can be understood in the everyday workings of our world, particularly within the different fields and spaces of education. The conference brought together researchers working within the fields of education, sociology and cultural studies to explore the different meanings given to interrogating the concept of intersectionality, and doing so with salient empirical examples. In writing and thinking about 'race', we both agree that 'race' is a contested concept and is not only problematic but also controversial and for this reason in this chapter we choose to use it with single quotes.

In writing about intersectionalities and difference, we both work and write from our own personal biographies: Kalwant's experience as a working-class (now middle-class) British Indian woman and John's experience as a White working (now middle-class also) man in the Academy. We are aware of how our own identities impact not only upon our daily lives but in world of the Academy. Kalwant's experiences of covert and sometimes overt racism resonate with the underlying aspects of difference, of being an outsider, of being 'othered'. John's experiences were fundamentally different in terms of racial positioning. From within whiteness, albeit an Irish, working-class whiteness on the periphery of 'middle-class Englishness', he was privileged. Working together we are also aware how we are both treated differently in the same space: John gaining from White privilege whereas Kalwant often disadvantaged because of her 'race' and gender. However, as formally working-class academics (and sometimes we admit we cling on to these identities) we also frequently find agreements in our positioning. The attachments of class/'race' and other intersectionalities are therefore complex and for many of the writers of this volume their personal and intellectual histories are interwoven.

The chapters in this book seek to locate dimensions of difference and identity within recent theoretical discourses such as Critical Race Theory, Judith Butler and 'queer' theory, poststructural approaches and multicultural models to analyse whiteness and the educational experience of minority ethnic groups (such as Trinidadian boys, Irish girls, Black women and Asian girls). The authors use intersectional approaches to specifically examine the inequalities and diversities of educational experiences. To do this, the chapters review existing research and present new and original evidence in a theoretically informed context-specific manner. Whilst there is considerable literature on social inequality and education, there is little which explores notions of *intersectionality* and how such difference is theorised. Given the gap in the literature on theorising difference it becomes all the more important to address the specificity of difference. This collection brings together major researchers in the field, united by an explicit goal of challenging both dominant perspectives on difference and institutional structures that underpin inequality.

Intersectionality has been used by feminists to address essentialist models of social theory by acknowledging that not all women's experiences are the same. Black feminist theory arose from the need for Black women and women of colour to question discourses of the concept 'woman', particularly to address the absence of Black women's experiences in relation to feminist struggles. The focus for Black feminism was to challenge White Eurocentric knowledge which was taken as the norm. There was a need to understand and deconstruct the concept of 'woman' and analyse this in relation to 'race', class, gender and sexuality (hooks 1990; Bhavnani and Phoenix 1994). In Britain, these discussions centred around women's political position and how they defined themselves in relation to being 'Black' (Grewal et al. 1988; Anthias and Yuval-Davis 1992; Brah 1996); this took place through challenges around the essentialist assumptions of racism (such as through employment, domestic violence and reproductive technologies). In discussing the everyday struggles of Black women, recent work on intersectionality has acknowledged, 'recognition that "race", social class and sexuality differentiated women's experiences has disrupted notions of a homogenous category "woman" with its attendant assumptions of universality that served to maintain the status quo in relation to "race", social class and sexuality, while challenging gendered assumptions' (Brah and Phoenix 2004, 82). This has also been emphasised by Collins (2005, 11), who views intersectional paradigms as mutually constructing systems of power which permeate all social relations, and Seidman (1994), who analyses the different facets of intersectionality through the multiple axes of social hierarchy. What is clear about this work is the need to focus on the *multiplicities* of identity and to acknowledge that experiences cannot be taken in isolation: 'We need to be more aware of how all of our experiences intersect and merge with one another' (Brock 1991, 14).

The pioneering work of Crenshaw (1989, 1994) in the US addressed the flawed essentialist model by arguing that a single axis analysis of 'race' or gender did not acknowledge the true experiences of Black women. Through legal cases of discrimination, Crenshaw argued that the one-dimensional approach did not take into consideration the multiple dimensions of an individual's experiences.

> Black women can experience discrimination in a number of ways and that contradiction arises from our assumptions that their claims of exclusion must be unidirectional. Consider an analogy to traffic in an intersection, coming and going in all four directions. Discrimination, like traffic through an intersection, may flow in one direction; it may flow in another (1989, 321).

More recent work by Floya Anthias has attempted to move away from the idea that certain groups or categories (of 'race' or gender, for instance) intersect; instead, she explores the influence of social locations and processes through the concept of *translocational positionality*. 'The concept of translocational positionality addresses issues of identity in terms of locations which are not fixed but are context meaning, and time related and which therefore involve shifts and contradictions' (Anthias 2008, 5). Anthias argues that translocations are not just about people moving to different locations (either spatially or culturally); rather, they are about crossing borders and defining and redefining boundaries associated within them. 'The notion of translocation references the idea of "location" as a social space which is produced within contextual, spatial, temporal and hierarchal relations around the "intersections" of social divisions and identities of class, ethnicity and gender (amongst others)' (2008, 9).

Poststructuralism has also attempted to analyse the concept of intersectionality. Crudely speaking, poststructuralists aim to deconstruct perceptions of the world and to challenge what appears to be 'normal' or 'natural'.

The perspective of poststructuralism is grounded in different types of analyses such as discourse theory, psychoanalysis and postcolonial theory. Consequently, the focus is on examining questions of intersectionality through historical relationships which are embedded in contesting fields of discourses and multiple subject positions. Here the concepts of 'agency' and power (Foucault 1972; Derrida 1974) are central. As a result, new ways of examining how difference is understood within the realms of intersectionality have developed (Butler 1990; Weedon 1996; Spivak 1999). Postcolonial studies, for example, have been used to examine the processes around colonial and postcolonial discourses surrounding the category 'woman'. In developing such approaches, some researchers have attempted to use the analysis of 'border theory' to explore how intersectionality works through time and place and the crossing of specific boundaries (Lewis 2000). Other theorists have used the concept of space to refer to diasporic identities. Brah (1996) uses the concept of diaspora space to analyse how identity is configured when individuals move from space to space through particular historic moments.

> Diaspora space is the intersectionality of diaspora, border and dis/location as a point of confluence of economic, political, cultural and psychic processes. It is where multiple subject positions are juxtaposed, contested, proclaimed or disavowed; where the permitted and the prohibited perpetually interrogate; and where the accepted and the transgressive imperceptibly mingle even while these syncretic forms may be disclaimed in the name of purity and tradition (1996, 208).

According to Brah, then, difference is conceptualised as part of an experience, that of subjectivity, identity and location. More recently, McCall (2005) has questioned the methodologies that are used to examine intersectionality and the difficulties associated with this. She outlines three approaches for the study of intersectionality: anticategorical complexity, intercategorical complexity and intracategorical complexity.

Critical Race Theory (CRT) and, in particular, Critical Race Feminism (CRF) frequently adopt intersectional theories to understand the dynamics of racial oppression. Despite the emphasis in CRT on the endemic nature of racism and White supremacy as a 'conspiracy' of White interests (Harris 1993; Gillborn 2005, 2006; Leonardo 2005), it has been sensitive to the interactions of other modes of oppression with racial oppression. Firstly, CRT has been nuanced by the specific dynamics of racial oppression in various cultural contexts, giving rise to offshoots such as Asian American CRT (AsianCrit), Latino CRT (LatCrit) and American Indian CRT (TribalCrit). These derivatives of CRT show how different racial oppressions are experienced and resisted by various 'racial' groups and point towards the specificity of intersectional racialized experience. Secondly, and particularly through CRF, the specificity of racialized and gendered experience and 'voice' is foregrounded. As the chapters by Gillborn and Leonardo (this volume) indicate, CRT also provides an entry point to considering the classed experience of both majoritarian and minoritarian groups and Chakrabarty indicates how CRF can attend to the specificities of racialized and gendered experience.

OUTLINE OF THE BOOK

The individual chapters and the collection as a whole are based on the premise that education is a controversial subject in which difficult and contested discourses are the norm. Individuals in education experience multiple inequalities and have diverse identifications that cannot necessarily be captured by one theoretical perspective alone. The book and the coherence of its arguments are dictated by an examination of controversial grounds, both empirical and theoretical debates, within educational research around issues of identity, culture and inclusion. Each of the chapters in different ways will 1) specifically examine areas of discrimination and disadvantage such as 'race', class, identity and gender within education as well as debating the difficulties of applying such concepts in relation to the experiences of students in education and 2) analyse contesting discourses of identity in different cultural contexts. By doing so, the book provides an engaging space in which to examine its themes and initiate debates about identity, 'race' and culture within a wider sociological context and beyond the simple confines of the educational sphere into an arena of sociological and cultural discourse.

David Gillborn in his chapter argues that 'race' and class inequalities cannot be fully understood in isolation. He explores their intersectional quality through two contrasting discourses examined from a historical perspective and through an analysis of contemporary British media during late 2008; a time of significant international financial meltdown, the essential values of neoliberalism were being examined and reasserted as natural, moral and efficient. Gillborn explores these approaches through two contrasting discourses. First, a *victim* discourse, which presents White working people, and their children in particular, as suffering because of minoritized racial groups and their advocates. Second, a discourse of *degeneracy*, which presents an immoral and barbaric underclass as a threat to social and economic order. He uses the 'interest-convergence principle' from CRT to argue that the discourses amount to a strategic mobilization of White interests where the 'White, but not quite' status of the working class provides a buffer zone at a time of economic and cultural crisis which secures societal White supremacy and provides a further setback to progressive reforms that focus on 'race', gender and equality. In this controversial and engaging chapter, Gillborn argues that contrary to the arguments of some class theorists (who dismiss CRT as blind to the situation of poor Whites), the existence of poor

White people is not only consistent with a regime of White supremacy; they are actually an essential part of the processes that sustain it.

Through a different theoretical strand and understanding of intersectionality, Deborah Youdell analyses Judith Butler's processes of subjectivation—by considering Althusser's notion of subjection and Foucault's notion of subjectivation and the possibility for discursive agency and performative politics. She does so by examining the relationship between subjectivation and the performative suggested in Butler's work by analysing how the performative is implicated in processes of subjectivation—in 'who' the subject is, or might be, subjectivated as. She explores the usefulness of understanding the subjectivating effects of discourse specifically for education and for educationalists who focus on interrogating educational inequalities. The empirical data for Youdell's chapter is based on a reading of an episode of ethnographic data generated in an Australian high school. Youdell in her enlightening chapter suggests that it is through specific subjectivating processes that Butler helps us to understand how some students are inside subjects and others are outside or what she refers to as 'outside student-hood'. Youdell's chapter enables the reader to engage in theoretical debate regarding the position of students within education and gives the reader the opportunity to explore this from an international student and education experience.

Zeus Leonardo in his chapter uses Marxist objectivism and 'race' theory's focus on subjectivity by integrating the two to argue that as a result of this integration both Marxism and 'race' analysis are strengthened in a way that maintains the integrity of each discourse. This benefits educational policy theory because praxis is the dialectical attempt to synthesize the inner and external processes of schooling. His chapter works from the premise that in educational policy theory, orthodox Marxism is known for its commitment to objectivism, or the science of history. 'Race' analysis is developed in its ability to explain the subjective dimension of racial oppression. The two theories are often at odds with each other. He argues that if both theories are integrated, it provides us with an understanding of how intersectionality, difference and diversity operate.

Alpesh Maisuria offers the reader an analysis of the CRT concept of 'White supremacy' as an organisational principle that pervades society. He does so by problematising CRT's assertion of 'White supremacy' by drawing on Derek Bell's 'Rules of Racial Standing'. By examining the conception that White people are a homogenous and empowered group, the chapter argues that 'whiteness' can be explained by the concepts of embourgeoisement and bourgeoisification, and in so doing intersect with social class and culture. Drawing on the Marxist theory of racialization, Maisuria offers an articulation of injustice that intersects 'race', culture and class. The main thrust of the argument focuses on the need for CRT to combine the culturalist perspective of 'White supremacy' with the role of class to allow it to make connections to the mode of production. This critique proposes an analysis that acknowledges class-based racialized relations of production in a neoliberal global capitalist society, and like Gillborn, Maisuria locates this within current global economic instability. The chapter engages with a critique of CRT by suggesting an analysis that locates racism within the socioeconomic mode of production.

Karl Kitching uses the work of Judith Butler, the tools of the decentred subject: recognition, viability, self, body and situated contexts to provide a critical discourse analysis of spatial divisons and bodlity boundaries to examine how anxieties and certainties through spatial divisions and bodily inscriptions might form part of an approach to understanding oblique forms of racism beyond unitary identities in schools. Kitching explores the subject's condition: maintaining/changing performed selves and/or contexts where possibility for redrawing inclusion lies. The chapter uses data from an ethnographic study conducted in a 'good school' with a recent migrant population in a White-Irish, socioeconomically mixed suburban region of Dublin, Ireland. By using one fragment of interview data, it analyses some classifications that two White-Irish 'respectable' girls make of their fellow students during one interview. Kitching explores ways of understanding how their viability as respectable (White) girls might be ensured and con-tested through bodily (physical) and symbolic (psychic) spaces, and to read possible anxieties, certainties and vulnerabilities that may accompany these processes. Kitching, by drawing on the work of Butler (2005), argues that understanding the vulnerability selves is ethically central to this notion of negotiating viability. The authority of the researcher to make judgements in discourse analysis is itself understood as a form of subjectivation. This perspective requires a vigilance to research subjects and to recognise their vulnerabilities, including when they are read as excluding others.

Namita Chakrabarty in her chapter uses Derrida's positioning of the ghost in the midst of binaries in *Specters of Marx* as a theoretical starting point. This chapter positions the role of the spectre within hierarchical organisations as having future agency. By using the lyrics and video of *If I Were a Boy* and associated YouTube online community comments, the chapter seeks to give an activist reading to the use of 'race', gender and homoeroticism with reference to a radical feminist analysis of racial and gendered hierarchies, psychoanalytical cultural theories and Critical Race Theory. The popular cultural text is used as a lens through which to view the role of struggle for equality specifically in the new American age of Obama by contrasting it with video footage of Michelle Obama's speech addressed to London schoolgirls during the G20 events in London in 2009. The chapter highlights the ghosts of militarism in both videos by suggest-ing that the lyrics 'if you thought I would wait for you, you got it wrong' (Knowles 2008) and the Michelle Obama 'high five' are a twenty-first-cen-tury continuity of the words of Malcolm X on education. In this engaging and topical paper, Chakrabarty explores the issues of heteronormativity and gender roles raised by both videos and the inherent lessons for an edu-cation beyond prevailing culture.

Ravi Rampersad provides the reader with new fascinating discourses of intersectionality by examining the concept of 'pigmentocracy'. Pigmentocracy is understood as a structuring of society where whiteness or lightness is afforded with a higher level of social capital; in a sense, the higher up in society you go, the lighter the skin colour (Hunter 2008). Rampersad uses the colonial history of Trinidad to argue that its continuing legacy facilitated the evolution of an education system which embodies this sense of pigmentocracy. The chapter explores how the symbiotic structuring of 'race' and social class is operationalised in terms of the access and achievement of Afro-Trinidadian boys at primary-school level. Rampersad uses the legal concept of the property value of whiteness as adapted in CRT discourse in education to argue that inherent flexibility of both CRT and the concept of the property value of whiteness allows for its adaptation to the postcolonial context of Trinidad. Empirical data from two primary schools in Trinidad are used to highlight how this pigmentocratic structuring is manifested and sustained in the daily experiences of education of different socially situated Afro-Trinidadian boys. Rampersad's work highlights how pigmentocracy works to associate colour with success or failure. Schools associated with the 'whiter' and 'lighter' middle and upper class are highly regarded as a centre of excellence and those linked with the 'darker' working class are stereotyped as a pathological place of failure.

Andrew Morrison uses the limitations of the Bourdieusian culturalist model of class analysis for explaining Black and Minority Ethnic (BAME) youth achievement by presenting an 'intersectionalist' model of 'race', class and gender. By focussing on BAME post-16 achievement, Morrison uses Sayer's (2005) distinction between 'identity-sensitive' and 'identity-neutral' forms of domination and subordination, and the recognition of their complex but contingent interdependency within 'lived' concrete relationships. He argues that this understanding of 'race', class and gender accommodates the insights offered by Bourdieu but offers the potential to go beyond a simplistic BAME category to consider how class and gender interact with 'race' in the development of minority youth educational identities. By using empirical findings from a recent study of youth postcompulsory educational decision making, Morrison argues for the workings of an 'ethnic capital' (Modood 2004), that is, the transmission of a normative ethnic identity through parental expectations and inter and intrafamilial educational competition. Morrison's paper highlights the complexity of the how class and gender intersect with ethnicity, particularly in the educational experiences and decision making of students and furthermore argues how the concept of BAME is problematic in this analysis.

Indra Dewan examines the power of class in determining the everyday educational experiences of young mixed-race people in London. She works from the premise that in public discourse mixed heritage people are, on the one hand, conceived as harbingers of a race-free and cosmopolitan society in which no correlation between ethnic/racial/class background and opportunity exists; on the other hand, mixed people are constructed as Black, from working-class backgrounds, educationally underachieving, and a group which has a high rate of school expulsion and family breakdown. Her empirical research reveals that students from middle-class backgrounds tended to reflect the cosmopolitan discourse of personhood—many had never experienced discrimination or unequal chances on account of being mixed race, and felt that it was an unproblematic and even a desirable identity. Those from working-class backgrounds, however, were much more likely to experience life through the lens of 'race' and conflict, and many struggled with the effects of stereotyping and prejudice. By drawing attention to the persistent salience of 'race' and class in some mixed people's lives, Dewan argues that despite the overriding societal discourses of multiculturalism, equality and meritocracy, there are few educational interventions which examine the experiences of young mixed-race people.

Farzana Shain's chapter explores the intersections of 'race', class, gender and identity in the social and political identifications of Muslim boys in England. She analyses this through an exploration of current public, political and academic discourses, particularly around the 'war on terror' and the fear of 'home-grown' terrorism. Shain argues that Muslim boys were previously stereotyped as being passive and law abiding, but are now construed as dangerous, violent and a threat to the social oirder of British society. Consequently, they have come under unprecedented surveillance and scrutiny. Furthermore, such stereotypes are gendered in which women and young girls are seen as victims and symbols of Muslim oppression. Shain argues that such discourses deny agency to Muslim young people and at the same time stereotyping and overemphasising the religious and cultural practices in relation to young Muslim people's experiences and identities. Drawing on her empirical data from her research in schools, Shain examines the educational identities of Mulsim boys to offer an alternative reading of their social and political identifications which focus on intersections of 'race', religion, gender and class in the context of their local schooling and neighbourhood experinces. Her data reveal that Mulsim boys challenge the dominant discourses on Muslim masculinity and there are a range of factors that shape their experiences of schooling, and their social and political identifications. By bringing together new empirical research on the intersections of difference, this book interrogates, challenges and questions notions of difference and the 'other'.

REFERENCES

Anthias, Floya. 2008. Thinking through the lens of translocational positionality: An intersectionality frame for understanding identity and belonging. *Translocations: Migration and Social Change* 4 (1): 5–20.

Anthias, Floya, and Nira Yuval-Davis. 1992. *Racialised boundaries: Race, nation, gender, colour and class and the anti-racist struggle.* London: Routledge.

Bauman, Zygmunt. 1992. *Modernity and the Holocaust.* Cambridge: Polity.
Beck, Ulrick. 1992. *Risk Society: Towards a new modernity.* London: Sage.
Bhavnani, Kum Kum, and Ann Phoenix. 1994. Shifting identities, shifting racisms. *Feminism and Psychology* 4: 5–18.
Brah, Avtar. 1996. *Cartographies of Diaspora: Contesting identities.* London: Roultedge.
Brah, Avtar, and Ann Phoenix. 2004. Ain't I a woman? Revisiting intersectionality. *Journal of International Women's Studies* 5 (3): 75–86.
Brock, Debi. 1991. Talking about a revelation: Feminist popular discourse on sexual abuse. *Canadian Women's Studies* 12: 12–15.
Butler, Judith. 1990. *Gender trouble.* New York: Routledge.
———. 2005. *Giving an account of oneself.* New York: Fordham University Press.
Collins, Patricia Hill. 2005. *Black sexual politics: African Americans, gender and the new racism.* New York: Routledge.
Crenshaw, Kimberlé. 1989. Demarginalising the intersection of race and sex. *University of Chicago Legal Forum* 139: 139–167.
———. 1994. Mapping the margins: Intersectionality, identity politics and violence against women of color. *Stanford Law Review* 24–38.
Derrida, Jacques. 1974. White mythology: Metaphor in the text of philosophy. *New Literary History* 6 (1): 5–74.
Foucault, Michel. 1972. *The archaeology of knowledge.* London: Tavistock.
Gillborn, David. 2005. Education policy as an act of white supremacy: Whiteness, critical race theory and education reform. *Journal of Education Policy* 20: 485–505.
———. 2006. Rethinking white supremacy: Who counts in 'whiteworld'. *Ethnicities* 6: 318–340.
Grewal, Shabnam, Jackie Kay, Liliane Landor, Gail Lewis and Prabita Parmar. 1988. *Charting the journey.* London: Sheba.
Harris, Cheryl I. 1993. Whiteness as property. *Harvard Law Review* 106 (8): 1707–1791.
hooks, bell. 1990. *Yearning: Race, gender and cultural politics.* Boston: Southend Press.
Hunter, Margaret. 2008. The cost of color: What we pay for being black and brown. In *Racism in the 21st century: An empirical analysis of skin color,* ed. Ronald E. Hall, 63–76. New York: Springer.
Leonardo, Zeus. 2005. The color of supremacy: Beyond the discourse of 'white privilege'. In *Critical pedagogy and race,* ed Zeus Leonardo, 37–52. Oxford: Blackwell.
Lewis, Gail. 2000. *Race, gender, social welfare.* Cambridge: Polity.
McCall, Leslie. 2005. The complexity of intersectionality. *Signs* 30: 1771–1800.
Modood, Tariq. 2004. Capitals, ethnic identity and educational qualifications. *Cultural Trends* 13 (2): 87–105.
Sayer, Andrew. 2005. *The moral significance of class.* Cambridge: Cambridge University Press.
Seidman, Steven. 1994. *Contested knowledge: Social theory in the postmodern era.* Cambridge: Blackwell.
Spivak, Gayatri. 1999. *A critique of postcolonial reason.* Boston: Harvard University Press.
Weedon, Chris. 1996. *Feminist practice and poststructuralist theory.* Oxford: Blackwell.

1 The Unhappy Marriage between Marxism and Race Critique
Political Economy and the Production of Racialized Knowledge

Zeus Leonardo

ABSTRACT

In educational theory, orthodox Marxism is known for its commitment to objectivism, or the science of history.[1] On the other hand, race analysis has been developed in its ability to explain the subjective dimension of racial oppression. The two theories are often at odds with each other. This chapter is an attempt to create an integrated theory by focusing on the intersection between Marxist objectivism and race theory's focus on subjectivity. This suggests neither that Marxism neglects the formation of subjectivity nor that race theory ignores material relations. It is a matter of emphasis and the historical development of each discourse. In attempting to integrate them, intellectuals recognize their frequent appearance on the historical stage together. As a result, both Marxism and race analysis are strengthened in a way that maintains the integrity of each discourse. This intersectional framework benefits educational theory because praxis is the dialectical attempt to synthesize the inner and external processes of schooling.

Heidi Hartmann (1993) once argued for a more progressive union in the 'unhappy marriage' between Marxism and feminism. Along the same lines, this chapter argues for a similar intersectional theory between race and class analysis in education. Often, when Marxist orthodoxy takes up the issue of race, it reduces race relations to the status of a reflex within class dynamics. In short, orthodox Marxism economizes the concept of race and the specific issues found within themes of racial identity, development and representation become subsumed in modes of production, the division of labour, or worse, as an instance of false consciousness. On the other hand, when race analysis takes up class issues, it sometimes accomplishes this by reifying race as something primordial or fixed, rather than social and historical. Indeed, in the social science literature there is both a general consensus that race amounts specifically to skin color stratification with black and white serving as the litmus test for other groups and more generally as a proxy for 'group' that includes any social identity under the sun, which could be construed as a race. The former perspective has been criticized for its dichotomizing tendencies, whereas the latter is guilty of too expansive of a definition of race. Moreover, uncritical engagement of class issues within race discourse fails to incorporate the historical explanations found in Marxism and ends up projecting the 'naturalness' or 'foreverness' of racial categories. In this chapter, I attempt to maintain the conceptual integrity of both Marxist and race discourses through a synthesis of their strengths, the first a material, objective analysis, the second through an analysis of subjectivity, or how the historical conditions of class are lived in existentially racial ways. In order to advance the theoretical understanding of educational analysis, I will pursue the historical and conceptual integration of race and Marxist discourse.

It is now a well-acknowledged social scientific fact that class status remains one of the strongest, if not the strongest, predictor for student achievement. In short, there is a positive correlation between the class status of a student's family and that student's success in schools. The higher the student's family class status, the higher the chances for school success. It is also an equally well-acknowledged fact that people of color disproportionately comprise the working-class and working-poor groups when compared to their White counterparts. In schools, Latino and African American students face the interlocking effects of racial, economic and educational structures. From the outset, this establishes the centrality of both class and race analysis concerning school outcomes and policies designed to address them (Leonardo 2002, 2003, 2009).

The field of orthodox Marxist studies is dominated by the elucidation of the objective conditions of capital at the expense of the subjective, or ideological, dimensions of race within capitalism. It covers racism not as a field of contestation among racial groups for power but as an ideological distraction from the inner workings of capitalism. In short, racism is not at all about race but capital. With the advent of Western Marxism, especially under the influence of Lukács' (1971) humanism, Gramsci's (1971) notion of a cultural revolution and Frankfurt critical theory, Marxist concepts about subjectivity came to the fore. In contrast, race theory analysis of the subjective experience of race has been developed at least as much as studies that map its institutional, material basis. Du Bois's (1989) concept of 'double consciousness' and Fanon's (1967) psychology of race are invoked as widely as talks of institutional 'discrimination' or 'segregation'. Du Bois's search for the 'souls of black folk' signals his concern for the subjective existence of a people whose worth is 'measured by the tape of another man' through a school system that denies their true participation as intellectual citizens. Similarly, Fanon's journey into the essence of the Black psyche, or his appropriation of Aimé Césaire's concept of negritude, finds this subjectivity routed through the distorting effects of a colonial education. Orthodox Marxism is conceptually silent on these issues because it brackets the subjective in order to explain the objective, much the same way Piaget brackets the objective to explain the subjective development of the child (Huebner 1981). Marrying Marx with Piaget, Huebner introduces a brand of 'genetic Marxism' as a way to bridge the objective and subjective correlates of history. It is through this synthesis that critical pedagogists arrive at the political economy of curricular knowledge. Huebner does not address the racial form of genetic Marxism but he is instructive in addressing the blind spots of orthodox Marxism and Piagetian epistemic theory. The marriage between objective and subjective analysis represents the cornerstone of educational praxis since at least as far back as Dewey.

LINKS BETWEEN ORTHODOX MARXISM AND RACE CRITIQUE

In the field of educational theory it is apparently unfashionable to revisit Bowles and Gintis's (1976) original insights because of the assumption that theoretical knowledge has advanced beyond their conceptual monism. The return to Bowles and Gintis is a fashionable *faux pas* as out of step as disco is in today's dance clubs, although one can expect the Gap clothing company to exploit it for nostalgia. In addition, with the popularity of various post-ism's, post-al's, or posties, Marxist structuralism appears imperialistic and conceptually flawed by its determinisms. Raymond Williams (1977) puts it best when he says that Marxism without determinations is a useless theory, but, were it to retain them in their current forms, Marxism would become a crippled intervention. That said, Marxist resiliency seems alive and well, judging from McLaren's (2000) reinvigoration of it in his book on Che Guevara and Paulo Freire; *Cultural Logic*, an online education journal dedicated to the vision of Marx; and countless claims that despite the marginalisation of Marxism in academe within the rise of neoliberalism, it maintains a privileged status as a revolutionary explanation and intervention, especially in these times of global economic instability. The neoconservative, neoliberal, and postmodern attempts to displace global critique of capitalism seems only to reinvigorate Marxist commitments to a perspective that responds with a vengeance, much like a boomerang that returns to hit its thrower in the face (see Harvey 1989; Eagleton 1996; Ebert, 1996; San Juan, Jr. 1999; Buroway 2000). No doubt, post-Marxism would be more attractive in a world of post-exploitation. But for now, Marxism is like blue jeans, refusing to fade away.

Under the structuralist wing of orthodox Marxism, schools are said to reproduce the social relations of labour through the correspondence between school and work structures (Bowles and Gintis 1976). Schools neither add nor take away from economic inequality at large; they reproduce labour relations through homology. Like a factory, schools welcome students as inputs to the juggernaut of capitalism, where they learn dispositions necessary for the reproduction of capital, then leave the school site twelve years or so later as outputs of the system. Bowles and Gintis share Althusser's (1971) theory of the reproduction of the relations of production. They provide an innovation within Marxist theory by emphasising the state apparatuses' ability to reproduce the division of labour not so much through material processes but through ideology. Although critiques of reproduction theory abound, this phenomenon does not refute the fact that reproduction occurs in schools (Leonardo 2000).

Students take their place in the work world and the economico-educational process that puts them there is depicted as relatively smooth and uninterrupted. Although they differ in their orientation toward economic determinism, such that Althusser (1969) believes the superstructure rebounds and affects the economic infrastructure (i.e., overdetermines it), Bowles and Gintis and Althusser commit to the science of Marxism, earlier defined by Lukács (1971) as the 'scientific conviction that dialectical materialism is the road to truth' (p. 1). Dubbed as 'critical functionalism' by Carnoy and Levin (1985), Bowles and Gintis's correspondence principle differs from the functionalism of Durkheim (1956, 1973) and Dreeben (1968) insofar as Bowles and Gintis are critical of capitalist structures and the general division of labour. However, critical functionalism shares a common conceptual assumption with structural functionalism to the extent that both discourses assume schools serve a predetermined social function. Although Bowles and Gintis focus on the school as their primary unit of analysis (a superstructural feature), they privilege the industrial labour force as the necessary, causal mechanism that gives form to school structures. It is for this reason that their perspective belongs to Marxist orthodoxy.

The role of race or racial groups in orthodox class analysis is significant but secondary, at best. The racial experiences of African Americans, Latinos and Asian Americans are determined by the economy, reduced to reflex status and fragmented by the effects of ideology. As Bowles and Gintis (1976) observe, 'Blacks certainly suffer from educational inequality, but the root of their exploitation lies outside of education, in a system of economic power and privilege in which racial distinctions play an important role' (p. 35). It would be a mistake to conclude that the authors trivialize the structures of race and racism; as Bowles and Gintis say, they play a 'role'. But as in a play, race and racism are not the star of the show. In effect, Bowles and Gintis conceptually dissolve race into class relations, a move common to other Marxists not necessarily from the Bowles and Gintis school of thought. Other Marxists may be more graceful in their uptake of race but nevertheless share Bowles and Gintis's problematic and commitments. It becomes clear that race relations are products, effects of and determined by the objective laws of economic processes. Though not usually perceived as a Marxist, Oakes (2005) later modifies this position through her studies of tracking by suggesting that 'school matters'. She finds that the institutional practice of tracking exacerbates, at times creates, class *and* race differences. She confirms Cornel West's (1994) simple but straightforward contention that 'race matters'.

From this, we can infer that working-class students of colour face 'double jeopardy' as they confront the specific interlocking conditions of class exploitation and racial stratification. Orthodox Marxist analyses of schooling pay respect to race as an important 'distinction', but not a decisive, certainly not a determining, one. Thus, they forsake the racial concepts that would otherwise help students make sense of their racialized class experiences.

The racialized experience, while possessing an objective character because it finds its form in material relations, strengthens the subjective understanding of class relations. In effect, race is a mode of how class is lived (Hall 1996). As such, class is lived in multiple ways, one of them being racial. Students of colour, like many scholars of colour, find it unconvincing that they are experiencing only class relations when the concepts used to demean and dehumanize them are of a racial nature. As Fanon (1967) finds, 'A white man addressing a Negro behaves exactly like an adult with a child and starts smirking, whispering, patronizing, cozening' (p. 31). Thus, it is not only understandable but reasonable that the orthodox branding of the racial imagination as 'false consciousness' does not sit well with non-White subjects. It occludes White power and privilege, and the interests that maintain them. It is conceptually misleading as well.

In Ladson-Billing's (1998) studies of colonial education from 'Soweto to South Bronx', African Americans experience daily psycho-cultural assaults that cannot be explained purely through economism because it does not propose a convincing explanation as to why African Americans and other students of colour should be the targets of deculturalization (see also Spring 2000). This has led Fanon (1963) to the conclusion that 'Marxist analysis should always be slightly stretched everytime we have to do with the colonial problem' (p. 40). Fanon's (1967) endorsement of Marxist critique is very clear when he says,

> If there is an inferiority complex, it is the outcome of a double process:
>   —primarily, economic;
>   —subsequently, the internalization—or, better, the epidermalization—of this inferiority (p. 11).

Stretching the conceptual tendons of orthodox Marxism makes it flexible in accommodating the subjective experience of students of colour as they navigate through an educational system hostile to their worldview. Although Fanon was speaking of the decolonisation struggle during the 1960s, his insights are valid today because internal colonies like ghettos, *barrios* and reservations bear the material and psycho-cultural marks of colonial education within a nation that daily reminds their subjects of the rightness of whiteness.

Like Hartmann's (1993) charge that orthodox Marxism's conceptual universe is 'sex blind,' one can lay a similar charge that it is also 'color blind'. Marxism lacks the conceptual apparatus to explain who exactly will fill the 'empty places' of the economy. Its discursive structure does not provide compelling reasons for women's relegation to housework or non-White overrepresentation in the working class, buttressed by an educational system that appears to reproduce the dispositions for such a sorting of workers. Regardless of their class status, students of colour show an incredible amount of resilience in an educational process that undervalues their history and contribution. Economic analysis conveniently forgets that when labour organizes itself into a subject of history, this subject is often constructed out of the White imagination (Roediger 1991). In other cases, White labour organizes to subvert the interests of people of colour, as in the case of the Irish, choosing their whiteness alongside their working-class interests, elbowing out Blacks for industrial jobs. It is a sense of naturalised entitlement that White labourers, even against the objective and long-term interests of the White working class, choose whiteness in order to preserve their subjective advantage, or what Du Bois calls Whites' 'public and psychological wages' (cited in Roediger 1991). The wages of White skin advantage is so pervasive, it is well-represented even within non-White communities. Hunter (1998, 2005) finds that the 'lighter the berry' the more privileges one garners, such as higher rates of education and status. In addition, lighter-skin-toned African American and Mexican American women bear the privilege of being regarded as beautiful, as in the case of *la güera*, or 'fair skinned'. Here, 'fair' takes on the double entendre of light and pretty. Of course, the point should be clear that they are not regarded as White subjects, but approximations of whiteness.

Race theory is not the only discourse to critique orthodox Marxism. With the development of neo-Marxist educational theory, Marxist economism becomes a target of cultural materialism. Arising out of the conceptual space that emphasises the superstructure rather than the base in historical materialism, neo-Marxists like Bourdieu (1977, 1984) and Lareau (2000, 2003) mobilize concepts, like 'cultural capital' and *'habitus*,' to explain the conversion of economic capital to cultural practices that favour the life chances of middle- to upper-class students. Here, the focus is less on the objective structures of labour and more on the rituals and cultural repertoire that reify class privileges. Said another way, neo-Marxism is concerned with cultural reproduction in schools rather than the social reproduction previously described by Bowles and Gintis. Thus, a latent correspondence principle is still at work and discursively in place, this time with culture as the operating principle. For example, Lareau documents the difference in school participation between modestly middle- and upper-middle-class parents. Appropriating Bourdieu's framework, Lareau finds that, among other consequences, modestly middle-class parents lack both the institutional confidence and cultural pedigree to influence the school bureaucracy during school activities, like open house or parent-teacher conferences. In contrast, upper-middle-class parents possess the cultural repertoire and resources that position their children in advantageous ways in school, such as the academic ability to help them with homework or having the occupational credentials that put them well above teachers in terms of status. Such an innovation provides scholars information about a much-ignored group within Marxist theory: the middle class, broadly speaking. Because public schools serve mostly working- and middle- to upper-class students, the cultural relationship between the 'have some' and 'have not' becomes an important site of understanding.

By and large, 'the haves' send their children to private schools and thus do not interact with their working- and middle-class counterparts. Bourgeois parents do not directly work with working- or middle-class people because they have associates they can deploy to deal with management concerns. As a result, everyday interactions in public schools and other public places are waged between working- and middle-class families, and the Bill Gateses of the world can afford (or pay) to avoid the fray. Thus, they become even more abstract to the working and middle class. In short, the capitalist class remains out of sight, out of mind. There are two concerns that strike the interests of this chapter with respect to the increased, conceptual attention toward the middle and upper classes. First, when conflict between working and middle to upper class becomes the focus of analysis, the original contradiction formulated by Marx with respect to the working and capitalist classes shifts or is displaced. Therefore, one may receive the impression that the primary contradiction is now between the working and middle class. It is indeed the case that middle-class students receive curricular matter fashioned in their image. Their linguistic capital and cultural codes form the basis of pedagogical knowledge and legitimate interactions in the classroom.

Now regarded as an apparatus of the middle class, public schools reproduce the value system of their privileged clients, who hold a monopoly over the legitimate power to correct others who fall out of line with 'the middle'. Bourdieu (1991) describes,

> Through its grammarians, who fix and codify legitimate usage, and its teachers who impose and inculcate it through innumerable acts of correction, the educational system tends, in this area as elsewhere, to produce the need for its own services and its own products, i.e. the labour and instruments of correction (p. 61).

In the institutional context of schooling, middle-class codes and values form the standard of correct *habitus*. It is at this point that the relational character of Marx's stress on the primary conflict should be invoked. The middle class may receive benefits or may even be the hegemons of the public schools, but this is different from saying that they benefit from the economic system at large and in an absolute way. With much of the analytical focus falling on middle-class privileges, the productive power of the capitalist class is obscured. Despite their relative power, the middle class is not the main problem within a divided labour force. They may be the favoured sons, but the father still controls the house. No doubt, as Marx reminds us, the middle class does not represent the revolutionary impetus for change, but neither are they the main target of critique. In fact, the everyday existential battles between the working and middle class over issues such as vouchers and other choice programs detract from a greater understanding of the role of the capitalist class in the educational system. Again, they remain out of sight, out of mind.

That said, like Bourdieu and Lareau, neo-Marxism finds a productive ground on which to develop, in a dialectical way, the relationship between objective structures and their sedimentation on parents and students' subjectivity, which is the central concern of this chapter. In particular, they provide direction for a study of the body because a theory of *habitus* explains the way institutional arrangements become grafted directly onto the embodied perceptions and dispositions of students. However, a second problem arises when one considers the issue of race. Bodies are not just material deposits of class relations; they are also racialized bodies. In his unrelenting critique of the Racial Contract, Charles Mills (1997) asserts that traditional contractarians project a social understanding of the world that is race blind. He proposes a theory of the Racial Contract that explains states and state apparatuses, such as the school, as mechanisms of White power in a herrenvolk democracy where the dominant White group experiences liberty at the expense of subordinate racial groups. Furthermore, he criticizes Marxism for its projection of a 'colorless class struggle' (p. 111). Bourdieuan analysis of schooling benefits from an integration of the race concept in order to provide an analysis of parental involvement, for example, that asks the extent to which parents of colour feel intimidated by White teachers or feel tentative during parent-teacher conferences and open-house night, even when both groups represent the same class. This would enrich Lareau's findings by modifying Bourdieu's influential concept of 'cultural capital' in terms of race.

RACISM AND THE PROBLEM OF EXPLOITATION

As Cornel West (1988) proclaims, 'The time has passed when the so-called race question, or Negro question, can be relegated to secondary or tertiary *theoretical* significance in bourgeois or Marxist discourses' (p. 18: italics in original). In the history of class-race relations in the United States there have been three conceptual ways to define the specific place of African Americans in the social formation. One, African Americans are subsumed into the working class. This strain ignores the specific experiences of African Americans outside of industrial labour or the workplace. Two, African American specificity is acknowledged within particular practices in the economy, such as discrimination. This perspective is not as reductionistic as the first but shares its economism. Three, and most influential, African Americans suffer general class exploitation within a national context. This acknowledges the importance of Black nationalism, is antireductionistic and antieconomistic. Although West is concerned with the specific plight of African Americans, he acknowledges its common features with other oppressed groups, such as Chicanos, citing Mario Barrera's (1979) powerful work *Race and Class in the Southwest*.

As we settle into the new millennium, race and class critique becomes more complex and specific. It is more complex because we must apply Marx's original insights to an economic system that is increasingly postindustrial, especially in first- and second-world nations. It is specific because the race question accounts for some of the unevenness in the economy, especially when we take into account the internationalisation of the labour force. The development of race critique benefits from Marxism's general focus on objective, historical developments. In particular, its emphasis on the 'real' provides race critique with a conceptual arm that guards against reification of the race concept. For example, Manning Marable's (1983) early polemic against racial essentialism blasts Black men and the Black petty bourgeois for their sexism and complicity with the exploitation of Black women. Marable exposes the spurious myth behind the suggestion of a 'black capitalism' or 'black bourgeoisie,' citing the fact that, in the beginning of the 1980s, only two hundred Black entrepreneurs account for the corporate core of American capitalism. Despite this, Black men occupy positions in the sexualized economy that far outrun the mobility of their female counterparts. The abuse of women, especially by certain sectors of the subproletarian world controlled by Black men, does not warrant all Black men an assumed racial solidarity with Black women because they contribute to the economic exploitation of women. This suggests that racial grouping does not equate with racial belonging.

That people of colour exploit each other on the basis of a subgroup's economic interest subverts the notion of an essential group affiliation based on identity. Exploitation is an objective phenomenon that does not ask questions about the colour of its perpetrator. On some level, the exploitation that people of colour suffer at the hands of Whites or other people of colour bears a material mark that looks and feels the same. On the level of meaning, the exploited person of colour may rationalize the exploitation as different, depending on the identity of its source. This perception may even attenuate the subjective experience of exploitation, that is, soften it, because of a sense of self-identification that the exploited feels toward the exploiter. This rationalisation is reasonable because it attests to the specific historical relationship between people of colour and Whites as opposed to intraminority politics. However, conceptually it is problematic and reifies the concept of race because it posits an essential subject of identity such that it performs an a priori assumption about sameness between members of a 'like' group. Exploitation by my sibling objectively alienates me as much as it would if it came from a complete stranger. If anything, the first case seems more of a betrayal than the second because there exists an assumed contract that is broken.

In light of this quandary, it is consequential that educators' definitions of racism become as complex as its subject matter. There are at least two ways to define racism: as a system of privilege or a system of oppression. In the first, a system of privilege depends on identity, or as Beverly Tatum (1997) explains, people of color can harbour racial prejudices, but do not earn the title of 'racist' because they possess neither the institutional power nor the means to enforce it. Within this discourse, only Whites benefit from racism in a direct and absolute way because they possess both racial power and institutional means. This is not untrue. People of colour can be just as hateful as Whites and perpetrate random acts of violence toward them, but they cannot be called racists. This definition has several advantages. It makes power central to the system of race and its problem: racism. Also, it makes clear who benefits from a racist formation: Whites. Moreover, it distinguishes between temporary, relative benefits from absolute benefits.

In education it is widely touted that Asian Americans, as a group, represent the model student (see Nakanishi and Nishida 1995). They are characterized as studious, obedient and educationally oriented. As the racial middleman group, Asian Americans act as a buffer between Whites and Blacks. As the buffer, Asian Americans may receive additional benefits, such as positive representations as the 'good minority'. First, I am not here to debunk the construction that Asian Americans, by and large, are studious. However, that this studiousness is due to their racial makeup—genetic, cultural or otherwise—is another matter. It is a known fact that Asian immigrants arrive into the United States already occupying a different class status when compared to their Latino or Black counterparts (Portes and Rumbaut 2006). Second, the relative benefits that Asian Americans receive as the favoured child of US paternalism keep them at bay with respect to race relations. In fact, this may explain why many Asian Americans resist applying racial analysis to their life experiences, choosing instead to hunker down and remain silent. Also, Asian Americans avoid race analysis because this would put them closer to the more vocal African American discourse on race and thus become more closely associated with Black rather than White in the American racial dichotomy. In the final analysis, the case of Asian Americans shows how relative success is used to discipline Latinos and African Americans on the 'fairness' of the US educational system because a minority group is apparently able to rise in ranks (see Wu 2002). Asian Americans benefit from this arrangement but, as Tatum suggests, this does not translate into institutional power.

Tatum's definition accomplishes its task, but not without conceptual trade-offs. It leaves underdeveloped or unexplained the responsibility and accountability of people of colour who do not help the cause of racial emancipation, or worse, perpetuate racist relations, such as Marable's discussion of the subproletarian economy. An alternative way to define racism is to demarcate it as *a system of racial oppression*. This differs from Tatum's identity-dependent definition because it is a politics unguaranteed by the agent's identity. It is not merely a discussion about the agent's inauthenticity and more about racial consequences and the upkeep of race relations. Just as Ebert (1996) makes it possible to call Camille Paglia a 'patriarchal feminist', it is also possible to say that the *actions* of people of colour are racist when they participate in the maintenance of a racist system. This does not suddenly put people of colour on a par with White subjects because Euro-White atrocities toward the other are more comprehensive, far-reaching and unparalleled (Said 1979). Also, attention to racist acts as opposed to racist people should not be confused as saying that all racist acts are the same, as if to call a Black person a 'nigger' is somehow the same as calling a White person 'honkey'. A sophisticated conceptual analysis arrives at the historically divergent material source of the meaning of each term—both are derogatory but different in force.

As an insightful student of mine once commented, phrases such as 'White trash' should not be mistaken as only a class-related slur disconnected from race. She reminds us that White trash is a stand-in for 'bad Whites,' a descriptor that assumes the existence of 'good whites'. By contrast, even 'good nigger' is a slur scripted through an act of distancing, of differentiating between frightful, militant-seeming Black students ('bad') and an accommodating Black student ('good'). Both 'types' of student belong to the discourse of distantiation through its construction of the generalized, rather than concrete, Black figure. They come out of a discourse of fear. In short, as another student concludes, Denzel Washington is still a 'nigger' in the White supremacist imagination, and for that matter, Jackie Chan just another 'chink', and James Edward Olmos another dreaded 'wetback'. Again, it should be clear that the speaker of racist semantemes matters, but this does not exonerate the act. Snoop Doggy Dogg or Tito of Power 106 on the Los Angeles music airwaves can just as easily act to perpetuate these structures.

In the 1990s, when Tito recounted the top four songs at 4:00 of any given afternoon with an exaggerated Mexican accent while Black and White disc jockeys alike have a hearty laugh, it is not conveniently set aside as an act of a colonized mind. Certainly Tito was being used as a pawn of racist capitalism, and this would have been enough. Millions of students in the L.A. basin inhale these negative messages as they do the smog in the air. The speech act belongs objectively in the space of White supremacist discourse. As David Theo Goldberg (1990) describes, racism is a field of discourse. It consists of expressions, acts, consequences, principles, institutions and a set of texts associated with subjects but not guaranteed by them. In other words, following Foucault, we may say that racist discourses maintain a certain autonomy from the subjects who utter them. Though it would certainly be a contradiction to discuss racism without reference to any racists, discursive analysis establishes the possibility that racist discourses work as easily through Whites as they do through people of colour, even if it works against the latter's interests. Certainly, we may bring capitalism into the fold as a reminder that racism sells and financially benefits Tito and his co-conspirators. But crack also sells and no self-respecting person of colour is rushing to encourage its promotion.

The discursive turn in social theory informs us of the social construction of identity. In a reading of identity as text, Stuart Hall (1996) explains the fragmentation of identity into ethnicity, sexuality and race. As such, the essentialist reading of identity in the forms of negritude or radical strains of feminism are compromised and filtered through the articulation of several formations within a given context. Rather than offering a stable and overreliable notion of selfhood, Hall offers certain articulations of difference that are inflected through a constellation of competing discourses. In other words, there is no universal subject of race that is not already interpenetrated by overlapping ways of being, like gender, ethnicity or class. This does not suggest that identity is neither meaningful nor useful. In fact, this does not prevent strong calls for the politicisation of identity as a basis for social movements. It is this variegated sense of politics that Gramsci, read through Hall, describes as the 'relations of force' that must be taken into account when applying Marxism to a particular social formation. Here we see the pragmatic suggestion of multiple levels of race analysis that resists its reification as an identity formed once and for all. Rather, through a *specific* engagement of the objective, historical conditions, Marxist race scholars understand that racialized subjects are inflected by a set of discourses struggling to define them. First and last, their determinants are not economic but a combination of material and ideological forces within a given social formation. For instance, the invention of postmodern racism is a material context where schooling becomes a denial of dialogue and becomes conscripted in incommensurable world-views unable to connect on important issues, like equality (Flecha 1999). The specific application of Marx's insights to the current objective conditions advances our understanding of an educational milieu fraught with decidable features, such as inequality.

Productive (rather than productivist) readings of race avoid the pitfalls of two positions: traditional identity politics and beyond identity politics. Identity may not be real (i.e., material) like the economy but it produces real consequences as racialized subjects act *as if they were real*. When White teachers act in patterned ways toward students of colour through tracking practices or the like, they behave in ways that produce real and racial consequences. Some students face these behaviours on such a consistent basis that they become formidable, material forces in their educational lives. When students of color resist 'official' school culture because they consider academic success as 'acting White' (Fordham 1988), they reproduce racial patterns in school outcomes. In short, racial politics exist, even if they are not real in the orthodox Marxist sense of the word. They exist as a material force that is objective and outside of individual control. The traditional sense of identity politics has been all but discredited in mainstream social theory. That identity *is* politics is a form of guarantee that even Walmart cannot redeem. However, this does not suggest the end of all talks of identity politics. In fact, something curious has happened to the discourse on identity politics.

On one side, Marxists reject the postmodern attempt to fragment class struggle into green politics, gay and lesbian liberation or multiculturalism. On the other side, postmodern theorists announce the annihilation of the unified subject at a time when the said groups were gaining momentum as social movements. Clearly, one receives a disjointed and confused picture. It is a bit like blaming the messenger for delivering someone else's message. Identity politics is quite old as discourses go. In other words, as a response to postmodern theorizing, the call for getting 'beyond identity politics' seems both conceptually muddled and historically misplaced with respect to race and/or ethnicity. On identity politics, Lipsitz (1998) has this to say:

> [W]ork often derided as identity politics . . . [finds that] attacks on immigrants and on affirmative action amount to little more than a self-interested strategy for preserving the possessive investment in whiteness, a politics based solely on identity. Conversely, the best ethnic studies scholarship . . . [is] aimed at creating identities based on politics rather than politics based on identities (pp. 56, 66).

Race scholars informed by a nonreductionist reading of Marx provide some of the best insights for analyzing the material basis of race, racism and ethnocentrism. By marrying Marxist objectivism with race critique, insurgent educators provide a language of critique that locates, rather than obscures, the beneficiaries of inequality in all its forms.

TOWARDS AN INTERSECTIONAL THEORY OF MARXISM AND RACE CRITIQUE

Without a critical language of identity politics, policy educators cannot answer convincingly the question 'Who will fill the empty places of the economy?' With it, they can expose the contradictions in the 'beyond identity politics' thesis, which is dependent on the concept of identity in its reassertion of the Euro-White patriarchal capitalism. However, without economic principles, educators also forsake an apprehension of history that maps the genealogy of the race concept. It is not uncommon that students of education project race into the past and equate it with the descriptor 'group' rather than a *particular way* of constructing group membership. For that matter, the Greeks of antiquity, Trojans of Troy, and Mesopotamians each comprise a race, much like today's African Americans or the African diaspora. There is enough consensus between social scientists about the periodization of race to disprove this commonsense belief (see Goldberg 1990; Mills 1997, 2003).

A progressive union between Marxist concepts and race analysis allows critical educators to explain that race is a relatively recent and modern phenomenon, traceable to the beginnings of European colonization and capitalist expansion. As a concept, race is coextensive with the process of worldmaking. Edward Said (1979) has explicated the process of Orientalism, or how the Occident constructed the *idea* of the Orient (or Near East) through discursive strategies in order to define, control and manipulate it. This does not mean that the Orient did not exist in a material sense, but that it was spatially demarcated and then written into a particular relationship with the West through scholarship and industries invested with economic resources. Cedric Robinson (1983) has mobilized a parallel oeuvre in what Robin Kelley (1983), in the foreword to *Black Marxism*, characterizes as a version of Black Orientalism, or how Europe constructed the idea of the black Mediterranean. In this sense, race is a process of cocreation—it creates an external group at the same time as it defines its creator. Likewise, Linda Tuhiwai Smith's (1999) *Decolonizing Methodologies* accomplishes a similar appropriation of Said for the Maori conditions in New Zealand.

Another popular reaction to race discourse is the preference for the concept of culture. Rejecting the race concept as purely socially constructed, educators opt for the cultural analysis route as a substitute. In short, whereas race is an abstraction, culture is real. Culture is comprised of rituals, practices and artefacts, whereas race is an idealist categorization of people based on phenotypes. Marginalized people have created rich inventories of culture, whereas race is imposed by White domination. Fearing the further reification of race, some scholars and students of education avoid the term altogether. They prefer race as ethnicity, race as class or race as nation (see Omi and Winant 1994). In other words, opposite race as an essence, race becomes an illusion. The cultural discourse benefits from a language of racial formation within a given historical context, or what Omi and Winant (1994) describe as 'the sociohistorical process by which racial categories are created, inhabited, transformed, and destroyed' (p. 55). Broadly speaking, racial formations evolve in the field of representations, or racial projects. Racial projects are also objective material processes that compete for the distribution of resources such as educational credentials.

Other problems arise when we override, rather than integrate, race with culture. First, the real/nonreal pairing between race and culture appears dichotomous, as if they were at odds with each other. With respect to certain groups, culture and race maintain such a close relationship that some forms of culture would not have evolved had specific racial structures been absent. In the case of African Americans, cultural practices such as slave narratives, blues and secretly jumping the broom at weddings evolved from the 'peculiar institution' of slavery. Cultural practices such as these are only real to the extent that they arose from the objective context of enslavement, the objectification of humans as chattel, and material arrangements such as Jim Crowism. Jumping the broom existed in Africa, but the context of its surreptitious practice in the US has a particular meaning related to the institution of slavery. Second, in order to make real their social experiences, slaves and their descendants objectified them in cultural forms, thereby producing history through material practices. The privileging of culture divorced from racio-economic evolution may regress to a feel-good concept that is at once celebratory and forgetful that 'More Americans are ill-housed, poorly educated, and without health care that ever before. The condition for the racial minorities of course is twice, even three times worse than for the general population' (San Juan, Jr. 1994, 60).

In fact, one finds this tendency in mainstream multicultural practice. San Juan, Jr. (1994) does not mince words when he writes, 'One outstanding example of multiculturalism in practice is the apartheid system in South Africa where racist theory and racialist practice insist on the saliency of cultural differences . . . where the hegemonic ideology valorizes differences to guarantee sameness' (pp. 70–72). When multicultural education does not pay critical attention to the commodification of culture via racist signification, it robs students of the liberating aspects of cultural training. A materialist outlook on culture and race understands that too much *pluribus* and not enough *unum* takes for granted differences that only lately walked onto the scene. That is, although a multiculturalist should surely fight against what Memmi (2000) calls 'heterophobia', or fear of difference, he or she should surely also reject differences that were constructed in order to create differences, rather than merely to observe them.

It is on this last note that I want to end this chapter. Spickard (1992) has acknowledged the illogic of American racial categories by pointing out its shifting meaning, blurry lines and sometimes inconsistent application. However, he admits that people of colour find meaning in race because it gives them a sense of common struggle based on a denominator of historical maltreatment. This brings up a question with respect to the future of the race concept, which I (2010) have taken up elsewhere. If the creation of race is dubious and coterminous with exploitation, then it begs the question: 'Why keep it?' A progressive education must risk the possibility of transcending the race concept only by going through it and not over it, just as, for a Marxist, it behooves us to transcend the class system. Martin Luther King's dream is, after all, David Duke's nightmare: a society free of racial strife only after full disclosure of its racio-economic essence.

NOTES

1. This essay first appeared under the same title in *Policy Futures in Education*, 2(3&4), 493–493.

REFERENCES

Althusser, Louis. 1969. *For Marx*. B. Brewster (trans). New York: Verso.
———. 1971. *Lenin and philosophy*. B. Brewster (trans.). New York: Monthly Review Press.
Barrera, Mario. 1979. *Race and class in the Southwest*. Notre Dame, IN: Notre Dame University Press.
Bourdieu, Pierre. 1977. Cultural reproduction and social reproduction. In *Power and ideology in education*, ed. Jerome Karabel and A. H. Halsey, 487–511. Oxford, UK: Oxford University Press.
———. 1984. *Distinction: A social critique of the judgment of taste*. R. Nice (trans. and ed.). Cambridge, MA: Harvard University Press.
———. 1991. *Language and symbolic power*. John B. Thompson (ed.). Gino Raymond and Matthew Adamson (trans.). Cambridge, MA: Harvard University Press.
Bowles, Samuel, and Herbert Gintis. 1976. *Schooling in capitalist America*. New York: Basic Books.
Burawoy, Michael. 2000. Marxism after communism. *Theory and Society* 29 (2): 151–174.
Carnoy, Martin, and Henry Levin. 1985. *Schooling and work in the democratic state*. Stanford, CA: Stanford University Press.
Dreeben, Robert. 1968. *On what is learned in school*. Menlo Park, CA: Addison-Wesley.
Du Bois, W. E. B. 1989. *The souls of black folk*. New York: Penguin Books.
Durkheim, Emile. 1956. *Education and sociology*. Glencoe, IL: Free Press.
———. 1973. *Moral education*. New York: The Free Press.
Eagleton, Terry. 1996. *Postmodernism and its illusions*. Oxford, UK: Blackwell.
Ebert, Teresa. 1996. *Ludic feminism and after*. Ann Arbor: University of Michigan Press.
Fanon, Frantz. 1963. *The wretched of the earth*. C. Farrington (trans.). New York: Grove Press.
———. 1967. *Black skin white masks*. C. Markmann (trans.). New York: Grove Press.
Flecha, Ramon. 1999. Modern and postmodern racism in Europe: Dialogical approach and anti-racist pedagogies. *Harvard Educational Review* 69 (2): 150–171.
Fordham, Signithia. 1988. Racelessness as a factor in Black students' school success: Pragmatic strategy or pyrrhic victory? *Harvard Educational Review* 58 (1): 54–84.
Goldberg, David Theo. 1990. The social formation of racist discourse. In *Anatomy of racism,* ed. David Theo Goldberg, 295–318. Minneapolis: University of Minnesota Press.
Gramsci, Antonio. 1971. *Selections from prison notebooks*. Quintin Hoare and Geoffrey Nowell Smith (trans. and ed.). New York: International Publishers.
Hall, Stuart. 1996. New ethnicities. In *Stuart Hall*, ed. David Morley and Kuan-Hsing Chen, 441–449. London: Routledge.
Hartmann, Heidi. 1993. The unhappy marriage of Marxism and feminism: Towards a more progressive union. In *Feminist frameworks*, 3rd ed., ed. Alison Jaggar and Paula Rothenberg, 191–202. Boston: McGraw Hill.
Harvey, David. 1989. *The condition of postmodernity*. Cambridge, MA: Blackwell Publishers.
Huebner, Dwayne. 1981. Toward a political economy of curriculum and human development. In *Curriculum & instruction*, ed. Henry Giroux, Anthony Penna and William Pinar, 124–138. Berkeley, CA: McCutchan Publishing Corporation.

Hunter, Margaret. 1998. Colorstruck: Skin color stratification in the lives of African American women. *Sociological Perspectives* 68 (4): 517–535.

———. 2005. *Race, gender, and the politics of skin tone.* New York: Routledge.

Kelley, Robin. 1983. Foreword to *Black Marxism.* Chapel Hill: The University of North Carolina Press.

Ladson-Billings, Gloria. 1998. From Soweto to the South Bronx: African Americans and colonial education in the United States. In *Sociology of education: Emerging perspectives*, ed. Carlos Alberto Torres and Theodore Mitchell, 247–264. Albany: State University of New York Press.

Lareau, Annette. 2000. *Home advantage.* Lanham, MD: Rowman & Littlefield.

———. 2003. *Unequal childhoods.* Berkeley: University of California Press.

Leonardo, Z. 2000. Betwixt and between: Introduction to the politics of identity. In *Charting new terrains of Chicana(o)/Latina(o) education*, ed. Carlos Tejeda, Corinne Martinez and Zeus Leonardo, 107–129. Cresskill, NJ: Hampton Press.

———. 2002. The souls of white folk: Critical pedagogy, whiteness studies, and globalization discourse. *Race Ethnicity & Education* 5 (1): 29–50.

———. 2003. The agony of school reform: Race, class, and the elusive search for social justice. *Educational Researcher* 32 (3): 37–43.

———. 2009. *Race, whiteness, and education.* New York: Routledge.

———. (2010). After the glow: Race ambivalence and other educational prognoses. *Educational Philosophy and Theory.* Published online September 10, 2010, DOI: 10.1111/j.1469-5812.2010.00645.x.

Lipsitz, George. 1998. *The possessive investment in whiteness.* Philadelphia: Temple University Press.

Lukács, Georg. 1971. *History and class consciousness.* Rodney Livingstone (trans.). Cambridge, MA: MIT Press.

Marable, Manning. 1983. *How capitalism underdeveloped Black America.* Boston: South End Press.

McLaren, Peter. 2000. *Ché Guevara, Paulo Freire, and the pedagogy of revolution.* Lanham, MD: Rowman & Littlefield.

Memmi, Albert. 2000. *Racism.* S. Martinot (trans.). Minneapolis: University of Minnesota Press.

Mills, Charles. 1997. *The racial contract.* Ithaca, NY: Cornell University Press.

———. 2003. *From class to race: Essays in White Marxism and Black radicalism.* Lanham, MD: Rowman & Littlefield.

Nakanishi, Don, and Tina Yamano Nishida, eds. 1995. *The Asian-American educational experience.* New York: Routledge.

Oakes, Jeannie. 2005. *Keeping track*, 2nd ed. New Haven, CT: Yale University Press.

Omi, Michael, and Howard Winant. 1994. *Racial formation in the United States: From the 1960s to the 1990s*, 2nd ed. New York: Routledge.

Portes, Alejandro, and Rubén Rumbaut. 2006. *Immigrant America: A portrait*, 3rd ed. Berkeley: University of California Press.

Robinson, Cedric. 1983. *Black Marxism.* Chapel Hill: The University of North Carolina Press.

Roediger, David. 1991. *The wages of whiteness.* New York: Verso.

Said, Edward. 1979. *Orientalism.* New York: Random House.

San Juan, Jr., E. 1994. Problematizing multiculturalism and the "common culture". *MELUS* 19 (2): 59–84.

———. 1999. *Beyond postcolonial theory.* Boulder, CO: Westview Press.

Smith, Linda Tuhiwai. 1999. *Decolonizing methodologies.* London: Zed Books.

Spickard, Paul. 1992. The illogic of American racial categories. In *The multiracial experience: Racial borders as the new frontier*, ed. Maria Root, 13–23. Thousand Oaks, CA: Sage.

Spring, Joel. 2000. *Deculturalization and the struggle for equality*, 3rd ed. Boston: McGraw-Hill.

Tatum, Beverly Daniel. 1997. *Why are all the Black kids sitting together in the cafeteria?* New York: Basic Books.

West, Cornel. 1988. Marxist theory and the specificity of Afro-American oppression. In *Marxism and the interpretation of culture*, ed. Cary Nelson and Lawrence Grossberg, 17–33. Urbana, IL: University of Illinois Press.

———. 1994. *Race matters*. New York: Vintage Books.

Williams, Raymond. 1977. *Marxism and literature*. Oxford, UK: Oxford University Press.

Wu, Frank. 2002. *Yellow*. New York: Basic Books.

2 The White Working Class, Racism and Respectability
Victims, Degenerates and Interest-Convergence

David Gillborn

ABSTRACT

This chapter argues that race and class inequalities cannot be fully understood in isolation: their intersectional quality is explored through two contrasting disciplinary tropes that circulate in popular and political discourse. These tropes are examined in historical perspective and through an analysis of contemporary British media during late 2008 (the timing is highly significant). While global capitalism reeled on the edge of international financial meltdown, the essential values of neoliberalism were reasserted as natural, moral and efficient through two apparently contrasting discourses. First, a *victim* discourse presented White working people, and their children in particular, as suffering because of minoritized racial groups and their advocates. Second, a discourse of *degeneracy* presented an immoral and barbaric underclass as a threat to social and economic order. Applying the 'interest-convergence principle' from Critical Race Theory (CRT), the discourses amount to a strategic mobilization of White interests where the 'White, but not quite' status of the working class (Allen 2009) provides a buffer zone at a time of economic and cultural crisis which secures societal White supremacy and provides a further setback to progressive reforms that focus on race, gender and disability equality. Contrary to the arguments of some class theorists (who dismiss CRT as blind to the situation of poor Whites), we can see that the existence of poor White people is not only consistent with a regime of White supremacy; they are actually an essential part of the processes that sustain it.

INTRODUCTION

Kimberlé Crenshaw, who is widely credited with coining the notion of intersectionality, is one of the foundational writers in Critical Race Theory (CRT). There is a common misconception that CRT imagines that all social inequalities, and indeed all situations, are reducible to racism. In fact, CRT has *always* been concerned with how raced inequity exists alongside, and in combination with, other forms of inequality (Crenshaw 2001). CRT sees race/racism as an ever-present feature of inequality in societies like the US and the UK but it does not imagine that racism operates the same way in every situation and at all times. A major strand in CRT, from its inception, has been to understand how racism works in, through and sometimes alongside other dimensions of inequality. Critical race theorists frequently use the notion of 'intersectionality' as the means by which these dynamics are analysed.

CRT is not interested in theory for theory's sake. In some circles the notion of intersectionality has become a buzzword devoid of critical content (see Davis 2008); the promise of intersectional CRT is that it might enable us to develop tools/concepts that help us to understand and oppose wider patterns of intersectional inequities. We can then use these tools as a basis upon which to:

- anticipate problems with reforms/policy innovations that may re-create, mask or transform inequities, and
- better interrupt and resist those intersections that generate, sustain and legitimate educational inequality.

The White working class have become flavour of the month for politicians and the media but this is by no means a *progressive* turn of events. This chapter explores the racialized and racist impacts of these discourses and their policy iterations.

Ordinarily, in an article fundamentally concerned with a particular social-class group (White working-class people), it would be sensible to begin with a definition of the group drawing on demographic data. In this case, however, the very nature of who/what 'counts' as working class is one of the key issues at stake in the discourses that I seek to analyse. The term 'White working class' is a shifting signifier (Apple 1992) whose boundaries are drawn differently according to the context and the writer. Hence, at times the 'working class' is positioned in popular and political discourse as an undifferentiated mass of nonelite people, but at other times a distinction is asserted between 'working class' and poor/underclass Whites. These distinctions are fluid and often deployed in highly contingent and contradictory ways. In this paper I explore how a regime of White supremacy benefits from popular discourses that present the working class as, on one hand, innocent victims of unfair racial competition and, on the other hand, degenerate threats to social and economic order. Using the CRT concept of 'interest-convergence', it is possible to document the very real material and symbolic violence that White working-class people experience, whilst recognizing that the existence of poor Whites is not only consistent with White supremacy; they are actually an essential part of the processes that sustain it.

Subsequent sections of this chapter examine the construction of the 'victims' and 'degenerate' discourses, both historically and currently. First it is useful to locate the discussion within wider debates about the nature of White supremacy in contemporary capitalist societies.

INTERSECTIONALITY IN THEORY AND PRACTICE

Critical Race Theory and Class/Race/Gender Intersections

CRT is a radical interdisciplinary approach to studying and resisting racial oppression. Having begun in US law schools in the 1970s and 1980s, the approach moved into US educational studies in the mid-1990s and is now established as a growing and important strand in UK antiracist scholarship (Ladson-Billings and Tate 1995; Delgado and Stefancic 2001; Crenshaw 2002; Preston 2007; Gillborn 2008). CRT places an understanding of White racism and the experiential knowledge of people of colour at the heart of its approach. Not surprisingly, this perspective has drawn concerted attacks from both left and right. In the UK the most vociferous critics have been a small group of self-proclaimed Marxist writers[1] (e.g., Cole and Maisuria 2007; Hill 2008, 2009; Cole 2009) whose critique trades on a narrow and highly caricatured version of CRT (see Stovall 2006; Warmington 2009; Gillborn 2009, 2010). CRT's detractors frequently assert that the perspective '*homogenizes all white people together as being in positions of power and privilege*' (Cole 2009, 113, original emphasis). This is simply untrue: CRT does not imagine that all White people are uniformly racist and privileged. However, CRT *does* view all White-identified people as implicated in relations of racial domination: White people do not all behave in identical ways and they do not all draw similar benefits—but they *do* all benefit to some degree, whether they like it or not (see Gillborn 2008, 34). None of which is to say that CRT is a complete and flawless approach; there are many internal dialogues and debates. One of the most important areas of continued discussion concerns the question of *intersectionality*, that is, how multiple dimensions of oppression (such as race, gender, class, sexuality, disability) work relationally, sometimes in unison, sometimes in conflict, sometimes in uncertain and unpredictable ways (Gillborn and Ladson-Billings 2010). As Patricia Hill Collins suggests, within a 'matrix of domination':

> Cultural patterns of oppression are not only interrelated, but are bound together and influenced by the intersectional systems of society (Collins 2000, 42).

The notion of intersectionality is increasingly being embraced, especially by minoritized feminist writers (see Brah and Phoenix 2004).[2] However, it is important to recognise that to *claim* an intersectional analysis is not necessarily to *accomplish* it. Serious critical work on intersectionality requires us to do more than merely *cite* the difficulties and complexities of intersecting identities and oppressions; it challenges us to *detail* these complexities and account for *how* categories and inequalities intersect, through what processes, and with what impacts (see Gillborn and Youdell 2009). This chapter is an attempt to add to the ongoing project of intersectional CRT by examining the discursive construction of the White working class in media and political debate, to show how apparently contradictory discourses (projecting the White working class as alternatively victimized and degenerate) maintain White middle-class interests, silence and demonize minoritized groups and reinforce traditional gendered and racialized notions of respectability and belonging.

What About Poor White People?

> Academics writing about class often make light of the racial privilege of the white poor. They make it seem as though it is merely symbolic prestige . . . Race privilege has consistently offered poor whites the chance of living a better life in the midst of poverty than their black counterparts. (hooks 2000: 114–115)

Critical race scholars will instantly recognize the phrase 'What about poor White people?' (Allen 2009). This phrase, or some version of it, is almost always present when White people are faced with CRT's understanding of *White supremacy*. It is important to point out that CRT uses this term very differently from its general understanding. Whereas 'White supremacy' is commonly understood to refer to individuals and groups who engage in the crudest, most obvious acts of race hatred (such as extreme nationalists and neo-Nazis), in CRT the term refers instead to a regime of assumptions and practices that constantly privilege the interests of White people but are so deeply rooted that they appear *normal* to most people in the culture. The most important, hidden and pervasive form of White supremacy lies in the operation of forces that saturate the everyday mundane actions and policies that shape the world in the interests of White people (Delgado and Stefancic 2001). Many critical race scholars view White supremacy, understood in this way, as central to CRT in the same way that the notion of capitalism is to Marxist theory and patriarchy to feminism (Stovall 2006). However, many (in my experience *most*) White people (and indeed some of their minoritized peers) find it impossible—or at least, too uncomfortable—to comprehend CRT's view of White supremacy. Whether students in class or academics at conferences and in print, even self-avowed radicals often struggle to reconcile the existence of poor White people alongside a regime of White supremacy. As CRT scholar Ricky Lee Allen argues, such a perspective touches upon some key intraracial dynamics:

'What about poor White people?' . . . [implies] that privilege cannot be assigned to all members of a particular group because some members of that group, in this case poor Whites, are not privileged. Therefore, privilege must be considered at the level of the individual, not the group . . . It also signifies that poor and nonpoor Whites share a close bond: nonpoor Whites stand up for poor Whites when poor Whites are not around to represent themselves. (Allen 2009, 210)

Race and class interests intersect so that, under certain conditions, both middle-class and working-class Whites benefit from a shared White identity. Indeed, contrary to the arguments of some class theorists (who dismiss CRT as blind to the situation of poor Whites), we can see that the existence of poor White people is not only consistent with a regime of White supremacy; they are actually an essential part of the processes that sustain it. This chapter develops and exemplifies this analysis by examining the discursive construction of the British White working class at a specific point in space and time when White elite interests were under grave threat because of a crisis of capitalism that saw the near collapse of global banking, and related neoliberal assumptions, in late 2008.

Interest-convergence and the White Working Class

An exegesis of 'What about poor White people?' that is rooted in CRT assumes that texts created by Whites must be scrutinized for their political race implications. As Leonardo (2002) argues, it is crucial that we 'dismantle discourses of whiteness' by 'disrupting . . . and unsettling their codes' (p. 31). (Allen 2009, 213)

In this chapter I focus explicitly on two contrasting discourses that project important popular and policy versions of the British White working class. In so doing, I aim to respond to Allen and Leonardo's entreaties to help disrupt, unsettle and dismantle the codes by which White supremacy operates. Before I turn to the specific discourses themselves, however, I need to outline a CRT concept that is crucial to understanding how such apparently contradictory discourses can be understood as complementary in terms of their consequences for the regime of White supremacy.

One of the central concepts in CRT is known as the 'interest-convergence principle'; put simply, this view argues that advances in race equality only come about when White elites see the changes as in their own interests. It is important to note that interest-convergence does not envisage a rational and balanced negotiation between minoritized groups and White power holders, where change is achieved through the mere force of reason and logic. Rather, history suggests that advances in racial justice must be won through protest and mobilization, so that taking action against racism becomes the lesser of two evils for White interests because an even greater loss of privilege might be risked by failure to take action. Derrick Bell, who created the concept, has always been clear that lower-class White interests are likely to be the first to be sacrificed; indeed, Richard Delgado has described the interest-convergence principle as a theory that 'explains the twists and turns of blacks' fortunes in terms of the *class* interests of *elite* whites' (Delgado 2007, 345; emphasis added):

> Racial remedies may . . . be the outward manifestations of unspoken and perhaps subconscious judicial conclusions that the remedies, if granted, will secure, advance, or at least not harm societal interests deemed important by middle and upper class whites. (Bell 1980, 253)

Hence, the interest-convergence principle is centrally about an intersectional analysis of race/class interests. It views *non*elite Whites as a kind of buffer, or safety zone, that secures the interests of elite Whites, especially when challenged by high-profile race equality/civil rights campaigns. We can hypothesize that the same processes might also operate to sacrifice working-class interests where elite interests are threatened (even in the absence of gains for minoritized groups): Such a moment was presented by the global financial crisis of 2008.

VICTIMS: THE WHITE WORKING CLASS AS RACE VICTIMS

Late 2008 saw global capitalism in crisis. Governments in the global 'north' pumped billions into a banking system that stood on the verge of collapse and major multinationals went bankrupt. The economy dominated news coverage but was by no means the *only* story. On December 12, 2008, Britain's national daily newspapers echoed to the sound of White anger as newly published education statistics were quoted as showing that 'poor' and/or 'working-class' White boys were among the lowest achieving groups in public examinations at the end of their compulsory schooling. The following headlines are from national daily newspapers:

> Poor white boys fall behind (*Daily Express*, p. 31)
> Poor white boys fall behind again at GCSE (*Daily Mail*, p. 17)
> Poor white boys lagging at GCSE (*Daily Mirror*, p. 6)
> Poor white boys falling further behind at school (*Daily Telegraph*, p. 16)
> White boys on free meals fall further behind in GCSEs (*The Guardian*, pp. 20–21)
> Poor pupils fail to make the grade (*The Times*, p. 25)

December 2008 also saw a slew of headlines *attacking* poor Whites as a threatening and degenerate presence (see below). The headlines about White working-class educational failure repeated a line of argument that has become familiar in the UK whenever educational statistics are published. I examine this discourse of educational victimization in detail later in this section, but first it is useful to place the discourse within its historical context: the idea of the White working class as victims of a minoritized racial Other is by no means a new idea.

Whites as an Endangered Majority in Historic Policy Discourse

A common thread in British political discourse has been the view that White people in general, and the White working class in particular, are at risk because of the presence of minoritized 'racial' groups. An especially strong element in this discourse has been the argument that, regardless of the facts, if the working class *believe* themselves to be disadvantaged, then the threat of unrest alone requires action against the minoritized groups.[3]

This line of argument first came to prominence in the modern era following the postwar rise in migration into the UK by people in the so-called New Commonwealth, especially the Caribbean and the Indian subcontinent (India, Pakistan and Bangladesh). In 1958 Nottingham and London witnessed a series of disturbances characterized by White violence against Black and South Asian people.[4] In both cases the episodes escalated over a period of days and weeks, with large gangs of White youths, sometimes numbering a thousand or more, gathering to engage in armed attacks that included systematic assaults on the homes of Black people (Ramdin 1987, 204–210). In both cities the police were clear that the violence was started by Whites, sometimes sparked by the involvement of far right/fascist groups. Over the following months public and policy debate began to focus on what was termed 'the colour problem'. Politicians on both sides of the House of Commons sought to excuse the actions of the White youths and the view grew that 'The trouble makers . . . were shouting what others were whispering' (Ramdin 1987, 210). Quickly the logic of the debate swung to constitute the migrants (the victims of racist violence) as the *cause* of the problems and, therefore, as in need of greater control, leading ultimately to the imposition of harsh immigration controls targeted explicitly at Black and South Asian groups (Finney and Simpson 2009).

In the late 1970s, Margaret Thatcher (in)famously sounded a similar chord when she argued that the *perception* of a threat to White interests was the most important reason for further immigration controls:

> People are really rather afraid that this country might be swamped by people with a different culture . . . if there is a fear that it might be swamped, people are going to react and be rather hostile to those coming in. (quoted in Barker 1981, 15)

Thatcher was not the first female head of state to invoke the fear of racist action by White people as a legitimate reason for racist action by the state itself: More than five hundred years ago Elizabeth I issued a proclamation calling for the expulsion of 'Negroes and blackamoors . . . who are fostered and relieved here, to the great annoyance of her own liege people who want the relief which these people consume . . . ' (quoted in File and Power 1981, 6).

The long history of this discourse is testament to its enormous popular appeal. Typically this line of argument is used to promote both more restrictions on the number of migrants able to enter the UK in the future, and to justify greater surveillance and/or control of minoritized people already in the population. Although immigration and policing are, therefore, the most prominent areas where such debates take place, the field of education is also an important battleground. As Sally Tomlinson has documented (1977, 2008), in education the most common theme is a dominant emphasis on teaching the English language. In the 1960s the primacy of White interests and sensitivities was made explicit when the Education Department sought to ensure that no school should have more than one-third of its population made up of 'immigrants':

> *It will be helpful if the parents of non-immigrant children can see that practical measures have been taken to deal with the problems in their schools, and that the progress of their own children is not being restricted by the undue preoccupation of the teaching staff with the linguistic and other difficulties of immigrant children.' DES circular 7/65*[5]

This 'dispersal' policy left many children and young people especially vulnerable to racist attacks because they were kept as a small minority in schools, often having to travel considerable distances from home (see Dhondy 1982). Significantly, dispersal was again embraced as a policy tool, in the late 1990s, by a Labour government keen to placate popular racist sentiments about asylum seekers. Since the 9/11 attacks in 2001 and the London bombings of 2005, education policy has mirrored the changing policy environment more generally, with 'multiculturalism' being pronounced a failure and a renewed emphasis on English-language teaching (Gillborn 2008, ch. 4). The most high-profile and persistent discourse currently surrounding race and education in contemporary Britain projects an image of White working-class children as victims of ethnic diversity.

Victims in the Classroom: Race, Education and White 'Working-class' Boys

For more than a decade discussions of educational inequality in England have given a prominent role to the experiences and achievements of boys. A variety of studies have sought to quantify and understand the generally higher average achievements of girls at the age of sixteen. Feminist researchers have been especially critical of the way that boys are often viewed as a single homogenous group, ignoring key differences in social class and ethnic origin (Arnot et al. 1998; Youdell 2006; Archer and Francis 2007). Since the mid-2000s a particular focus of popular discourse (in radio, TV and newspaper coverage) has been White *working-class* boys. This is how the second-highest selling national newspaper reported official data on exam results in 2007:

White boys falling behind
White, working-class boys have the worst GCSE results

Just 24 per cent of disadvantaged white boys now leave school with five or more good GCSEs.

This compares with 33.7 per cent for black African boys from similar low-income households.

There were fears last night that the figures could hand votes to the far-Right British National Party [BNP] because additional funding is available to help children from ethnic minorities. (*Daily Mail*, 13 January 2007)

There is a great deal of ideological work going on here, even in so short a quotation. First, note the misleading assertion that 'additional funding is available to help children from ethnic minorities': In fact, local authorities and schools have to *bid* for dedicated funding towards minority education projects; any additional funds are not simply handed out, automatically privileging minoritized children, as the story seems to suggest. Second, the story argues that the results could fuel support for extreme political parties like the BNP. This repeats the familiar racist argument of previous decades (and centuries) when a perceived threat to White interests is used to discipline minority groups: by warning of the danger of inflaming support for racist parties, politicians and commentators to invoke the threat of racist violence as a means of re-centring White interests and rejecting calls for greater race equality. This can be seen clearly in the following quotation from the specialist educational press:

Cameron Watt, deputy director of the Centre for Social Justice . . . said: 'There's a political lobby highlighting the issue of underachievement among black boys, and quite rightly so, but I don't think there's a single project specifically for white working-class boys. I don't want to stir up racial hatred, but that is something that should be addressed.' (*Times Educational Supplement*, 12 January 2007)

It is important to recognise what is happening here. Official statistics reveal that most groups in poverty achieve relatively poor results *regardless* of ethnic background. As Figure 2.1 illustrates, the achievement gap between White students in poverty (using receipt of free school meals—FSM—as an indicator) and more affluent Whites (non-FSM) is more than *three times* bigger than the gaps between different ethnic groups who are equally disadvantaged: there is a 32 percentage point gap between N-FSM and FSM White boys, compared with a 9.7 percentage point gap between FSM White boys and the most successful of the Black FSM boys (categorized as Black African). And yet it is the race gap that is highlighted both in the *Daily Mail* story and in the *Times Educational Supplement*. It is significant that despite the larger income-related inequality, media commentators and policy advisers do not warn of an impending class war: They do not raise the spectre that failure on this scale will promote action against private schools or the 'gifted and talented' scheme, which receives millions of pounds of extra funding and is dominated by middle-class students (see Gillborn 2008). The *race* dimension is deliberately accentuated in the coverage.

The media image of failing White boys goes further than merely highlighting a difference in attainment; it includes the suggestion that White failure is somehow the *fault* of minoritized students and/or their advocates. This is implicit in the newspaper coverage (above) but was explicit in other parts of the media including, for example, an award-winning news and current-affairs programme.

Described as 'one of the success stories in the recent history of British broadcasting' (Tolson 2006, 94), *Radio 5Live* is a national radio channel run by the BBC. The BBC enjoys exceptionally high levels of public trust in relation to its news content, receiving more than five times the rating of its

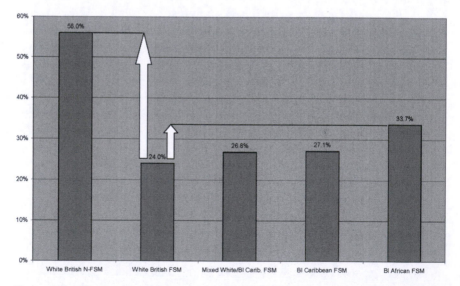

Figure 2.1   Five or more higher-grade (A*–C) GCSEs (any subject) boys by ethnic origin and free school meal status, England 2006.
Source: DfES (2006a): Table 32.

nearest rival (YouGov 2005). The BBC's news coverage is, therefore, highly significant; it is the most trusted news provider and caters to a national audience. In addition, the programme in question (Radio 5Live's *Breakfast Show*) is held in high regard professionally: It won the Sony Radio Academy Award for the Best News & Current Affairs Programme (Sony 2007). On June 22, 2007, the programme led its news bulletins with a story claiming that white 'working-class' boys were now the lowest-achieving group in English schools. At around 6 am, Nicky Campbell, one of the programme's two main hosts, interviewed a researcher who was introduced as having contributed to the study behind the headlines:[6]

Nicky Campbell: Isn't the problem that—the race relations industry has, some would argue, *compartmentalized* people. And if we had *less* concentration on race, more on *individuals*, we took colour out of the equation: it wouldn't be 'oh Black boys do this, white boys do that, Chinese boys do this, Asian'—it should just be looking at children *as individuals*. Isn't race part of the problem here in a sense?

Despite the host's suggestion that 'the race-relations industry' (a derogatory name for race-equality professionals that portrays them as living off, and possibly manufacturing, race conflict) is somehow culpable, the researcher responded that ethnicity is an important variable and should not be ignored. Nevertheless, Campbell returned to the same theme an hour later when he interviewed a London head teacher about the story:

Nicky Campbell: There's the inescapable conclusion, according to some of our listeners, a . . . a . . . and indeed according to some experts too, that the school system has been focusing *disproportionately* . . . *too much* on children from other ethnic backgrounds.

The host's analysis was now backed by the invocation of 'some of our listeners' and 'some [unnamed] experts too' but again the interviewee failed to support the idea. Undeterred by his guests' refusal to confirm the editorial line, at 8 am the same topic led the news headlines and was explored with new guests, including Professor Gus John (one of Britain's leading campaigners on race equality):

Nicky Campbell: 'Professor Gus John—'
Gus John: 'Good morning.'
Nicky Campbell: 'Some are saying that too much attention has been given to African and Caribbean boys to the *detriment* of young white boys.'
Gus John: 'Well the facts don't bear that out you see. An . . . and I think this discussion is pretty *distorted*, certainly as far as facts are concerned.'

The interviewee steadfastly rejected the proposal that White boys' low achievement was somehow the fault of Black students. But the damage was already done. Listeners and unnamed 'experts' had been cited to support the argument and its constant repetition made it a key aspect of the morning news broadcast. At 9 am the *Breakfast Show* was followed by an hour-long phone-in on educational failure and the presenter read out a familiar-sounding view:

> *Presenter:* [reading from listeners' text messages] 'Somebody else says, er, "White youngsters fail because PC [politically correct] teachers and the media are more interested in Black and Asian children".'

In this way the country's most trusted news service effectively promoted the view that White children are the *victims* of ethnic diversity in general and race equality in particular.

A tendency to present White people as race victims has been commented upon by writers in both the US (Delgado and Stefancic 1997; Apple 2001) and the UK (Preston 2007; Rollock 2007). The particular manifestation of White victimology in recent media analyses of examination performance is especially dangerous for several reasons. The discourse presents Whites as the victims of race-equality measures. Consequently, moves that have been inspired by a commitment to social justice become recast as if they represent a competitive threat to White people; social justice campaigns are thus redefined as a sectional (racialized, even racist) activity. Simultaneously, this refrain of racial competition has the effect of erasing from sight the possibility that members of *all* ethnic groups might excel in a single educational system. The prominence given to these arguments and the strategic citation of far-right groups (such as the BNP) has the clear effect of sounding a warning to everyone involved in education: *Make sure that White children are catered for—don't let race equality go too far.* The threatened price of de-centring White children is racial violence—both symbolic (in threats and insults) and physical (it is known, for example, that racist harassment often increases after prominent news stories on race issues).[7]

What goes unreported in the news coverage is that the statistics which dominate stories of White *working-class* failure actually relate to the *most disadvantaged fraction* of the working class: every one of the news stories cited above (in the newspapers and the radio coverage) relate exclusively to the attainments of children in receipt of free school meals (FSM). A good deal of educational research uses FSM as a crude measure of disadvantage, mainly because the information (which is routinely collected by schools) is easily accessed and analysed. But FSM does not equate to what most people imagine when they hear the phrase 'working class'. For example, the *Daily Mail* story (above) drew on official data where 13.2 per cent of all pupils were in receipt of free school meals (DfES 2006a: Table 32). And yet 57 per cent of UK adults described themselves as 'working class' in a recent survey by the National Centre for Social Research (BBC News Online 2007). The discursive slippage from 'free school meals' to 'working class' has the effect of inflating the significance of the data: Statistics on a relatively small group of students (13% of the cohort) are reported in a way that makes it appear descriptive of more than half the population (57%): a slippage that reoccurs even in broadsheet headlines:

> White working-class boys are the worst performers in school
> *Independent*, 22 June 2007

> Half school 'failures' are white working-class boys, says report
> *The Guardian*, 22 June 2007

The focus on pupils in receipt of free school meals has become increasingly pronounced in recent years. The media's exclusive use of the FSM statistics reflects the way that the data are presented by the Education Department itself. In 2006, for example, the department published a 104-page digest of statistics on race and education (DfES 2006b). Amid the nineteen tables and forty-eight illustrations, the document focuses a good deal on the significance of FSM and, for example, includes *three* separate illustrations detailing different breakdowns of exam attainment among FSM students (DfES 2006b, 65–68): In contrast there is not a single table or illustration giving a separate breakdown for non-FSM students. This absence is highly significant because the image of White students as relative underachievers cannot be sustained when the focus moves to the 86.8 per cent of the school population who do not receive FSM. In the official data that supplied the basis for the *Daily Mail* story, for example, White British students who do not receive free meals are more likely to attain five higher grade passes than their counterparts of the same gender in several minoritized groups— including those of Black Caribbean, 'Mixed (White/Black Caribbean)', Pakistani, Black African and Bangladeshi heritage. Clearly, race inequality of the more familiar variety (where minoritized students achieve less well) remains a key characteristic of the English education system and affects students of *both* genders.[8] The largest inequalities relate to Black Caribbean N-FSM students, where girls are 9.7 percentage points less likely to achieve the benchmark than their White N-FSM peers and the difference for boys is 17.2 percentage points.

An exclusive focus on FSM students, therefore, has the effect of erasing from sight the very significant inequalities of achievement that remain for most minoritized groups (N-FSM). In addition, the FSM statistics provide the basis for media and political commentators to repeat a view of White 'working-class' boys as a racially victimized group who need urgent attention for fear of generating support for extreme racist political causes. Those arguing for greater race equality in education find themselves rendered silent by a discourse that rewrites reality; if White children are racial victims, then moves to address race inequity for minoritized groups are not only redundant but dangerous. Antiracist and multicultural education initiatives are positioned as a problem, their funding threatened, and a new focus on White students is promoted. This focus is now reflected in policy debates and promoted via numerous special initiatives. In 2009, for example, a parliamentary debate on '*White Disadvantaged Pupils*' was told by a Birmingham MP that:

> White pupils are the largest underachieving group in Birmingham and across the UK. . . . If we stop talking about proportions and start talking about real numbers, the picture is even more disturbing. Why? Because quite simply there are a lot of white pupils. (*Hansard* 19 May 2009: Column 397WH).

In reply, the government spokesperson agreed on the importance of highlighting White students in need and, just two years since Cameron Watt lamented the absence of White-focused projects, they listed several initiatives aimed exclusively at them:

> I agree that we need to acknowledge the problem of underachievement among white children from disadvantaged backgrounds and to make the issue more visible at national and local level . . . examples of good practice in supporting disadvantaged communities are included in the "Breaking the link" document, in the recent Ofsted report "White boys from low-income backgrounds: good practice in schools" and in the National College for School Leadership publication "Successful leadership for promoting the achievement of white working class pupils". (*Hansard*, 19 May 2009: Column 401 WH–402WH)

DEGENERATE: THE WHITE WORKING CLASS AS THREATENING OTHER

Part of the enormous power of Whiteness comes from a façade of apparent obviousness and naturalness which hides a reality of complex and shifting political identifications. History offers numerous examples of groups (such as the Irish and Jews in the US) who have 'become' White, not in the sense that their biological skin tone (or any other phenotypical marker) has changed but in the sense that they have been welcomed within the White camp by the White elite that defines and polices the borders of Whiteworld (Ignatiev 1995; Bonnett 1997; Brodkin Sacks 1997). Similarly, the White poor have long existed on the boundaries of Whiteness, what Ricky Lee Allen (2009, 214) terms 'White but not quite'.

In this part of the chapter I trace both the historic and contemporary manifestations of discourses that project an image of White working-class people as a potentially threatening, deviant—even degenerate—presence. At first sight this might seem to be entirely at odds with the discursive projection of the White working class as victims (above). However, just as the White middle class benefit from the individualised perspective and denial of race-equality claims that is engendered by the *victim* discourse, so too the White middle class benefit from the *degenerate* discourse which promotes docile, hardworking visions of a compliant ('respectable') working class in opposition to the supposedly deviant ('undeserving') poor.

Respectability and the White Working Class in History

No single definition of social class enjoys universal agreement: Raymond Williams traces the emergence of the 'modern' use of the term to the industrial revolution of the late eighteenth and early nineteenth centuries (Williams 1983, 61). Although the term is used a great deal in social research, there are multiple competing definitions. Nevertheless, official statistics testify to the significance of 'class' in relation to what Michael Apple (2001, 63) calls the 'gritty materialities' of life. For example, in the UK people in the lowest income levels are less likely to attend high-achieving schools, more likely to die as infants and more likely to experience all major forms of crime (from burglary to physical violence) (ONS 2008). The lack of a single clear definition of social class signals its fundamental quality as a discursively constructed and regulated phenomenon:

> Class is a discursive, historically specific-construction, a product of middle-class political consolidation, which includes elements of fantasy and projection. (Skeggs 1997, 5)

These constructions have very real impacts on the ways in which people think of themselves (and Others) and constrain the range of policy directions that are considered possible/desirable. As Beverley Skeggs notes, these 'representations . . . are not straightforwardly reproduced but are resisted and transfigured in their daily enactment' (1997: 6). One of the most important elements in providing a critical understanding of how class is defined discursively at different historic moments is to understand how such representations serve the perceived interests of middle-class people. Skeggs (1997, 42–49) shows how the regulation of women's bodies and attitudes was central to Victorian discourses that sought to distinguish between '*respectable*' working-class folk on one hand and, on the other hand, the '*undeserving*' poor. Both Finch (1993) and McClintock (1995) have explored the gendered and racialized elements that were powerfully at work in the development of the Victorian cult of domesticity which defined the 'respectable' working class as sexually restrained, hardworking and docile insofar as they accepted their role in servicing their supposed middle-class 'betters'. By presenting the alternative as morally bankrupt, questions of *structural oppression* and conflict were discursively erased and replaced with questions of *personal responsibility*:

> Respectability was closely tied to the domestic ideal—a standard imposed from a very different social positioning—which was promoted as a way of displaying difference from women who were positioned as pathological, polluting and poisonous . . . By transferring the debate from one of revolutionary threat onto questions of familial and moral responsibility the structural and social relations of class could conveniently be ignored and attention could be shifted onto specific aspects of working class organization (Skeggs 1997, 13, 43–44).

Writing in the late 1990s, at a time when middle-class interests were well served by credit-fuelled capitalism, Skeggs documents a 'retreat' from class-based discourses as politicians focused on an individualized understanding of the world, where class no longer mattered and individual effort was celebrated as the key to success (thereby encouraging all to buy into the boom). In late 2008, however, as world banking came to the brink of total financial meltdown, the British press began a frenzied attack on what it described as a form of 'underclass'. Once again, middle-class interests were well served; the working class was subjected to disciplinary discourses of respectability that shifted blame for the harsh economic situation away from a crisis in capitalism and focused instead on the supposed moral and economic cost of undeserving, lazy and feral working-class people.

Feral, Feckless and Promiscuous: The Uncertain Whiteness of the White Working Class[9]

In December 2008, two criminal prosecutions dominated the national news agenda and became the platform for a sustained attack on a section of the working class who were portrayed as welfare-dependent, dangerous and criminal.[10] The first case concerned Karen Matthews, a thirty-three-year-old woman from the north of England, who was jailed for eight years for her part in the faked kidnapping of her nine-year-old daughter Shannon. Shannon had been reported missing on 19 February 2008, sparking a major police investigation and generating spontaneous searches of neighbouring areas by up to two hundred members of the local community desperate to help find the missing girl (BBC News Online 2008a). Shannon was discovered alive twenty-four days later in the flat of Michael Donovan, a relative of Shannon's stepfather. The 'abduction' had been staged by Donovan and Karen Matthews in the hope of generating money. Chemical analysis revealed that Shannon had been given sedatives over a prolonged period, possibly to make her less demanding of attention during breaks from school (BBC News Online 2008a). Much of the press coverage focused on Karen as a welfare-dependent, immoral and abusive mother. The most important aspect, however, was not the portrayal of Matthews as an individual but as a symbol of a presumed 'underclass' threatening the very fabric of economic and social order:

> Karen Matthews is the personification of that terrifying growing phenomenon: a feckless, amoral, workshy, benefit-dependent underclass. All this woman has done with her life is make money out of her children. She's had seven children by five or six fathers (she's lost count) because to her, children mean cash. (Platell 2008)

The second case concerned 'Baby P'—the court pseudonym given to a seventeen-month-old boy who died after months of vicious abuse at the hands of his mother, her partner and a male lodger. After the trio were jailed, more details were released into the media and it emerged that the child had died despite being on the 'at-risk' register and having sixty contacts with police, health and social-work professionals over the last eight months of his life (BBC TV 2008). Baby P's killers were jailed while the Matthews prosecution was still in court and press coverage initially focused on the mismanagement of the case by the child-protection services. However, when Karen Matthews's verdict was announced (just over three weeks after Baby P's killers were jailed), the case reemerged in the news media and was frequently cited as further evidence of the threat posed by a growing immoral and cruel underclass.

The dominant discourses surrounding these cases replicate the familiar historic tropes of attacks on the social dangers posed by working-class people. Sexual promiscuity, laziness and criminality were all present as the police, media and politicians scrambled to proclaim their disgust not merely at the two individual cases but at what they asserted was a growing national presence. An especially important element in the development of the story was the repeated assertion that these two extraordinary cases were, in fact, merely the tip of an iceberg of depravity.

The rush to cite Matthews as a symptom of a wider social problem was started by the police officer in charge of the investigation. In a TV programme charting the case, and aired to coincide with the court's verdict, the chief constable of West Yorkshire, Norman Bettison, stated that Matthews lived 'without the sense of having to answer for the consequences of her actions':

> 'They aren't socialised in the way that society is generally socialised in terms of norms of behaviour.' He said their normal standard of behaviour was 'whatever they could get away with'. Mr Bettison added: 'You see flotsam and jetsam drifting in, people who are sort of feckless and

sort of ambitionless coming in and plonking themselves down on the sofa, having a can of beer.' (BBC News Online 2008b)

Significantly, in a language that directly echoes Victorian distinctions between 'respectable' (hardworking, disciplined, compliant) and 'undeserving' poor, Bettison appears keen to distinguish between such 'feckless' and 'ambitionless' folk and 'good people' whose ambition marks them out for praise:

'There are good people bringing up kids as you and I would recognise is a right way to bring up kids,' Mr Bettison said . . . 'Being poor, does not make people bad. I've been in many poor households where children are brought up wonderfully well and given, right from birth, the idea of right and wrong. And given the hope and ambition to strive.' But he said that a dependence on benefits was partly to blame for Matthews' behaviour. 'The more kids you have, the more welfare you get, the less opportunity there is to contribute to society and to the economy and the less you need to,' he said. (BBC News Online 2008b)

Bettison's comments on welfare dependency were gleefully repeated and extended by the right-wing press. In its editorial column, the *Daily Mail* explicitly combined the two cases as evidence of an 'ever-growing subculture':

On council estates, children who have never known their fathers are being brought up in an ever-growing subculture of neglect, violence, drugs, pornography, crime and unemployment. Consider that brutal, filthy, feckless woman Karen Matthews, churning out seven children by six fathers and subjecting her daughter Shannon to years of abuse before kidnapping her in the hope of cash for more drink and drugs. The more children she had, the more money she got from the state. Consider the couldn't-care-less mother of Baby P, who allowed her child to be tortured to death for the gratification of a sub-human yob with whom she happened to be sleeping. (*Daily Mail* 2008)

Predictably the women in the cases are singled out for special attention, with open revulsion at a woman 'churning out' children following sex with different men. This became a key issue—an unquestionable mark of deviance—a fact so powerful that it often featured in *headlines* as if the mere fact alone was disgusting:

Shannon's mother and seven babies by six men (Platell 2008)

Seven children, six fathers (and a ring from Argos): lazy, sex-mad Karen Matthews symbolises broken Britain (Brooke 2008)

The *Daily Mail*'s editorial continued in this vein but extended the attack to blame the supposed 'subculture' for virtually every social ill, neatly removing structural inequalities and systems of raced and classed oppression from the scene:

> Behind the overwhelming majority of cases of child abuse, crime, educational failure, drug addiction and teenage pregnancy lies a pattern of wantonly irresponsible parents and broken homes . . . far from rescuing children from the feral underclass, too often our welfare system traps them in it for life. The tax and benefits system offers no inducements to responsible behaviour. On the contrary, it rewards fecklessness and promiscuity, while penalising married couples. (*Daily Mail* 2008)

And so it was that two extraordinary cases became the platform for the construction of a moral panic asserting the dangers posed by a growing 'underclass' whose personal lack of responsibility and effort were asserted as the cause of 'educational failure' (among other things) and where the obvious solution is to reform tax laws (benefitting the middle class) and reduce social assistance (disciplining the working class). This theme was taken up by numerous right-wing commentators, including Melanie Phillips, who added an attack on feminism to the trope of a welfare-fuelled underclass. Describing child benefit as 'the seminal link [sic] between man-hating feminism and welfare dependency', she argued that:

> By providing welfare payments for women on the birth of every child, regardless of whether or not they were married, it [child benefit] became the biggest single incentive for lone parenthood . . . it is clear that child benefit, and all the multifarious other welfare incentives to irresponsibility, are intrinsically linked to the emergence of households where, in truth, civilisation has given way to barbarism. (Phillips 2008)

It is worth remembering that this 'biggest single incentive for lone parenthood' currently stands at £20 per week for the first/only child and falls to £13.20 a week for each subsequent child—hardly a passport to financial security. Once again the disciplinary tropes of 'respectable' versus 'undeserving' are mobilized against working-class women (especially those who dare to be unmarried and have children). Significantly, Phillips still found space mid-rant to acknowledge the existence of *some* respectability even among lone parents:

> Such [feral] children are concentrated in housing estates where two-thirds of households are occupied by lone parents and—notwithstanding those who do a heroic job single-handedly raising their children properly and lovingly—where children are many times more likely to suffer abuse as a result. (Phillips 2008)

The 'notwithstanding' caveat is so brief as to barely interrupt the flow of invective but its presence is important because it maintains the vital argument that this attack is not on working-class people per se, but merely on deviant (unambitious, unmarried, unemployed) working-class people. Indeed, the frequent use of the term 'underclass' offers a neat discursive trick to those whose bile might be taken personally by their readers—after all, as I noted earlier, more than half the UK population consider themselves 'working class'. Writing in the best-selling (Murdoch-controlled) newspaper *The Sun*, John Gaunt was at pains to repeat the centuries-old distinctions:

> Whole estates are infested by this underclass. They are not working class—the clue is in the title—they don't and won't work. They have no pride in their homes or areas. They have no respect for themselves, let alone their neighbours or children. They have a moral code that would make an alley cat blush. They have a lawyer's expert knowledge of their rights but, sadly, no idea of their responsibilities to their kids or society in general. This is an underclass . . . these people aren't equal to you and me, and they need to be told so before they are allowed to breed another generation that will only be more irresponsible and useless. (Gaunt 2008)

All the hallmarks of the historic respectable/undeserving discourse are present: the respectable working class contribute to society (they have pride and a moral code) whereas the undeserving merely take (they know their rights and claim benefit). Gaunt also managed to include a particular national and racial inflection to his views. Although the guilty parties in both the Matthews and Baby P cases were White people,[11] he went on to include 'new arrivals' among those who must no longer burden 'the decent majority of Brits':

> Only those who have paid into the system through NI [National Insurance] or tax contributions should be allowed to claim anything out of the pot. If this were applied, it would soon rule out junkies, new arrivals or people like Karen Matthews. . . . These people have chosen a life of benefit dependency because they have been allowed to do so. *Never before, with the world in economic crisis, has there been such a need for urgent reform.* With hard-working people facing the prospect of losing their homes and their savings, I don't see why the decent majority of Brits should shoulder the responsibility of the bone idle any longer. (Gaunt 2008, emphasis added)

Gaunt's reference to a 'world in economic crisis' is telling; attacking poor White people (alongside 'new arrivals') identifies a useful scapegoat at a time when White middle-class interests are directly threatened.

Politicians were no less ready to seize the initiative and use the cases to promote their own—already existing—policies. David Cameron, leader of the (then opposition) Conservative Party, used the Matthews case to simultaneously present every person in receipt of a state benefit as a potential 'Karen Matthews' while also repeating his party's education proposals. In an article entitled '*There are 5 million people on benefits in Britain. How do we stop them turning into Karen Matthews?*' he stated:

> The verdict last week on Karen Matthews and her vile accomplice is also a verdict on our broken society. The details are damning. A fragmented family held together by drink, drugs and deception. An estate where decency fights a losing battle against degradation and despair. A community whose pillars are crime, unemployment and addiction. . . . Another challenge is reforming our schools. . . . Turning this around won't happen overnight—it needs long-term change. Not just tougher discipline and stronger standards, but radical reform. That's why we're planning 1,000 new academies with real freedoms, and why we'll allow people with a passion for education to set up their own schools. (Cameron 2008)

The facts contradict both Cameron's analysis *and* his solution: the 'community whose pillars are crime, unemployment and addiction' provided a clear picture of a close-knit and generous spirit when more than two hundred locals spontaneously organized searches for the missing child. Similarly, the academies that Cameron sees as a panacea are known to accept a shrinking proportion of FSM children—precisely the group he expects them to reform (PriceWaterhouseCoopers 2006, 9). Academies also exclude students at twice the rate of other maintained schools, including a disproportionately high number of Black young people (Gillborn and Drew 2010).

The Labour Party (which was then in government) also sought to use the prevailing mood as a chance to push ahead with its chosen policies, not least by introducing tougher rules on benefit eligibility by arguing that, in the words of a minister, 'virtually everyone has to do something in return for their benefits' (BBC Online 2008c). Part of these changes, a new sickness-benefit test, raised the threshold for people with disabilities to qualify for additional support. The following year initial figures, leaked to the press, suggested that the previous pattern (where around 65 per cent of applicants were approved) had been reversed, with 'more than two thirds of applicants . . . being rejected' (Barker 2009).

It is clear, therefore, that police, right-wing commentators and politicians (from both main parties) each indulged in a contemporary version of the centuries-old disciplinary discourse of 'respectable' working class versus 'undeserving' poor. The flexibility of the discourse, its lack of precision, is one of its strengths. Hence, even in the midst of the most vitriolic of attacks, there was frequently a caveat noting the existence of a respectable section of the working class. But the caveats are vague and shifting in a world where the negative class signifiers encompass an increasingly large proportion of the 'working class' and where *any* welfare benefit can become a sign of deficit. In the summer of 2009, for example, another right-wing national newspaper, the *Daily Express*, ran the following front page headline:

SHAMELESS: *60% of council house tenants don't pay rent* (Hall 2009)

The story pressed all the familiar rhetorical buttons, describing 'a benefits-dependent underclass' enjoying a 'massive benefits handout' which 'is costing hard-working middle-income families a total of £10 billion a year' (Hall 2009, 1). Hence, everyone in receipt of housing benefit (including disabled people and low-paid workers) is implicated in a parasitic underclass. The underclass/undeserving label is a sliding signifier which serves a disciplinary purpose. It is not a simple descriptor of any single class fraction (with or without jobs); it is a tool whereby any proportion of the working class can potentially find themselves Othered.

The *Daily Express* story (above) also highlights the fact that the degenerate discourse was not generated by the Karen Matthews/'Baby P' cases but rather used them as convenient hate figureheads. The degenerate discourse has a centuries-old track record and its latest iteration has continued to be deployed as a new Conservative–Liberal Democrat coalition government seeks to impose the biggest cuts in state spending since the Second World War. In an article for the *Daily Mail*, for example, the government's leading advisor on addressing poverty lamented the loss of a culture of 'respectability' and 'dignity' that had resulted in 'what I call 'toe-rag parents'' who haven't got a clue how to raise children, and delegate the role of breadwinner to the social security system' (Field 2010).[12] The story's Web page carries a picture of a young White woman, with four small tattoos on her arm, holding a young child: Its caption reads 'Vicious downward spiral: Bad parents can only lead to more feckless offspring' (ibid.).

CONCLUSIONS

Historically there is ample evidence to show that the bodies of the British urban poor were regularly compared with African natives of Empire in terms of physique, stature, posture, facial mannerisms, intelligence, habits, attitudes and disposition . . . The designation of the British working classes as white is then a *modern* phenomenon. (Nayak 2009, 28, 29).

The constitution of the White working class is a much more fluid and complex matter than is usually recognized. In this chapter I argue that critical race theory offers important insights into the present construction and deployment of the White working class in popular and political discourse. In late 2008, as global capitalism reeled from an international banking crisis unlike anything experienced since the Great Depression of the 1930s, it seemed as though neoliberalism had been dealt a catastrophic blow. And yet, within the British media, apparently contrasting discourses focused on the White working class as by turns victims and deviants. At one moment White working-class pupils (especially boys) were victims of political correctness, the forgotten backbone of a country that needed special attention if they were not to be 'left behind' and driven into the arms of fascism. The next moment these same children were 'being dragged up in a life of grime that leads to a life of crime' (Gaunt 2008), their parents (especially their mothers) vilified as welfare-dependent, immoral scroungers who breed for money and live without ambition or effort. These discourses are superficially very different but their effects are powerful and flow in a unified direction:

- *White middle class normality is celebrated*: The White middle class is assumed to represent the normal, moral core of society providing economic and social leadership despite the burden of lesser groups.
- *Anti-minority*: Statistical slippage between a small group (13% in receipt of free school meals) and the majority (who self-define as 'working class') provides the basis for a rejection of race equality policies in education while resources are focused on the newly underachieving 'White' group. Race-equality issues are not simply marginalised; they are erased from the policy agenda.
- *Anti-immigration*: A romanticized picture of the respectable working class, pushed towards far-right sympathies as they see 'their' country alter around them, blames immigration for changing Britain, lowering standards and multiplying the burden on 'the decent majority of Brits' (Gaunt 2008).
- *Patriarchal assumptions are re-centred*: Both the 'victims' and 'degenerate' discourses are highly gendered. The first places male achievement at the top of the education policy agenda whereas the second repeats centuries-old disciplinary tropes that focus on the regulation of women's labour and sexuality.
- *A neoliberal worldview is reasserted as economically and morally essential*: Emphasis on personal responsibility and respectability positions state aid as corrupting and dangerous. 'Good people', we are told, work hard and have ambition; inequality is therefore due to personal (often moral) failings not structural matters of class, race, gender and disability.

The CRT concept of interest-convergence is useful here because it helps explain the operation of these victim/degenerate discourses that seem at one level to split the White group and yet, ultimately, they help secure White supremacy overall. For the *White middle classes* the benefits are clear and unambiguous; the resurgent neoliberalism of personal responsibility and individual effort means that their privilege merely reflects their greater merit; race inequality is erased from the policy agenda; and moves to cut welfare payments promise tax breaks in the future. The benefits for the *White working class* are more mixed but, on balance, remain clear: They may face a tougher time qualifying for benefits but they know that their interests will be secure against those of minoritized groups because the solidarity of the White middle classes ensures that the spectre of racial violence (both symbolic and real) will be mobilized if, for example, their educational or employment prospects dip below those of key (especially Black) minoritized groups. In addition, this group can always console themselves that they are part of the respectable class fraction rather than the degenerate section.

For *minoritized racial groups*, the consequences of the discourses are also clear: educational policy and practice becomes even more aggressively White-focused (including special programmes exclusively targeting White students) and social welfare cuts will have a disproportionately negative impact on minoritized groups (because a higher proportion of Black children live in single -parent households, often with carers holding down several low-paid jobs). Although the 'degenerate' discourse trades on images of the *White* working class, therefore, the policy impacts will likely hit minoritized groups the hardest.

In conclusion, an intersectional analysis reveals that far from ignoring social class inequalities, CRT provides an important lens for understanding the shifting and sometimes contradictory discourses that might seem to show Whites fundamentally divided along class lines while actually strengthening White supremacy. The White working class are beneficiaries of Whiteness (seen clearly in the 'victims' discourse) but also at times in a liminal position, where they can be demonized when necessary or useful: 'White but not quite' (Allen 2009, 214), they provide a buffer, a safety zone that protects the White middle classes.

ACKNOWLEDGEMENTS

An earlier version of this chapter appeared in the *British Journal of Educational Studies* 58 (1): 3–25. My thanks to James Arthur for permission to reuse the piece and for his help and encouragement throughout the writing process. I also wish to thank the following colleagues for their insightful comments on earlier versions of the analysis: Michael Apple, Alice Bradbury, Richard Delgado, Charles Mills, Nicola Rollock, Carol Vincent, Deborah Youdell and Terezia Zorić.

NOTES

1. It has been argued that Marx himself demonstrated considerably more complexity than is sometimes evident in work done by those who claim his legacy (Leonardo 2009; Mills 2009).
2. I use the term 'minoritized' in preference to the more usual 'minority ethnic' because the former draws attention to the social processes by which particular groups are defined as lesser or outside the mainstream.
3. It is significant, of course, that racist logic dictates that action be taken against the minoritized groups rather than the majority group that is threatening unrest.
4. By 'Black' I mean those people who would most likely self-identify according to this term: In the UK presently that usually includes people with family origins in Black Africa and/or the Caribbean.
5. Quoted in Swann (1985, 194; original emphasis).
6. All quotations from *Radio 5 Live* are my own verbatim transcriptions from an audio recording of the programmes. I use standard transcription notations:
   . . . denotes that speech has been edited out;
   italicized text denotes that the speaker stressed this word/phrase;
7. 'Officers in the Race and Violent Crime Task Force . . . were shocked to discover a direct relationship between political rhetoric, such as Tory leader William Hague's "foreign land" speech, and an increase on attacks on asylum-seekers' (Ahmed and Bright 2001, 1). The British playwright, novelist and film director Hanif Kureishi recalls similar reactions on the street and in school when he was a child (Kureishi 1992, 3–10).
8. Students of Chinese and Indian ethnic heritage are the only principal minoritized groups who are *more* likely to achieve five higher grade passes than their White N-FSM peers: For a detailed account of these groups and an analysis of racism within their school experiences, see Gillborn (2008, ch. 7).
9. Feral, feckless and promiscuous are labels attached in a single comment piece in the *Daily Mail* (2008).
10. I want to make clear that I am not, in any way, questioning the seriousness of the horrific crimes that were committed by the imprisoned adults in these cases. Rather, my concern is to examine the wider 'degenerate' discourse that was built upon these two exceptional cases.
11. It is symptomatic of how Whiteness is created and sustained that, although the media's chosen 'underclass' hate figures were White, the 'underclass' itself was never referred to in racial tones: Whiteness can be invoked as an all-encompassing *victim* identity but not a universalizing *negative* one.
12. The *Oxford English Dictionary* defines toe-rag as 'a tramp or vagrant; a despicable or worthless person'.

REFERENCES

Ahmed, Kamal, and Martin Bright. 2001. Labour failing to meet pledges on race. *The Observer*, April 22, p. 1.

Allen, Ricky Lee. 2009. What about poor White people? In *Handbook of social justice in education* , ed. William Ayers, Therese Quinn and David Stovall, 209–230. New York: Routledge.

Apple, Michael W. 1992. Do the standards go far enough? *Journal for Research in Mathematics Education* 23 (5): 412–431.

———. 2001. *Educating the 'right' way.* New York: RoutledgeFalmer.

Archer, Louise, and Becky Francis. 2007. *Understanding minority ethnic achievement*. London: Routledge.

Arnot, Madeleine, John Gray, Mary James, and Jean Rudduck, with Gerard Duveen. 1998. *Recent research on gender and educational performance*. London: The Stationery Office.

Barker, Martin. 1981. *The new racism*. London: Junction Books.

Barker, Alex. 2009. New test raises bar for sickness benefits. *Financial Times*, July 13, p. 1.

BBC News Online. 2007. What is working class? http://news.bbc.co.uk/1/hi/magazine/6295743.stm (accessed 7 September 2007).

———. 2008a. Shannon Matthews timeline. http://news.bbc.co.uk/1/hi/uk/773 3586.stm (accessed 24 October 2009).

———. 2008b. Simple motive of 'filthy lucre.' http://news.bbc.co.uk/1/hi/england/west_yorkshire/7765176.stm (accessed 24 October 2009).

———. 2008c. Benefit claimants 'must do more.' http://news.bbc.co.uk/1/hi/uk_politics/7775361.stm (accessed 24 October 2009).

BBC TV. 2008. Panorama: What happened to Baby P? http://news.bbc.co.uk/1/hi/programmes/panorama/7732125.stm (accessed 3 October 2009).

Bell, Derrick. 1980. Brown v. Board of Education and the interest-convergence dilemma. *Harvard Law Review* 93: 518–533.

Bonnett, Alastair. 1997. Constructions of whiteness in European and American anti-racism. In *Debating cultural hybridity: Multi-cultural identities and the politics of anti-racism*, ed. Pnina Werbner and Tariq Modood, 173–192. London: Zed Books.

Brah, Avtar, and Ann Phoenix 2004. Ain't I a woman? Revisiting intersectionality. *Journal of International Women's Studies* 5 (3): 75–86.

Brodkin Sacks, Karen. 1997. How did Jews become White folks? In *Critical White studies*. Ed. Richard Delgado and Jean Stefancic, 395–401. Philadelphia: Temple University Press.

Brooke, Chris. 2008. Seven children, six fathers (and a ring from Argos): Lazy, sex-mad Karen Matthews symbolises broken Britain, *Mail Online*, http://www.dailymail.co.uk/news/article-1092012/Seven-children-fathers-ring-Argos—Lazy-sex-mad-Karen-Matthews-symbolises-broken-Britain.html (accessed 22 October 2009).

Cameron, David. 2008. There are 5 million people on benefits in Britain. How do we stop them turning into Karen Matthews? *Mail Online*, http://www.dailymail.co.uk/news/article-1092588/DAVID-CAMERON-There-5-million-people-benefits-Britain-How-stop-turning-this.html (accessed 28 October 2009).

Cole, Mike. 2009. The color-line and the class struggle. *Power and Education* 1 (1): 111–124.

Cole, Mike, and Alpesh Maisuria. 2007. 'Shut the f*** up', 'you have no rights here': Critical race theory and racialisation in post-7/7 racist Britain. *Journal for Critical Education Policy Studies* 5(1), http://www.jceps.com/?pageID=article&articleID=85 (accessed 4 June 2007).

Collins, Patricia Hill. 2000. *Black feminist thought*. 2nd ed. New York: Routledge.

Crenshaw, Kimberlé Williams. 2002. The first decade. *UCLA Law Review* 49: 1343–1372.

Daily Mail. 2007. White boys falling behind. January 13.

———. 2008. Plea for the victims of welfare Britain, http://www.dailymail.co.uk/news/article-1092390/MAIL-COMMENT-Plea-victims-welfare-Britain.html (accessed 26 October 2009).

Davis, Kathy. 2008. Intersectionality as buzzword: A sociology of science perspective on what makes a feminist theory successful. *Feminist Theory* 9 (1): 67–85.

Delgado, Richard. 2007. *The law unbound! A Richard Delgado reader*. Ed. Adrien Katherine Wing and Jean Stefancic. Boulder, Co: Paradigm Publishers.

Delgado, Richard, and Jean Stefancic, eds. 1997. *Critical White studies.* Philadelphia: Temple University Press.
———. *Critical Race Theory.* 2001. New York: New York University Press.
Department for Education and Skills (DfES). 2006a. *National Curriculum Assessment, GCSE and equivalent attainment and post-16 attainment by pupil characteristics in England 2005/06 (provisional).* SFR 46/2006, London: DfES.
———. 2006b. *Ethnicity and education: The evidence on minority ethnic pupils aged 5–16.* Research topic paper: 2006 edition. London: DfES.
Dhondy, Farrukh. 1982. Who's afraid of ghetto schools?, in *The black explosion in British schools* ed. Farrukh Dhondy, Barbara Beese and Leila Hassan, 36–42. London: Race Today Publications.
Field, Frank. 2010. The biggest crisis facing Britain? Too many parents don't have a clue how to raise children. *Daily Mail,* August 10, http://www.dailymail.co.uk/debate/article-1301747/Britains-biggest-crisis-Too-parents-dont-know-raise-children.html (accessed 7 September 2010).
File, Nigel, and Chris Power. 1981. *Black settlers in Britain 1555–1958.* London: Heinemann.
Finch, Lynette.1993. *The classing gaze: Sexuality, class and surveillance.* St Leonards, NSW: Allen & Unwin.
Finney, Nissa, and Ludi Simpson. 2009. *Sleepwalking to segregation?* Bristol, UK: Policy Press.
Gaunt, Jon. 2008. More Shannons in Benefits R Us hell. *The Sun,* December 5, http://www.thesun.co.uk/sol/homepage/news/columnists/john_gaunt/article2006202.ece (accessed 24 October 2009).
Gillborn, David. 2008. *Racism and education: Coincidence or conspiracy?* London: Routledge.
———. 2009. Who's afraid of critical race theory in education? *Power and Education* 1(1): 125–131.
———. 2010. Full of sound and fury, signifying nothing? A reply to Dave Hill's 'Race and class and in Britain: A critique of the statistical basis for critical race theory in Britain'. *Journal for Critical Education Policy Studies* 8 (1): 78–107, http://www.jceps.com/?pageID=article&articleID=177.
Gillborn, David, and David Drew,. 2010. Academy Exclusions. *Runnymede Bulletin* 362 (Summer): 12–13.
Gillborn, David, and Gloria Ladson-Billings. 2010. Critical Race Theory. In *International Encyclopedia of Education,* ed. Penelope Peterson, Eva Baker and Barry McGaw, Vol. 6: 341–347. Oxford: Elsevier.
Gillborn, David, and Deborah Youdell. 2009. Critical perspectives on race and schooling. In *The Routledge international companion to multicultural education,* ed. James A. Banks, 173–185. New York: Routledge.
Hall, Macer. 2009. SHAMELESS: 60% of council house tenants don't pay rent. *Daily Express,* August 19, p. 1.
Hill, Dave. 2008. A Marxist critique of culturalist/idealist analyses of 'race', caste and class. *Radical Notes,* http://radicalnotes.com/index2.php?option=com_content&do_pdf=1&id=68 (accessed 24 October 2009).
———. 2009. Race and class in Britain: A critique of the statistical basis for Critical Race Theory in Britain and some political implications. *Journal for Critical Education Policy Studies* 7(2): 1–40, http://www.jceps.com/?pageID=article&articleID=159.
hooks, bell. 2000. *Where we stand: Class matters.* New York: Routledge.
Ignatiev, Noel. 1995. *How the Irish became White.* New York: Routledge.
Kureishi, Hanif. 1992. The Rainbow Sign. In *London kills me: Three screenplays and four essays.* New York: Penguin Books.

Ladson-Billings, Gloria, and William F. Tate. 1995. Toward a critical race theory of education. *Teachers College Record* 97 (1): 47–68.

Leonardo, Zeus. 2002. The Souls of White folk: Critical pedagogy, whiteness studies, and globalization discourse. *Race Ethnicity & Education* 5 (1): 29–50.

———. 2009. *Race, whiteness, and education.* New York: Routledge.

McClintock, Anne. 1995. *Imperial leather.* London: Routledge.

Mills, Charles, W. 2009. Critical Race Theory: A reply to Mike Cole. *Ethnicities* 9(2): 270–281.

Nayak, Anoop. 2009. Beyond the pale: Chavs, youth and social class. In *Who cares about the white working class?* Ed. Kjartan P. Sveinsson, 28–35. London: Runnymede Trust.

Office for National Statistics. 2008. *Social Trends* 38. Basingstoke, UK: Palgrave Macmillan.

Oxford English Dictionary Compact Edition. 1989. 2nd ed. Oxford: Clarendon Press.

Phillips, Melanie. 2008. Shannon's mother, a crude culture of greed and why we must abolish child benefit." *Daily Mail*, December 8, http://www.dailymail.co.uk/news/article-1092740/Shannons-mother-culture-greed-abolish-child-benefit.html (accessed 26 October 2009).

Platell, Amanda. 2008. Shannon's mother and seven babies by six men. *Daily Mail*, December 6, http://www.dailymail.co.uk/news/article-1092401/AMANDA-PLATELL-Shannon-8217-s-mother-seven-babies-men.html#ixzz0Ug3A9d5B (accessed 24 October 2009).

Preston, John. 2007. *Whiteness and class in education*, Dordrecht, Netherlands: Springer.

PriceWaterhouseCoopers. 2006. *Academies evaluation: 3rd annual report.* London: DfES.

Ramdin, Ron. 1987. *The making of the Black working class in Britain.* Aldershot, UK: Wildwood House.

Rollock, Nicola. 2007. *Failure by any other name?* London: Runnymede Trust.

Skeggs, Beverley. 1997. *Formations of class & gender.* London: Sage.

Sony Radio Academy Awards. 2007. The News & Current Affairs Programme Award, http://www.radioawards.org/winners/?awid=74&awname=The+News+%26+Current+Affairs+Programme+Award&year=2007 (accessed 7 September 2010).

Stovall, David. 2006. Forging community in race and class: Critical race theory and the quest for social justice in education. *Race Ethnicity & Education* 9(3): 243–259.

Swann, Lord. 1985. *Education for all: Final report of the Committee of Inquiry into the Education of Children from Ethnic Minority Groups.* Cmnd 9453. London: HMSO.

Tolson, Andrew. 2006. *Media talk.* Edinburgh: Edinburgh University Press.

Tomlinson, Sally. 1977. Race and education in Britain 1960–77. *Sage Race Relations Abstracts* 2(4): 3–33.

———. 2008. *Race and education: Policy and politics in Britain.* Maidenhead, UK: Open University Press.

Warmington, Paul. 2009. Some of my best friends are Marxists: CRT, labour, culture and the 'figured worlds' of race. C-SAP Critical Race Theory Conference, Institute of Education, London.

Williams, Raymond. 1983. *Keywords.* London: Fontana.

Youdell, Deborah. 2006. *Impossible bodies, impossible selves: Exclusions and student subjectivities.* Dordrecht, Netherlands: Springer.

YouGov. 2005. *Press Gazette* poll: The most trusted news brands. London: YouGov.

3 Interrogating Pigmentocracy

The Intersections of Race and Social Class in the Primary Education of Afro-Trinidadian Boys

Ravi Rampersad

ABSTRACT

Pigmentocracy is understood as an intertwining structuring of society based on race and social class, where lightness is afforded with a higher level of capital; in a sense, the higher up in society you go the lighter the skin colour. It is argued that the colonial history of Trinidad and its continuing legacy facilitated the evolution of an education system which embodies this sense of pigmentocracy. The result is the constitution of the dual system of prestige versus stereotyped government schools. This chapter aims to engage with the operationalisation of this symbiotic structuring of race and class in terms of access and achievement of Afro-Trinidadian primary boys in the dual system. In so doing, the legal concept of the property value of whiteness as adapted in Critical Race Theory (CRT) in education is employed. It is noted that CRT was developed in engaging with issues of race and racism in a North American and White majoritarian context. However, it is argued that the inherent flexibility of both CRT and concepts of the property value of whiteness allows for its adaptation to the postcolonial and non-White majority context of Trinidad.

The study proceeds through analysis of qualitative data collected at two primary schools in Trinidad over the course of one school term. The schools were chosen to represent opposite ends of the achievement differential; a major concern was to avoid the traditional focus solely on failing Black boys in favour of a comparative approach. Subsequently, one school is associated with the 'whiter' and 'lighter' middle and upper class and is highly regarded as a centre of excellence; and the other, linked with the 'darker' working class, is stereotyped as a pathological place of failure. The data reveal how pigmentocracy is manifested, embodied and sustained through human agency in shaping the quality and quantity of education in different socially situated schools of the dual system.

INTRODUCTION

Trinidad is part of the twin island republic of Trinidad and Tobago; the focus on Trinidad owes to a difference in colonial history, racial composition and racialized engagement in Trinidadian society as compared to Tobago (see Meighoo 2003). Equally, this study marks a challenge to the simplistic and pathological constructions of Black failure symbolised in the labelling of Afro-Trinidadian boys as the lowest academic achievers.

The Context of Race in Trinidadian Discourse

It is pertinent to firstly establish a context of how race and skin colour are portrayed and consumed in popular discourse, enabling a more nuanced appreciation of the dynamics and machinations of pigmentocracy. Bonilla-Silva and Dietrich (2008, 152) suggest that countries in the Americas, such as Trinidad, follow an 'ostrich approach' to racial matters, 'that is, they all stick their heads deep into the social ground and say, we don't have races here. We don't have racism here.' Lowenthal (1967, 580), in his seminal piece on race and colour in the West Indies, similarly asserts that

> central to this image is the notion that West Indians enjoy harmony and practice tolerance among manifold races, colors, and creeds. In the outside world, Caribbean race relations are often termed exemplary. Local governments industriously promote this impression to attract foreign investments, to emphasize social progress, and to vaunt their achievements. Guyana, once the "Land of Six Peoples," now proclaims it is "One People, One Nation"; Trinidad's coat of arms reads "Together We Aspire, Together We Achieve," and the ruling party's slogan is, "All o' we is one"; Jamaica proclaims "Out of Many, One People."

In Trinidad, anecdotally, proof of either harmonious race relations or the marginality of race altogether is touted in the relatively high number of people of mixed race (Khan 1993), accounting for just under 15 per cent of all households (Central Statistical Office 2003). These views on race arguably contribute to the dearth in literature and the lack of open dialogue on race in Trinidad and the Caribbean (Coppin 1997; Bonilla-Silva and Dietrich 2008). Consequently, this perspective empowers a dynamic which accuses those that raise issues of race as being themselves racist rabble-rousers.

Defining Pigmentocracy

Pigmentocracy is a 'system that privileges the lighter skinned over the darker-skinned people within a community of color', affording greater social opportunities (Hunter 2002, 176). Pigmentocracy should not be viewed as an independent racialized process, but one that is intimately interwoven with class and other structures of domination. Thus in the context of Trinidad, middle- and upper-class status are concomitantly associated with whiteness and lightness in a measure making the terms interchangeable. Hunter (2008, 65), in reference to pigmentocracy in the US, suggests that

> skin color is not an equal opportunity discriminator. In fact, on all major socioeconomic indicators, such as income, occupation, education, and housing, dark-skinned Blacks and Latinos (and increasingly Asians) pay a steep price for their tone. When measuring money and resources, light-skinned people of color are consistently advantaged.

In interrogating the intersections of race and class in education, this chapter firstly attempts to establish historical context for the discussion. It is argued that the role and legacy of colonialism are crucial in the constitution of pigmentocracy and its manifestation in education as the dual system of prestige versus stereotyped government schools. Secondly, the article continues in elucidating the overarching theoretical framework, one based on an adaptation of Critical Race Theory (CRT) in education to a non-White postcolonial context. Following this, there is a brief discussion of the research study in Trinidad. Data were collected at two primary schools representative of the extremes of the dual system: St. George's Boys and Pinehill Boys Government. The data collected were analyzed through a reformulation of Harris's (1993) CRT-framed concept of the property value of whiteness revealing the operationalisation of pigmentocracy in the Trinidadian education system.

Colonialism and Pigmentocracy

A major facet of slavery and the colonial system was the embedding of colour consciousness. Skin colour, while not the only marker of somatic image, took on great significance in the social ordering of society. Johnson (2004, 62) argues that

> in the Caribbean and Latin America, caste systems were loose enough to provide mobility between the groups directly above and below one, but functioned to keep most dark-skinned Africans from entering middling or elite society.

In attempting to control the masses, the colonial White elite used skin colour as a commodity of social capital, thereby affording lighter skinned non-Whites more opportunities. This facilitated the evolution of a racialized class structure from one based on *absolute* categories to the modern pigmentocratic manifestation.

Similarly, Fanon (1967, 14) argues that 'the colonized is elevated above his jungle status in proportion to his adoption of the mother country's cultural standards. He becomes white as he renounces his blackness, his jungle.' This concept of White supremacy is emphasised by Trinidadian social theorist C. L. R. James, writing that

> there are the nearly whites hanging on tooth and nail to the fringes of white society, and these . . . hate contact with the darker skin far more than some of the broader minded whites. Then there are the browns, intermediates, who cannot by any stretch of the imagination pass as white, but who will not go one inch towards mixing with people darker than themselves. (James 1932, 15)

Equally, colonialism's 'end' did not mark the final chapter of whiteness and its dominance (López 2005) in the Caribbean, but rather its reformulation in response to the new demographic reality. Arguably, over time White supremacy in the Caribbean would come to reflect a privileging of whiteness and increasingly lightness.

The Rise of the Dual System

Under British dominion, education was envisaged as an imperialist tool for social control over the darker-skinned masses (Brock 1982; London 2002; Bacchus 2005). A two-tiered school system was constructed to provide separate education for Whites and non-Whites, thereby ensuring that the dual system was racialized from the outset.

Trinidadian independence in 1962 did not significantly alter the nature of the dual system and it operates today as a structure of polar opposites. Firstly there are the prestige schools, typically denominationally managed and widely regarded as centres of excellence and the platform for entering the professions and corporate Trinidad (Campbell 1997). The other type of school is state run and pejoratively referred to as government. This carries a stigma of delinquency and underachievement and exacts a heavy burden on graduates with a collective weight of low expectations.

Whereas a Black-governed Trinidad could not appear to privilege whiteness in education, the intersections of race and class in the form of pigmentocracy meant that racialized outcomes in education could be scripted by references to class and individual diligence. Accordingly, the postcolonial movement of non-Whites into a numerical majority in prestige education can be taken as a sign of a nonracialized even playing field. However, it is argued that this movement was pigmentocratically structured, where White and lighter-skinned groups have been able to secure and maintain disproportionate access to prestige schools (Jules 1994). The Jules (1994) report confirms this pigmentocratic divide in access to prestige schools, highlighting statistical overrepresentation of Whites, Chinese and Syrians (groups disproportionately represented in the upper classes) and underrepresentation of the co-majority groups of Afro and Indo-Trinidadians. At the same rate, attendance in government schools appears to be indicative of the working class and decidedly Afro and Indo-Trinidadian based (Jules 1994).

The Theoretical Framework: The Intersections of Property and Race in Education

In understanding how the system of pigmentocracy operationalises the intersections of race and class in education, the legal concept of the property value of whiteness as adapted in Critical Race Theory (CRT) discourse in education is employed. Harris (1993, 1709) contends that in the US 'whiteness, initially constructed as a form of racial identity, evolved into a form of property'. Property is constructed more along the lines of a status and psychological asset that accompanies whiteness and which only Whites can fully possess and benefit from.

It is asserted that CRT, despite being of American design in analysis of a White majoritarian society, is flexible enough to be applied to a post-colonial non-White country such as Trinidad. For instance, in support of an adapted use of the property value of whiteness, Harris (1993, 1714) suggests that there is an inherent fluidity due to the dictates of historical process, adding that

> after legalized segregation was overturned, whiteness as property evolved into a more modern form through the law's ratification of the settled expectations of relative white privilege as a legitimate and natural baseline.

This statement is important for the application of this concept to the context of Trinidad. Historically, the facilitated rise during colonialism of a light-skinned buffer middle class against the Afro and Indo-Trinidadian masses (Brereton 1979) necessitated the early blurring of the property value of whiteness and its expansion into a system that not only valued and socially rewarded whiteness but now also lightness (Hunter 2008).

In understanding the impact of the intersections of property and race on education in the US, Ladson-Billings and Tate (2006) adapt Harris's work. The themes they adapt from Harris's (1993, 1731) exposé on the property functions of whiteness include: *the rights of disposition, rights to use and enjoyment, reputation and status property* and *the absolute right to exclude*. Adjusting for the historical and contemporary context of the property value of whiteness and lightness in Trinidad, these themes are applied in understanding the pigmentocratic structure of the dual system of schools.

THE STUDY—A TALE OF TWO SCHOOLS

St. George's Boys, a state-assisted denominational managed institution, is a high-achieving school with a lineage of achievement that spans many decades and is publicly perceived as a centre of excellence. Its competitive nature is evident in a system of streaming into three achievement brackets: A, B and C. As a matter of routine, students from the school place among the nation's top achievers at the SEA (Secondary Entrance Assessment). It is located in a quiet and fairly affluent suburb of the capital city. The stability, academic achievement, teacher quality and legacy of the school attract many parents, from middle- and upper-class professionals to civil servants.

Alternatively, there is Pinehill Boys Government, a fully state-funded and -managed school, situated physically and psychologically in the heart of the Pinehill area. The area is socioeconomically depressed; high unemployment, youth delinquency, drug abuse and violent crime are plaguing issues. Pinehill Boys receives students from the surrounding community and rarely any from outside of the area. Parents most often send their children to this school because of the convenience and reduced financial burden of enrolling their children in a school within walking distance and not because of its academic standing. The principal, Mrs. Watts, sums up the situation of Afro-Trinidadian boys and achievement at Pinehill:

> Academically they are not where I would like them to be, alright . . . it is just a minute bit, just about say. . . . I would say about ten percent of the school population would be at the level we would like them to be.

Methods

The research design called for a qualitative approach. In a sense, this owes to the CRT dictate of amplifying and centring the voice of the minoritised, which has been traditionally marginalised and deemed illegitimate. With this, data were collected at both schools over the course of one term using a trio of methods; observation, group discussions and interviews. The research participants included the standard four Afro-Trinidadian boys (typically 8 to 10 years old), their teachers, head teachers and parents. In both schools the boys were organised into three groups (A, B, C) of three to six boys each based on achievement within the school. By analysing differential achievement in both schools, the pathological pitfall of focusing solely on failing boys is avoided (Dei et al. 1997; Codjoe 2001, 2006).

Arranging and maintaining access and cooperation was quite straightforward because the administration in both schools signalled a willingness to facilitate research into the achievement of Afro-Trinidadian boys, a topic which held the public's gaze for many years. However, Mrs. Watts, the principal of Pinehill, iterated that discussing race was largely a 'no go' area for many people and that I should tread very carefully, reinforcing this author's perspective that race is an 'absent presence' (Tomlinson 2008) in Trinidad. As such, educational issues faced by Afro-Trinidadian boys were not deemed racialized, but subsumed under colour-blind discourses on gender, culture and family. This presented ethical issues in engaging with racialized issues with participants. To this I attempted to be sensitive to the mind-set of participants and also to provide frank and honest information about the study through leaflets.

THE RIGHTS OF DISPOSITION

In a legal sense, property rights are generally understood as alienable, that is, transferable, initially making it difficult to envisage whiteness as property (Harris 1993, 1731). However, Harris (1993) stresses that the alienability of certain property is limited, without diminishing its status as property. For instance, in the context of divorce, professional degrees held by one party and financed by the other are considered marital property and are subject to valuation by the court (Harris 1993). Thus Harris (1993, 1733) argues that

> a medical or law degree is not alienable either in the market or by voluntary transfer. Nevertheless, it is included as property when dissolving a legal relationship.

Decuir-Gunby (2006, 102) stresses this paradoxical point, suggesting that the transferability of whiteness facilitates its transmission from one generation of Whites to the next; in so doing, this actually ensures the inalienability of whiteness, essentially precluding it beyond bodies socially constructed as White. This disposition is inherently a status-protecting mechanism which constructs certain behaviours and patterns as indicative of White (Ogbu 2004) or lighter-skinned upper-class groups, packaging it as normative and ideal, while portraying 'otherness' as its antithesis. This thereby ensures the transference of these rights, privileges and advantages to the next generation of these groups and not to those constructed as 'other'.

The Family and Achievement

In Trinidad the nuclear family is heralded as a core determinant of achievement. What is crucial is how achievement becomes associated in a linear manner with the nuclear family and the middle and upper classes and thus whiteness and lightness. This construction of the nuclear family as beneficial and possessive of normative and heteronormative values is necessarily linked with another construction, the stereotyping of the single-mother home. Single-mother homes are typically labelled working class (Chant 2009) and thus perceived as endemic and pathological in darker-skin bodies and ultimately an indicator of underachievement.

This was emphasised in my discussions with Mr. Baptiste, an Afro-Trinidadian with many years of experience in the teaching service; he is currently the teacher of the C class at St. George's. Mr. Baptiste related his experiences at a government school in Laventille, a working-class area of North Trinidad, infamous for its violent crime. Teaching in Laventille exposed him to certain social issues, he explained: 'Many of those homes don't have both parents. . . . lack of fathers in the home'.

He goes on to add that in Laventille,

> a lot of them don't see their mom . . . ummh . . . if they had a father, they had somebody to fall back on to show them their homework, assist them . . . because the mom holding down two and three jobs, so that social fabric is broken up.

As far as instilling discipline, he believes that

> the father would be the one to ummh . . . be firm, so some of them you recognise they come into the classroom setting and they don't have that authority level there.

With this, Mr. Baptiste begins to create an image of single-mother homes reminiscent of deficit-thinking models (Valencia 1997) and contrary to heteronormative values. He pathologises this family type as lacking male role models, discipline and direction for children and where the parent has little direct involvement in their children's education (see Chevannes 1999; Parry 2004; Reynolds 2009).

The way in which achievement becomes linked with the nuclear family appears more obvious when Mr. Baptiste discusses the difference between the A, B and C classes at St. George's. He reflected that Afro-Trinidadian boys do exceedingly well at his school, particularly the A and B classes. In comparison, he admitted that his C class traditionally did less well. He also pointed out that the majority of the A and B classes come from the middle and upper classes, whereas the figure was much less for his C class—implying that many or most of his class is from the working class. When I enquired as to his opinions on why he thought these achievement patterns existed, he asserted the 'level of parental involvement' was directly related to how well a student performed. Despite admitting there were exceptions, he stressed that 'the majority of them who are successful have both parents, so the institution is alive'.

Consequently, it is understood, without Mr. Baptiste explicitly stating it, that he believed the below-par performance of his C class, much like boys at schools in areas such as Laventille, is linked to the working-class and single-mother homes, whereas success is tied into the values and patterns evident in the nuclear family and the middle and upper classes. This perspective was supported by the principal of St. George's, an Afro-Trinidadian, Mrs. Marsh.

Concomitantly, these ideas are corroborated with data collected at Pinehill. For instance, the principal Mrs. Watts, also an Afro-Trinidadian, confirms the predictive pattern of single-mother homes as normative of the working class, insisting that

> most of the children in this school come from single parent families or the extended . . . there are very few children who come from the nuclear family.

She also engages in latent stereotyping of single mothers where she asserts in connection to achievement and parental roles at Pinehill that 'some people are just downright lazy . . . they just lie down in their bed until whatever time'.

Mrs. Watts's point is qualified by her recollection that despite growing up in a 'rough' neighbourhood she and her siblings were shepherded towards academic and professional success by diligent hardworking parents, once again alluding to the benefits of the nuclear family.

Altogether, these statements reflect the structural manifestations of the intersections of race and social class; it is important to bear in mind that in a pigmentocracy social class and skin colour are relatively transposable. In this case, educational success is equated with the nuclear family concurrently with middle- and upper-class status; this is seen as the normative and moral baseline. Consequently, this view would render academic achievement as equally connected to white and light skin colour, whereas underachievement becomes associated with single-female-headed homes, the working class and ultimately darker skin. As such, as this racialized construction is consumed, embodied and enacted by various social actors, it reveals a perception of superiority and preference for things constructed as white and light.

Rights to Use and Enjoyment

> As whiteness is simultaneously an aspect of identity and a property interest, it is something that can be both experienced and deployed as a resource. (Harris 1993, 1734)

In education this functionality of whiteness and lightness essentially allows for a greater use or access to higher quality educative resources. In Trinidad, this is seen on two levels in the school system: through the exclusivity of private international schools and in the dual system.

Private International Schools—Worlds Apart

This exclusivity is exemplified in the case of the International School of Port of Spain, a school which offers the American curriculum and charges fees that only expatriates and the local upper class can afford (see http://www.isps.edu.tt/Fees.aspx). The fee structure ensures that the student population would be majority White and less so lighter skin non-White. The benefits of enrolment include: a high teacher-to-student ratio and small class sizes, a well-equipped and staffed library, onsite student counsellors, a dedicated computer lab and a dynamic sports programme (source: http://www.isps.edu. tt/Welcome.aspx). When this is compared to Pinehill and even St George's (a solidly middle-class school), the differences are significant. For instance, at St. George's teachers are routinely asked to conduct classes of over forty students crowded into small classrooms. Neither school has a fully functioning library or computer lab, much less a trained librarian or information-technology specialist on staff. Student support and counselling is another area of deficiency at both schools. Mrs. Watts at Pinehill laments the problems faced in accessing quality counselling services for her students, who are often exposed to guns, violence and drugs, stressing that,

> thank God I was exposed to a bit of counselling and I often have to take up that role when needed. . . . Ok, well last week and this week . . . I actually had to counsel two boys, there was one, his brother was killed and another his uncle or cousin.

The Dual System and Quality Differential

With the dual system the difference in facilities and material resources between schools is not always evident. This is the case with Pinehill and St. George's. However, with these two schools there is a marked difference in the quality and commitment of teachers and ultimately curriculum delivery. With the lineage and status of a school such as St. George's, a significantly higher level of staff retention is almost ensured; conversely, the stereotyping of the Pinehill community, school and its students guarantees a higher teacher turnover. As a result, according to Mrs. Watts, many of the potentially useful programmes implemented at Pinehill tended to 'fall apart due to high staff turnover'. She believed that a Ministry of Education practice of posting teachers from distant areas, particularly young inexperienced teachers, led to their high attrition rate. Mrs. Watts added that this was compounded by deficient teacher training in areas of social and community issues, which arise in areas like Pinehill. Arguably, the combination of these two factors contributes to the relatively lower quality and commitment of teachers at Pinehill compared to St. George's. For example, at Pinehill, first-time teacher Mr. Gopaul, an Indo-Trinidadian, conveyed that he usually takes two to three hours (on uncomfortable public transport) to get to work. Mrs. Watts further explains,

> by the time they come here . . . especially as today's nice and cool, but on a hot day, by the time they get here they're tired . . . low productivity and then you're focusing on what time am I getting home in the afternoon.

This helps to provide context in understanding the frustration and aggressiveness Mr. Gopaul displayed in his pedagogical approach. Consequently, Mr. Gopaul suggested that Pinehill held no future for him beyond accruing experience and financial resources to facilitate a career move.

Conversely, at St. George's teachers would have actively applied for a post at the school, signifying a willingness and ambition to work at this particular institution. The teachers tended to be comparatively more experienced and committed, their pedagogical skills being honed through years of teaching at other primary schools, often in areas such as Pinehill. It was observed that the general approach to their classes was supportive, nurturing and based on dialogue, particularly Mr. Baptiste. For instance, students were not chided for wrong or delayed answers as in Mr. Gopaul's class or told 'just shut up and sit down' in Ms. John's class at Pinehill.

This section does not argue that skin colour has a direct impact on education, as it would in an apartheid-type system. Rather, skin colour can be said to operate indirectly on education through cumulative effects on a student's ability to access quality education, in the form of international or prestige schools. Equally, attendance at these schools is connected to income, social class and residential patterns reflective of middle- and upper-class families (Jules 1994; Campbell 1997), patterns pigmentocratically associated with lighter skin colour (Hall 2008).

Reputation and Status Property

Decuir-Gunby (2006, 104) argues that construction and maintenance of the identity and status of whiteness 'as superior requires blackness as its inferior opposite'. Ladson-Billings and Tate (2006, 23) write of the US that

> in the case of schooling, to identify a school or program as non-white in any way is to diminish its reputation or status.

Accordingly, this section looks at how status and reputation are achieved and maintained in the pigmentocratic process and how they are manifested in human agency; that is, in sustaining either the superior image of whiteness and lightness or the much maligned constructions of blackness or darkness. To this end, two areas are examined: firstly, the significance of a school's location and its subsequent ascription of pigmentocratic status. Secondly, the weight of expectations looks at the way in which stakeholders consume and embody the pigmentocratic discourse resulting in differential expectations of communities, schools and students.

The Significance of Location

In explaining how status becomes imbued and sustained in a school, one can start at location. The location of a school in a particular community confers a level of status and thus expectations of those in attendance. For instance, St. George's is situated in a quiet suburban district, which was originally settled by the White colonial elite. Despite postcolonial demographic change, the area remains firmly middle class, mostly non-White. Accordingly, the school shoulders a collective weight of an area historically identified as White and lighter skinned, colonial, middle and upper class, and thus steeped in societal success, status and power. Alternatively, for many, Pinehill, a school firmly entrenched in the working class, mirrors a community in the throes of socioeconomic stagnation. As a community, Pinehill has traditionally been identified as Black and working class and thus appears to suffer perceptually from this association with blackness; this leads to a general stereotyping of the community and everything within it, including schools and students, as delinquent, pathological and other.

The Weight of Expectations

The location of a school in itself cannot reinforce status and expectation; this must come from human agency as stakeholders act upon their expectations of these schools and environments. A comment by a mother at Pinehill, based on her son's account of a teacher, illustrates this point. She lamented that

> now you teaching a class . . . you have a CD on . . . you have it in your ears and you playing gangsta music and 50 cents music, it loud and the children singing along with it . . . now tell me if that make any sense as a teacher.

Arguably, this teacher's behaviour is symptomatic of his level of expectation of the community, school and students. Additionally, this parent's view is subsumed within an overall negative image and expectation of teachers and the quality of the school.

Mr. Gopaul at Pinehill provides another useful example of how status and reputation impact expectations. Even though Mr. Gopaul was new to the school, he appeared to have formulated an approach to the boys and the school in general premised on low expectations of the community on the whole. Conversations with him revealed an outlook which stereotyped the community and the boys as displaying anti-school attitudes. This deficit thinking situated failure evident in the community in cultural traits believed to value education as secondary (Valencia 1997). Subsequently, he perceived Pinehill to be a 'party' area, saying that

> this is a fêting area no doubt about it . . . if a car passes outside playing music, they'll stop and start to dance.

He goes on to convey that

it is very, very difficult to get them to concentrate, all it needs is one person to start singing one song or start doing some ridiculousness, some total idiot and the entire class will just follow and for me to bring back . . . to get them away from that, very, very difficult, because this is the society they grow up in, is all about society and this society does not show them that academics is worthwhile . . . everything here is a party and a jam.

With this subscription to deficit thinking, Mr. Gopaul holds little hope for the future of many boys in his class, an attitude that filters into his teaching and the learning experience of the boys. He believes that a minority will progress onto prestige secondary schools and the majority onto low-achieving government schools. He suggested that he had 'at least five prospects for lifelong centres, persons who can't read or write'. This fatalistic perspective appeared to both reflect and reinforce an overall school ethos of failure and low expectations.

On the other hand, the status and reputation inherent at St. George's is manifested in a different range of expectations, mostly positive. Mr. Baptiste's level of expectation is measured in his views on the potential of the A and B class compared to his C class. His overall view of the school and students is ultimately shaped by the prestige and status imbedded in social constructions of race and class as they are played out in the school. He constructs a praiseworthy image of the A and B classes as representative of the White and lighter middle and upper classes and normative familial and cultural patterns. Conversely, pathology appears implicit in his social constructions of the C class as socially positioned more towards the Black and darker working class.

I believe Mr. Baptiste's pathological perspective is not incompatible with his supportive pedagogical approach because his opinions did not foster a pessimistic or lax approach. Rather, his perspective appeared to act as a motivator in counterbalancing the social issues perceived to be endemic in the families and communities of his C class. One such issue was emphasised in his habit of calling his students 'son' in the classroom. His belief in the lack of father figures and male role models seemed to underpin his strategy in adopting a position as a surrogate father figure; this allowed him to construct a supportive and nurturing environment.

It is seen that the reputation and status of whiteness and lightness in education is connected to the perception of the school's classed and raced identity within the pigmentocratic continuum, which in turn shapes attitudes and expectations towards those in attendance. Mrs. Marsh, the principal of St. George's, highlights how a school may protect its prestige and status. She disclosed that in one year group, seven boys out of approximately one hundred were forced to repeat because they failed to achieve the required grade. What is of interest is the remedial measures instituted; she stated that we were able to pull these seven boys out and place them in a class by themselves; we didn't fit them back into the mainstream classes where they could work at their own pace and where they could get specialised attention.

In the same discussion, she relates the problems of teacher shortages precipitated by the high demand for the school and burgeoning student numbers. As such, allocating seven boys their own classroom and teacher appears paradoxical, perhaps alluding to another less altruistic aim. Arguably, in maintaining the school's status and reputation as high achieving and prestigious, this strategy could have two goals; firstly, it could be designed to raise the achievement of these boys and thus prevent any potential damage to the school's reputation. Secondly, it could be regarded as a form of academic quarantine. By isolating these boys as a contaminant, it removes the potential for 'infection', especially for the A and B classes, thus helping to preserve their achievement record and the school's status.

The Absolute Right to Exclude

Harris (1993, 1736) argues that

> the right to exclude was the central principle, too, of whiteness as identity, for mainly whiteness has been characterized, not by an inherent unifying characteristic, but by the exclusion of others deemed to be "not white."

The historical unfolding of the absolute right to exclude in Trinidad actually follows a similar three-phase pattern to that of the US (see Ladson-Billings and Tate 2006). Firstly, during slavery, education and literacy were largely deemed dangerous and forbidden in most cases for fear of the slave's critical construction of his subordinated status as morally, spiritually and legally wrong.

The ending of slavery led to the second exclusionary phase with the creation of separate schooling for Whites and non-Whites, in Trinidad referred to as the dual system. Education devoted to the White elite in both Trinidad and the US was oriented towards status quo maintenance. This restricted the newly emancipated and non-White immigrant masses to low-quality and terminal educational services structured more towards ensuring their docility and compliance (Bacchus 1994, 2005). Relatively speaking, this second phase began the process where certain schools, created based on exclusivity, became identified with whiteness and lightness and concomitantly the middle and upper classes. However, it is important to note that this structure was only possible with the simultaneous construction of 'otherness' or darkness in opposition to the normative ideal in education, where 'other' schools were unduly saddled with low expectations of the darker-skinned masses.

With the third exclusionary phase, it is seen that despite the removal of legal racial restrictions, schooling has remained largely segregated, but now by choice. Arguably, this choice by White and lighter parents in the middle and upper classes stems from the overall property value in their whiteness and the relative low property value of blackness or otherness. Hence the mixing of whiteness and blackness in schools would devalue the worth and experience of education for Whites and the lighter skinned. In Trinidad these sentiments may not be conveyed directly in such a manner, but perhaps more along the lines of a class-based argument. Again, in Trinidad the intimately interwoven nature of race, skin colour and class would make such an argument equally a raced one.

Ladson-Billings and Tate (2006) also highlight that this absolute right to exclude exists within schools via the system of tracking or streaming, which through institutional and social barriers ensures that non-Whites are disproportionately barred from 'gifted' programs and courses. CRT views the permanence of racism in its ability to hide in plain sight (Taylor 2009); that is, through an outward portrayal of a society's social structure as colour-blind, masking the everyday privilege that accompanies whiteness as normative and mainstream (Bell 1992).

As schools are legally desegregated, maintaining racial exclusivity is difficult beyond residential patterns and zoning; this is not always practical given the small size of Trinidad. Once more it is asserted that the racial exclusivity of Trinidadian schools is equated with class exclusivity. So how does a school enforce this racial and classed exclusivity without appearing to be racist? The answer may be 'streaming', as is the practiced at St. George's; this contradicts claims of meritocracy. For instance, if the C class according to Mr. Baptiste and Mrs. Marsh is understood as reflecting the working class and all its social issues, then this class is inherently constructed by them as Black, darker and 'other' in comparison to the A and B classes viewed as coming from more normative and ideal backgrounds. Thus in an education sense, the prestige, status and expectation that are attached to students from a White or lighter middle- or upper-class background reinforces the dictate whereby their intermixing with 'others' will in effect dilute their progress. Subsequently, this aspect of racial and class exclusivity remains in systems of streaming as it becomes subsumed into the daily consciousness of the population as an example of meritocracy at work and in no way construed as a racialized outcome.

CONCLUSION

In the Caribbean, the relative failure of boys is constructed more as a concern of gender, particularly associated with socialisation and not linked with socio-historically mediated racialized structures. Arguably this discourse is owed to a postcolonial mentality whereby the ascension of peoples of colour into the corridors of political power is seen as an end to the 'reach' of whiteness, something constructed as only evident in White bodies (López 2005). Whereas it is indeed recognized that many Afro-Trinidadian boys are performing poorly (see Jules 1994), it is traditionally viewed as a nonracialized outcome pathologically linked to deficient cultural and familial values. An understanding of culture and socialisation practices may be important; however, the lack of accounting for their genesis inadvertently marginalises the racialized structural processes at the heart of societal development. What this chapter has shown is that the intersections of race and class, constituted as pigmentocracy, and manifest and operationalised in the dual system, structure the differential education received by Afro-Trinidadian boys. As such, pigmentocratic status as either lighter or darker facilitates or restricts access to quality educative resources as far as school infrastructure and resources, teacher quality and commitment and school ethos.

Whereas this paper is based on analysis of data collected for a study into the achievement of Afro-Trinidadian primary boys, the ideas advanced reflect a specific angle in understanding the racialized nature of education in Trinidad. Similarly, this chapter does not purport to answer or provide a holistic conceptualisation of all these social issues but, rather, specifically how the intersections of race and class, that is, pigmentocracy, are manifested in education. Essentially, this chapter revolved around four core themes: *the rights of disposition, the rights to use and enjoyment, the reputation and status property of whiteness* and *the absolute right to exclude*. These were elucidated through an adaptation of Harris's (1993) CRT scholarship on the property value of whiteness into a schema that interrogates both educational structures and the pervasiveness of skin colour in the postcolonial context of the two schools, Pinehill and St. George's. To this end, the research data highlight a constant thread: skin colour matters, challenging the assumption of meritocracy and colour blindness in the dual system as it maintains White and light privilege and supremacy.

A Call for Dialogue and Further Research

What this chapter has done is address and hopefully create academic space for invigorated interrogation of three issues: the application of CRT and this concept of pigmentocracy to different contexts, pigmentocracy and intersectionality and the discourse on race and education in Trinidad.

Firstly, it is understood that CRT was developed to scrutinize the US structuring of race (Gillborn 2005, 2006). However, Gillborn (2006, 19) does suggest that

> there is no reason, however, why the underlying assumptions and insights of CRT cannot be transferred usefully to other (post-) industrial societies such as the UK, Europe and Australasia.

Additionally, this study highlights that CRT, with some adjustments, can be used outside of White-majority countries and in postcolonial settings. In particular, the historical impetus of CRT and its perspective on racism as an evolving adaptive system congruently facilitate its use in contexts such as Trinidad. This study also alludes to the possible application of pigmentocracy as an organising principle of race and class in White majority countries such as the UK; this type of analysis has increasingly been used in the US (see Hunter 2007, 2008; Hall 2008).

Whereas pigmentocracy engages with intersections of race and class, other aspects of identity intersectionality do intercede, such as gender and disability. This I believe warrants further investigation in understanding how pigmentocracy may have a differential in its impact within racialized groups. For instance, Harrison et al. (2008) argue that darker skin affects women and men differently in the job market; for women, it may represent a 'triple jeopardy'—their gender, race and skin colour may disadvantage them as unattractive and lacking capability (Hersch 2006). Looking at Pinehill, it is also possible to conceptualise that within pigmentocracy there is a discourse of disability which ascribes pathologically to darker-skinned bodies a sense of lesser or impaired ability.

Lastly, there were two typical responses from Trinidadians on hearing my research topic. They generally suggested, 'Why a specific focus on Afro-Trinidadian boys?' or, 'Yes, good, we need to know why Afro-Trinidadian males are always failing and causing so much trouble.'

These differing perspectives centre a discourse on race and education, which either marginalises the salience of race altogether or constructs the relationship as pathological in Afro-Trinidadian bodies, families and cultural patterns. Therefore, in Trinidad, as in much of the Americas, a discourse on race is either an 'absent presence' (Tomlinson 2008) or an exercise in deficit thinking, imbuing the culture of the oppressed as illegitimate (Bonilla-Silva and Dietrich 2008). These perspectives on race inevitably limit or cloud potential analyses of related issues whereby the relative lack of race-focused studies engenders or allows a view of homogeneity in reference to minoritised groups. In this way, one may contend that this research marks a timely contribution in challenging the traditional academic discourse on race and education in Trinidad. It also amounts to a call to the academy for further and deeper engagement in analysis of pigmentocratic structures.

REFERENCES

Bacchus, M. Kazim. 1994. *Education as and for legitimacy: Developments in West Indian education between 1846 and 1895.* Waterloo, Ontario, Canada: Wilfrid Laurier University Press.
———. 2005. *Education for economic, social and political development in the British Caribbean colonies from 1896 to 1945.* Waterloo. Ontario, Canada: The Althouse Press.

Bell, Derrick A. 1992. *Faces at the bottom of the well: The permanence of racism*. New York: Basic Books.

Bonilla-Silva, Eduardo, and David R. Dietrich. 2008. The Latin Americanization of racial stratification in the U.S. In *Racism in the 21st century: An empirical analysis of skin colour*, ed. Ronald E. Hall, 151–170. New York: Springer.

Brereton, Bridget. 1979. *Race relations in colonial Trinidad 1870–1900*. Cambridge: Cambridge University Press.

Brock, Colin. 1982. The legacy of colonialism in West Indian education. In *Education in the Third World*, ed. Keith Watson, 119–140. London: Croom Helm.

Campbell, Carl C. 1997. *Endless education: Main currents in the education system of modern Trinidad and Tobago 1939–1986*. Kingston, Jamaica: University of the West Indies Press.

Central Statistical Office. 2003. *Pocket digest*. Port of Spain: Ministry of Planning and Development, Government of the Republic of Trinidad and Tobago.

Chant, Sylvia. 2009. Women-headed households: Poorest of the poor? Perspectives from Mexico, Costa Rica and the Philippines. *IDS Bulletin* 28 (3): 26–48.

Chevannes, Barry. 1999. What we sow and what we reap: Problems in the cultivation of male identity in Jamaica. In *The GraceKennedy Foundation Lecture Series*. Kingston, Jamaica: The GraceKennedy Foundation.

Codjoe, Henry M. 2001. Fighting a 'public enemy' of Black academic achievement: The persistence of racism and the schooling experiences of Black students in Canada. *Race Ethnicity and Education* 4 (4): 343–375.

———. 2006. The role of an affirmed Black cultural identity and heritage in the academic achievement of African-Canadian students. *Intercultural Education* 17 (1): 33–54.

Coppin, Addington. 1997. Color in an English-speaking Caribbean labor market. *Journal of Developing Areas* 31 (3): 399–410.

Decuir-Gunby, Jessica T. 2006. "Proving your skin is white, you can have everything": Race, racial identity, and property rights in whiteness in the Supreme Court case of Josephine DeCuir. In *Critical race theory in education: All God's children got a song*, ed. Adrienne D. Dixson and Celia K. Rousseau, 89–112. New York: Routledge.

Dei, George Jerry Sefa, Josephine Mazzuca, Elizabeth McIsaac, and Jasmin Zine. 1997. *Reconstructing 'drop-out': A critical ethnography of the dynamics of Black students' disengagement from school*. Toronto: University of Toronto Press.

Fanon, Frantz. 1967. *Black skin, white masks*. New York: Grove Press.

Gillborn, David. 2005. Education policy as an act of White supremacy: Whiteness, Critical Race Theory and education reform. *Journal of Education Policy* 20 (4): 485–505.

———. 2006a. Critical Race Theory and education: Racism and anti-racism in educational theory and praxis. *Discourse: Studies in the Cultural Politics of Education* 27 (1): 11–32.

———. 2006b. Critical Race Theory beyond North America: Towards a trans-Atlantic dialogue on racism and antiracism in educational theory and praxis. In *Critical Race Theory in education: All God's children got a song*, ed. Adrienne D. Dixson and Celia K. Rousseau, 241–265. New York: Routledge.

Hall, Ronald E., ed. 2008. *Racism in the 21st century: An empirical analysis of skin color*. New York: Springer.

Harris, Cheryl I. 1993. Whiteness as property. *Harvard Law Review* 106 (8): 1707–1791.

Harrison, Matthew S., Wendy Reynolds-Dobbs and Kecia M. Thomas. 2008. Skin color bias in the workplace: The media's role and implications towards preference. In *Racism in the 21st century: An empirical analysis of skin color*, ed. Ronald E. Hall, 47–62. New York: Springer.

Hersch, Joni. 2006. Skin-tone effects among African Americans: Perceptions and reality. *The American Economic Review* 96 (2): 251–255.

Hunter, Margaret L. 2002. "If you're light you're alright": Light skin color as social capital for women of color. *Gender and Society* 16 (2): 175–193.

———. 2007. The persistent problem of colorism: Skin tone, status, and inequality. *Sociology Compass* 1 (1): 237–254.

———. 2008. The cost of color: What we pay for being black and brown. In *Racism in the 21st century: An empirical analysis of skin color*, ed. Ronald E. Hall, 63–76. New York: Springer.

James, C. L. R. 1932. *Life of Captain A. A. Cipriani*. Lancashire, UK: Nelson. Quoted in B. Brereton, 1979, *Race relations in colonial Trinidad 1870–1900*. Cambridge: Cambridge University Press.

Johnson, Tekla Ali. 2004. The enduring function of caste: Colonial and modern Haiti, Jamaica, and Brazil—the economy of race, the social organization of caste, and the formulation of racial societies. *Comparative American Studies* 2 (1): 61–73.

Jules, Vena. 1994. *A study of the secondary school population in Trinidad and Tobago: Placement patterns and practices*. St. Augustine, Trinidad and Tobago: Centre for Ethnic Studies, University of the West Indies.

Khan, Aisha. 1993. What is 'a Spanish'?: Ambiguity and 'mixed' ethnicity in Trinidad. In *Trinidad ethnicity*, ed. Kevin A. Yelvington, 180–207. London: Macmillan Press Limited.

Ladson-Billings, Gloria, and William F. Tate. 2006. Towards a Critical Race Theory of education. In *Critical Race Theory in education: All God's children got a song*, ed. Adrienne D. Dixson and Celia K. Rousseau, 11–30. New York: Routledge.

London, Norrel A. 2002. Curriculum convergence: An ethno-historical investigation into schooling in Trinidad and Tobago. *Comparative Education* 38 (1): 53–72.

López, Alfred J. 2005. Introduction: Whiteness after empire. In *Postcolonial whiteness: A critical reader on race and empire*, ed. Alfred J. Lopez, 1–30. New York: State University of New York Press.

Lowenthal, David. 1967. Race and color in the West Indies. *Daedalus* 96 (2): 580–626.

Meighoo, Kirk. 2003. *Politics in a half made society: Trinidad and Tobago 1925–2001*. Kingston, Jamaica: Ian Randle Publishers.

Ogbu, John U. 2004. Collective identity and the burden of "acting white" in black history, community, and education. *The Urban Review* 36 (1): 1–35.

Parry, Odette. 2004. Masculinities, myths and educational underachievement: Jamaica, Barbados, and St. Vincent and the Grenadines. In *Interrogating Caribbean masculinities: Theoretical and empirical analyses*, ed. Rhoda E. Reddock, 167–184. Kingston, Jamaica: University of the West Indies Press.

Reynolds, Tracey. 2009. Exploring the absent/present dilemma: Black fathers, family relationships, and social capital in Britain. *The ANNALS of the American Academy of Political and Social Science* 624: 12–28.

Taylor, Edward. 2009. The foundations of Critical Race Theory in education: An introduction. In *Foundations of Critical Race Theory in education*, ed. Edward Taylor, David Gillborn and Gloria Ladson-Billings, 1–13. New York: Routledge.

Tomlinson, Sally. 2008. *Race and education: Policy and politics in Britain*. Berkshire, UK: Open University Press.

Valencia, Richard R., ed. 1997. *The evolution of deficit thinking: Educational thought and practice*. London: Falmer Press.

4 A Critical Appraisal of Critical Race Theory (CRT)
Limitations and Opportunities

Alpesh Maisuria

ABSTRACT

In 1993, one of the founders of Critical Race Theory (CRT), Richard Delgado, urged delaying appraisal of CRT, suggesting that scholars needed time to 'nurture it, get to know it, observe and interact with it' because it was only a few years old (Delgado 1993, 346). It has now been over twenty years since the inception of CRT and it has become a major tool of analysis in the US, and this trend is continuing overseas. This chapter has been written as a critical interpretation of CRT that raises important questions about its contributive potential, the analytical strength of CRT, and its capacity for intersectionality.

Over the course of the last twenty years, Critical Race Theory (abbreviated to CRT henceforth) has been a popular theoretical tool adopted by scholars examining racial injustice in the US. More recently, many scholars outside of the US, particularly in the UK and Australia, are using CRT. It is therefore timely that CRT is itself defined and problematised in order to make judgements about its contributive potential and scope for intersectionality.

This chapter has been inspired by the angry response I received to a critique of CRT I presented at the American Educational Research Association (AERA) 2010 annual conference where, during the plenary, I was told by a member of the audience that as a person born in England (incidentally of African/Indian origin) that I did not understand the analytical strength that CRT had in capturing racism because of its specificity to the sociohistorical context of the US. Furthermore, another member of the audience told me that Marxist-inspired critiques, such as mine, missed the point of CRT. To address this criticism, this chapter is designed to do three things: 1) to open up a debate about what CRT is conceptually comprised of; 2) outline a critical interpretation of CRT, which can then be used contribute to debates about the efficacy of it outside of the US; 3) use this critical interpretation to gage the potential for using CRT in combination with Marxism.

I begin by firstly introducing CRT and its major conceptual propositions. I will then outline some of the analytical positions of CRT and offer a review of the opportunities and limitations of CRT. I conclude with some thoughts on why intersectionality is important for emancipatory action.

SECTION 1: A BRIEF INTRODUCTION TO CRITICAL RACE THEORY

For a number of years CRT has been offering insight into struggles and conflicts of a racial nature in the US, especially for those who reject the Marxist tradition of critiquing political economy. CRT has its roots in Critical Legal Studies (henceforth CLS). CLS was a broad movement of predominantly Black scholars in Legal Studies that set about challenging the pattern of inequity that Black Americans faced in the US legal system. CLS scholars claimed that since the gains from the civil rights movement, 'people of colour' were being treated with less fairness because of a colour-blind liberalist approach to civil justice (Ladson-Billings 1998; Delgado and Stefancic 2000). Also, scholars such as Derek Bell (1987) claimed that CLS placed too much emphasis on social class to explain inequities, and the law and other civic institutions did not recognise the deep-seated racist undercurrents of society and therefore 'race' as a tool of oppression was missing at the expense of social class. So the issue for Bell and others was about the juxtaposition of structural racism versus structural classism. The assumption was that each could be analytically separated and posed in relation to the other. In essence, this meant that the entire US legal system was inherently treating 'people of colour' unequally by not accounting for the structural racism that was woven into the fabric of US society.

In a challenge to this social injustice, a collection of reformist lawyers and judges, led by Derrick Bell and including Alan Freeman, Richard Delgado, Kimberlé Crenshaw, Angela Harris and Charles Lawrence (Delgado and Stefancic 2000; DeCuir and Dixson 2004, 26), came together to mobilise a movement to draw attention to the centrality of 'race' and the role it played in the justice system. CRT literature has grown exponentially and is recognised as a major theoretical contribution to many disciplines in the academy and is now widely used across the US as an analytical, methodological and conceptual approach to study and resist racial injustice.

It is challenging to characterise CRT because it is a large and diverse intellectual formation, with many offshoots, for example, 'Lat Crit' that deals specifically with Latino racism. However, as a point of departure for critique, I will use Richard Delgado and Jean Stefancic (2000, 7–9), two of the key scholars of CRT literature, to define the six overarching tenets that are central to CRT. These are:

1. Racism is ordinary and structured by White-supremacy.
2. 'Race' is a social construction.
3. Intersectionality and anti-essentialism are necessary.
4. People of colour need to be given a voice.
5. People of colour are racialized.
6. Interest convergence.

These six tenets invite much critique of their analytical strength; however, due to space constraints, I will focus on CRT's fundamental overarching principles: the centrality of 'race', voice and counter-storytelling, the rules of racial standing. It is only after outlining these building blocks of CRT that an effective appraisal and judgement can be made about the sharpness of CRT as an analytical tool.

CRT Beyond the US

Recently there have been moves to export CRT to outside of the US. More than twenty years after CRT was initially established in the US, the first ever major CRT conference in the UK took place in 2006 at Manchester Metropolitan University in England. In the few years since then, CRT has been gaining positive recognition in Europe, largely through the efforts of David Gillborn, John Preston and Kevin Hylton (see, for example, Gillborn 2002, 2005, 2006a, 2006b, 2008a, 2009a, 2009b, 2010a, 2010b; Preston 2007, 2009; Hylton 2009) and others, including Lorna Roberts, Nicola Rollock, Andy Pilkington and Namita Chakrabarty.

In 2009 there were several high-profile UK-based CRT events and symposiums at large conferences organised with the aim of introducing CRT and establishing a British contingent of CRT scholars. Most notable was one entitled 'CRT: What Is It and How Can It Transform Research and Educational Practice and Pedagogy *beyond* the US?' (my emphasis). These conferences are important because they indicate that CRT has already gained ground outside of the US, and will continue to do so, which must be accompanied with appropriate critique.

Despite the emerging popularity in the UK over recent years, there are indications that the transfer of CRT from the US context has not been embraced uncritically. There has been growing scholarship problematising CRT's centralisation of 'race' and mainstreaming of the tenet of White supremacy in the UK and US, for example, E. San Juan, Peter McLaren, Randall Kennedy, Sandy Grande, Brian Brayboy, Gregory Meyerson, Mike Cole and Dave Hill. It is noteworthy that British CRT scholars themselves have reflected on the efficacy of a North American-centric theory in a UK context (Preston 2007, 2009); and others have been examining how CRT could potentially be compatible with nonvulgar interpretations of Marxism and building on works from, inter alia, Robert Miles, Ambalavaner Sivanandan, Cedric Robinson and Oliver Cox (Maisuria 2011).

This section has outlined the premises and provenance of CRT. In the following sections of the chapter, I will take specific aspects of CRT for review, and provide a critical interpretation focussing on conceptualisation and application of each aspect. The next section will discuss 'race' in CRT.

SECTION 2: THE CONCEPTUALISATION AND APPLICATION OF 'RACE' IN CRT

I now turn my attention to questioning some of the fundamental conceptualisations of CRT by drawing on the notion that the most effective form of appraisal may be one that penetrates its object and produces challenges from within the object, the object here being the central tenets of CRT.

One of the building blocks of CRT is the centralisation of 'race'. CRT proponents argue that 'race' has to be centred in analyses of injustice. 'Race' for CRT scholars is sacrosanct and explanatory theory would need to focus on the concept of 'race' either exclusively or predominantly in relation to class (or other identity formations) when seeking to explain inequities. As Darder and Torres (2004, 98) put it, CRT uses ' "race" as the central unit of analysis'. In an educational context, UK-based CRT scholar David Gillborn is clear on the centrality of 'race'. He suggests that

> CRT offers a challenge to educational studies more generally, and to the sociology of education in particular, to cease the ritualistic citation of "race" as just another point of departure on a list of exclusions to be mentioned and then bracketed away. CRT insists that racism be placed at the centre of analyses (Gillborn 2006a, 27).

Elsewhere, Gillborn has been more forthright about the role of 'race', unequivocally stating that 'class is used to silence debates about "race" ' and 'class is a smoke screen to promote racist action' (Gillborn 2008b). Furthermore, Gillborn has stated that 'we know, historically, that an overwhelming focus on social class tends to obliterate any concern with race equality' (Gillborn 2009b, 8).

Although more contemporary writings on CRT have attempted to intersect 'race' with other identities and draw out the complexities (cf. Preston 2007, 2009; Leonardo 2009), the vast bulk of, especially seminal, literature on CRT places an 'uncompromising insistence' on centrality of 'race' (Darder and Torres 2004, 98). However, Haney-Lopez has profoundly pointed out some time ago that '[r]ace may be . . . [the] single most confounding problem, but the confounding problem of race is that few people seem to know what race is . . . ' (Hanley-Lopez 1994, 5–6). Given that 'race' is a central feature of CRT, it is important to examine how CRT conceptualises it, and apply an exegesis of this. Doing this will allow for an analysis of the efficacy of CRT, and it will open the space for exploration of the opportunities and challenges for intersecting 'race' with social class and other identities.

Conceptualisations of 'race' have a long and contested history. Generally, there are two broad ways that 'race' has been articulated in the social sciences: as a biological category and a social construction. These long-standing terrains of argument have parallel manifestations in CRT and they will be problematised later, but before that, it is useful to explain the historical trajectory of these conceptualisations of 'race' to set out the problematic nature of deploying the term.

The Biological Conceptualisation of 'Race'

In the biological conceptualisation, 'race' is used to identify genetically given phenotypes that can be used to distinguish people from one another to establish taxonomies of 'race'. 'Race' in this conceptualisation is a scientific category that is determined by DNA makeup. Following this conceptualisation of 'race', explorer Francis Galton (1882–1911) established the eugenics movement (Chitty 2001). The proposition was that some 'races' were genetically dispositioned to inferiority in every aspect of being a human being. Humans, in this way, were born with a given quota of superior or inferior traits, and categories of 'race' were used to differentiate between these. Adherents to this scientific conceptualisation of 'race' claimed that some people were *naturally* predetermined to be culturally, socially, educationally and physically in deficit compared to others. Eugenics, it seemed, had a revolutionary mission, which was not only to preserve racial purity through selective breeding (Chitty 2001, 115) but also 'to improve the innate quality of the human race' (Chitty 2009, 51). The eugenics movement became the mainstream of the academy and politics and it influenced many governments' decisions about issues such as sterilisation, even in traditionally progressive countries in Scandinavia. This was even after the National Socialists in Germany in the 1930s and 40s used it to justify a hierarchy of Aryan supremacy based on somatic features, such as skin colour, shape of nose, size of skull, which culminated in six million Jewish people perishing. In sum, the basic idea of eugenics was that the human gene pool had to be protected from bastardisation by allowing breeding between the weak and fit. The profound effects of this human interference with nature begged for appraisal, and eugenics, as a form of social Darwinism, became the subject of critique itself.

THE SOCIAL CONSTRUCTION OF 'RACE'

Despite the then mainstreaming of eugenic theory, the controversial biological basis to the conceptualisation of 'race' prompted many scholars to explore the legitimacy of the science behind claims concerning deficit models of 'race'. Scholarly research that had led to the creation of a differentiation of weak and fit 'races' was being reevaluated and questions were being raised about its validity (UNESCO 1952). For example, it was deemed that Carl Linnaeus's valuable research on plant categorisations was being misused, which was significant because it had the unfortunate effect of creating four taxonomies of the human 'race': White Europeans, Red Americans, Yellow Asians, Black Africans. Similarly, when irrationally generalised, Baron Cuvier's *Natural History* (1890) laid the foundation for human 'race' as being divided into four categories: American Indian, Caucasian, Mongol and Negro. However, the scientific credibility of these broad categorisations was being questioned universally by the 1950s, and eventually these taxonomies had become obsolete by the 1970s. The prevailing accepted position after the 1970s was that DNA makeup did not suggest biological predestination and ultimately the science behind hundreds of years of research into 'race' was rejected.

The conceptualisation of 'race' as a social construction, rather than a biology, became officially doctrinal when the United Nations declared that 'the biological fact of race and the myth of "race" should be distinguished' and that 'it would be better when speaking of human races [*sic*] to drop the term "race" altogether and speak of ethnic groups'. 'According to present knowledge there is no proof that the groups of mankind differ in their innate mental characteristics' (Banton 2010, 137). In other words, 'race' was declared to be only skin deep—a social construction and to denote its problematic conceptual basis it was used within quotation marks, to signify a nuanced but crucial point being made—that 'race' is a social construction.

CRT and 'Race'

The section above, which provided a *general* account of 'racc' as a concept used as a tool of categorisation, herein lays a *specific* challenge to CRT, which needs explication. Within CRT scholarship, despite the crucial centrality of 'race', the specific conceptualisation of 'race' is unclear because some authors use it within quotation marks to denote that it is a problematic term, but most of the key writers do not, for example, Delgado and Stefancic (2001), Ladson-Billings (1998) and Leonardo (2009). The inconsistent use of quotation marks raises questions about how CRT conceptualises 'race' and is significant for theorisation. The options for CRT scholars are: 1) 'race' is not a social construction or 2) 'race' is a social construction. If the former conceptualisation is to be used by CRT scholars, then is the biological conceptualisation of 'race' being deployed and is 'race' therefore being reified? Without denoting its problematic nature by using quotation marks, 'race' becomes an a priori scientific truth, which is widely discredited, associated with far-right movements, and as of having no history. Without inverted commas, 'race' exists as a historically abstracted autonomous function *in itself* not related to axes of class, gender and other identities. 'Race' goes from existing only as a pseudoscience designed to differentiate people to one which acquires a 'phantom objectivity, an autonomy that seems so strictly rational and all-embracing as to conceal every trace of its fundamental nature: the relation between people' (Lukacs 1967 [1923], 1). 'Race' in this way is conceptualised as a fixed reality in time and space; it bestows on itself its own an axiomatic hegemony from 'science', separate from being rooted historically or contemporaneously in class or other causal relations. It harbours itself as an autonomous entity and not related to the process of social intercourse (for example, see Crenshaw's deployment of 'race', 1988, 1373).

Furthermore, in relation to a lack of conceptualisation, it is significant to note that despite centuries of scholarship on 'race' and racism, the two are not adequately 'separated' and the relationship between them is not articulated (Bernasconi and Lott 2000, vii). This is a fundamental question that relates to the conceptualisation of 'race' that is underdeveloped by CRT scholars. In CRT literature 'race' is conflated with racism, and often the two are used interchangeably. It is not clear what utility 'race' has for the mobilisation of racism.

To illustrate the problematic nature of not conceptualising 'race' as a problematic construction and not articulating its connection to racism, I will quote Gillborn (2010b, 2):

> [c]ritical race theorists are fully cognisant of the fact that race is a social construction; this is actually a cornerstone of the approach [here he is citing Delgado and Stefancic 2001]. However, a key point is that the constructivist nature of race makes it no less *real* in terms of its social, political and economic consequences.

He goes on to respond to challenges to this proposition: '[Are critics] really suggesting that racist inequities are not 'real, historical, material relations?'

There are two problems with the internal dynamics of Gillborn's (2010b) statement. Firstly, if all CRT scholars are unified with Delgado and Stefancic's third principle of CRT that 'race' is an imagined entity *existing only* in social intercourse and not detached from this (2001, 7), then why is 'race' not put into quotation marks to denote that it is a social construction based on a historically conditioned pseudoscientific conceptualisation? The fundamental issue here is that there is a lack of coherence between conceptualisation ('race' is a social construction) and application (not using quotation marks) in CRT scholarship.

To add to this conceptual underdevelopment of 'race', according to Ladson-Billings (2009) in the US and Warmington (2009) in the UK, 'race' has become 'more embedded and fixed than in a previous age' (Ladson-Billings 2009, 19). My contestation is not with the claim itself, which may or may not be true, but rather I argue that if statements like this are to be made, then explication is needed in regards to how/why 'race' has changed its permutation, and this has to be demonstrated theoretically. To do this, CRT scholars must clearly identify two things. What are the characteristics, mechanisms and workings that make 'race' something more than an imagined formation and into something that is materially existent? If 'race' becomes material during the process of social intercourse, then this process needs to be explicated. Secondly and crucially, CRT scholars must identify how their deployment of 'race' is different from the pseudoscientific formulation of 'race'. These are the fundamentals of CRT that need development to make it a more sophisticated and analytically rigorous tool for analysis.

The point of this chapter is to raise fundamental questions about the properties of CRT, and prompt exegesis in future scholarship, which in turn would aid judgements about its analytical strength. In sum, intellectual progress begins with posing problems and in this vein I am challenging the *detail* and *workings* of CRT's internal structure. For example, I have raised issue with the conceptual basis of 'race' within CRT scholarship, concluding that there is vagueness about how CRT articulates 'race' with racism. This problematic is a fundamental one, and its ambiguity and lack of clarity as it stands potentially undermine the structures of the theory itself.

SECTION 3: VOICE AND COUNTER-STORYTELLING IN CRITICAL RACE THEORY

One of the tenets of CRT is the use of 'voice' as a technique to capture subjective data from people of colour; however, there are substantive issues of tension and contradiction. I offer a critique in this section. I will start by introducing CRT's utilisation of 'voice' before moving onto a critical appraisal of how this is deployed.

CRT and Voice

CRT has borrowed the tool of 'voice' from Carol Gilligan's work reported in her influential book *In a Different Voice* (Farber and Sherry 1993). In this book, Gilligan proposes that men and women reason in different ways, with women being more contextual and approaching issues trying to understanding the subjective nature of the discourse. On the other hand, men tend to objectivise and universalise issues. The crucial point being that men and women not only provide different *perspectives*, but these different perspectives shape the *understanding* of issues (Farber and Sherry 1993). In a similar vein, CRT utilises the tool of voice to capture stories of personalised experience of oppression that are characterised by racial subordination (Matsuda 1989; Delgado 1989). The idea is that only Black people can account for Black people's reality because only they have been on the receiving end of the psychological 'spirit-murdering' and physical exclusion, discrimination and marginalisation (Delgado 1993, 345). For example, Patricia Williams's much-celebrated *Benetton Story* recounts an experience when she was rejected entry into a Benetton's clothes store, but only after the attendant had seen that she was Black (Williams 1991). The point is that a White person could not have told this narrative because White people cannot *feel* the racial subordination that Black people experience at the hands of White oppression.

One of CRT's founders, Richard Delgado (1995), argues that the stories of Black people come from a distinct vantage point. Delgado (1995) goes on to suggest that this *experience* is one that is underpinned by ubiquitous racism, and that this gives Black people a perspective that is different from the dominant representation of racism provided by White people, who have not lived that social reality. Therefore, granting a voice through storytelling is deployed to 'analyze myths, presuppositions, and received wisdoms that make up the common culture about race and that invariably render blacks and other minorities one-down' (Delgado 1995, xiv). Dixson and Rousseau (2005, 10) define this as 'the assertion and acknowledgement of the importance of the personal and community experiences of people of color as sources of knowledge'.

In this section I have so far sought to *define* 'voice' in CRT scholarship, but it is notable that the *application* of the 'voice' is not fixed and CRT scholars deploy it in two common ways. Firstly, it is believed that the narratives of Black people will expose the deeply ingrained privilege of White people. It provides a route to uncovering White supremacy and exposes the 'white world' (Gillborn 2008b). Counterstories are designed to unmask how White people dominate all spheres of public life, and assert their perspective on the issue of 'race'. It is claimed that although the White person's view is only one perspective, it becomes the dominant narrative because of the inherent White supremacy in social life. The White supremacy discourse becomes hegemonic in which the White perspective on 'race' is perpetuated and sustained (Delagdo 1993).

It is important to note that the term 'White supremacy' in CRT is deployed in a wider sense than its common usage, which refers to Nazi-type movements mobilised by the conscious aim of creating a racial hierarchy. CRT is built on the assumption that White supremacy is structurally all pervasive and perpetuated unconsciously as well as consciously. Leonardo suggests 'privilege conjures up images of domination happening behind the backs of whites, rather than on the backs of people of colour' (2004, 138). Adding to this, Mills (2003, 190) goes further, suggesting that White people are not so innocent because they are actually aware and culpable of involvement in 'pervasive patterns of not seeing and not knowing—structured white ignorance, motivated inattention, self-deception, historical amnesia, and moral rationalisation'. In sum, the position that CRT scholarship promulgates is that all White people are, by default, implicated in preserving White supremacy.

In order to analyse and challenge these 'permanent' (Bell 1992) power relations and the effect they have on the social reality of Black people, CRT employs parables, chronicles and anecdotes to account for the operation of 'race' in everyday life. Delgado (1993, 343) succinctly captures this by stating: 'Counterstory focuses not on helping a white understand a black, but on helping a white understand a *white* (original italics).' The idea therefore is to raise 'race' consciousness and the privilege that all Whites benefit from.

Secondly, and related to the first way that voice is deployed in CRT, it is a method to empower Black people. It is claimed that privileging the Black voice, which has been silenced by White people, will highlight the social reality of being Black and the racial subordination this entails (Bell 1992). The simple act of exposé has profound effects that may instigate transformative action. In addition, CRT scholars claim that Black people have a special affinity for storytelling as a form of emancipation. For example, Delgado (1993, 340) claims that counterstories are emancipatory because they 'reveal the contingency, partiality, and self-serving quality of the stories on which we have been relying to order our world'. It is claimed that storytelling has a rich and long history in the Black tradition (Farber and Sherry 1993). It has been used as a form of communication to keep alive historical memories, which are handed down through generations. Storytelling has therefore developed into a medium to convey a type of communication (Delgado 1995) which cannot be translated by dominant forms of language that have been devised by White people for the purpose of racial subordination (Farber and Sherry 1993). Thus, 'those [voices] drawn from the downtrodden have a special claim on our attention' (Farber and Sherry 1993, 321). This has been termed the 'different voice thesis'.

Critical Examination of Voice and Counter-storytelling

The different voice thesis is a central characteristic because CRT emerged in 1989. However, the concepts of voice and counter-storytelling have been subjected to little critical treatment. In this section I outline specific challenges about the quality and generalisability of counterstories that questions its efficacy.

The first challenge is based on the notion that legitimacy and academic rigour are central to research and scholarly activity. As noted above, in CRT counterstories are concerned principally with conveying experiences and emotions of Black people to unmask White supremacy. However, there are general principles of scholarship that appear to sit uneasily with the different voice thesis as conceived in CRT. Firstly, counterstories may simply be exaggerations and/or misinterpretations of actual events and experiences. People may provide falsified accounts, either wittingly because they have an agenda to pursue or unwittingly because of lapses in memory. In addition, the experience may be atypical. Therefore, there is the question of reliability, validity and quality, which in turn impacts the legitimacy of accounts. At worse, if counterstories are doctored to fit the theses of CRT, this is serious malpractice and even fraud (Farber and Sherry 1993).

Another technique in CRT is the use of fictitious stories to illustrate mechanisms of racial subordination. According to Gillborn (2008a, 4), 'the use of *imagined* characters to debate issues and exemplify real-world problems has become a hallmark of some of the best legal scholars of CRT' (my emphasis). Taking the critical cue from Katherine Abrams's work on feminist voice in 'Hearing the Call of Stories' (Abrams 1991), the question then is 'How are these stories about racial subordination reliable accounts of real-world contexts?' Despite being contested terrain in academia, arguments in social research and scholarship are subject to scrutiny in terms of illegitimacy and unreliability unless they are sustained by conventions of academic practice. Such parameters are not a demand for 'objectivity'; rather, they are to allow for judgements to be made on the strength contributions to the existing body of academic knowledge. These parameters are not a part of counter-storytelling and therefore there remains a question about the quality of contribution counterstories have, in spite of the noble essence of their goal for supporting racial justice.

CRT scholars such as Delgado (1993) have claimed that conventions of academic practice that safeguard academic integrity are designed by White scholars, perhaps as a deliberate strategy, to subordinate the Black voice to affirm hegemonic White supremacy. It is Delgado's assertion that scholarship from Black people is different from that of White people. In fact, Delgado argues, it is so different that it cannot be judged by the same quality and standards as White people's scholarship. As Farber and Sherry (1993) note, this assertion does not have any evidence to support it, and it could also be seen to be demeaning to Black people because the inherent insinuation that could be interpreted in this claim is that Black people cannot attain the same (high?) standards as White people. This is a serious point that could actually disempower Black people, and therefore needs development in CRT scholarship.

The second part of my critique draws on the notion of generalisability of counterstories and the prioritisation of certain voices. In one of the seminal CRT texts, Delgado (1991, 11) writes about the socially constructed nature of knowledge, where 'truths only exist for this person [of colour] in this predicament at this time in history'. If, as Delgado suggests, gathering data through counter-storytelling that captures racial domination is context and subject specific, then how can individual voices be generalised beyond that person and also articulated with structural forces other than 'race'? Linked to this, a key criticism of CRT may be that, whilst claiming to be intersectional, the overwhelming emphasis on 'race' overshadows all other explanations of injustice. For example, can

CRT articulate with an account of the capitalist mode of production with the stories that are told? In other words, is CRT adaptable to connect the subjective micro with the objective macro? If it can't make a correspondence between structures and agents, then it postulates the futility of resistance against the racist structure of society. Accounting for the structure of society is essential when examining social reality and social conditions of existence of individuals. On the other hand, if CRT scholarship can account for structural forces, then how does it do this and what are the mechanisms that allow for the connection between the agent and the structural forces of society? The charge that can be made against CRT is that voice alone cannot be used as an effective analytical tool because it rests on what may be superficial and thin, *descriptions* of subjective realities falling short of social structural *explanation* (Miles 2009), which in turn cannot be generalised beyond that time and context. On this view, it could be argued that counter-storytelling is no more than therapy falling short of tightly reasoned analytical and informed arguments.

Furthermore on the challenge of generalisability, how can CRT judge between competing accounts from various vantage points, for example, the Black person's story that provides a positive spin on an experience that was negative for another Black person? Equally, if the White voice is not heard, then how can analytical judgements be made about whether the story from one perspective has legitimacy? The privileging of the Black voice means that CRT is working against the notion of democratising the voice of all those who are seen as 'others' who are oppressed, for example, the poor Whites by privileging one element (the Black voice) in what is likely to be a complex emergent reality structured by external forces beyond, as well as 'race'. Leonard Pitts succinctly illustrates this point:

> [W]e talk about black poverty or Hispanic poverty. Less often do we speak of white poverty and even less than that do we simply talk about poverty, period . . . If the poor ever recognized [*sic*] this, got mad about it and began to coalesce irrespective of race, they could realign politics as we know it, require the nation to grapple with, and construct remedies for, their suffering. This was Martin Luther King's last dream. (McLaren and Scatamburlo-D'Annibale 2010, 123)

On the back of this point, criticism of the exclusivist deployment of voice in CRT is that it segregates rather than unites. Separating people by binary colour categories, when they are united in the struggle for justice, seems incomprehensible. Delgado, in his influential article 'Mindset and Metaphor' (1990), indicates that systems of belief are based on 'race', and refers to the Black person literally having a different mind-set from the White person. Following this, he suggests that Black people's stories provide 'representations [that] help us explain and deal with the unfamiliar and troubling by likening them to that which we know' (Delgado 1990, 1874). This quote is indicative of the problematic homogenizing nature of CRT—not only by the implication of the Black against White struggle implicit, but also the use of exclusionary language ('us', 'we'). It is also problematic because the insinuation is that all Blacks are able to speak about racial subordination. Farber and Sherry (1993, 316) ask how middle-class Black people 'whose occupation confers social and economic privilege, and who may come from privileged backgrounds similar to their White counterparts'—have a special claim to represent the view of poor blacks in urban ghettos'. In other words, there is a crudely exclusivist 'us'-and-'them' distinction that does not account for intergroup differences. More fundamentally and related to the problematic lack of conceptualisation of 'race' outlined above (in section 2), postulating the notion that all Black people speak from a singular 'voice', adds further confusion about how CRT deals with the complex concept of 'race' which reifies categories of people based on pseudoscience.

SECTION 4: THE WHITE WORLD AND THE RULES OF RACIAL STANDING

One of the key aspects of CRT is the prominence it affords to 'Black issues' to resist the 'whiteworld' (Gillborn 2006b). The claim is that it builds a sense of common understanding and empathy amongst Black people. This may be the case, but it is also problematic to give special attention to Black issues exclusively if it is at the expense of *all* oppressed groups, for example, the oppressed Whites. At a CRT conference at the Institute of Education, University of London, in 2009, on the back of a presented paper entitled *'Don't Trust "Whitey"? Articulations of the "Black Voice" in the Academy'*, the majority of the contingent of the CRT scholars in the room called for the establishments of 'safe spaces' where 'people of colour' organise themselves segregating from White people. An interpretation of this proposal is that all White people are dangerous, untrustworthy and racist. This is a crude and simplistic assumption made about the morality and mind-set of White people (Cole and Maisuria 2007, 2010; Maisuria 2011).

Given the foregrounding of 'race', CRT theorists would contextualise inequity in terms of an account of racial discrimination, and not couched in the discourse of *social* injustice per se, inferring a totalising of all forms of discrimination as *racial* injustice in the form of Black victims and White perpetrators. My point is not that only one group should be victimised; rather, the call is to recognise that victims (and oppressors) are not a homogenous group along colour lines. Establishing a colour-bar practice for Black people is exclusionary, separatist and divisive, which would create resentment and localised apartheid. Formal colour-coded networks such as Black-only spaces are falsely reacting against *all* White people. It could be argued that this type of separatism is no different from the separatism that the far-right 'British National Party' advocated when they tried to illegally disallow non-White people to join the party; or the 'Christian Identity Movement' in the United States, who are constituted by some groups who equate a non-Christian American Identity as akin to Satanism. Furthermore, one may demur in astonishment at the insinuation that *all* White people are racist, either wittingly or unwittingly. This position will potentially hinder building alliances to create solidarity between all those, despite skin colour, fighting for justice. A meaningful debate between scholars of social justice has to ensue in order to work intersectionally to unite against discrimination in all its forms and parameters.

A Critique of The Rules of Racial Standing

Derek Bell is one of the founders of CRT and his work on 'race', racism and American law has been considered to be pioneering (Taylor 2000) and continues to be influential in what is known as 'whiteness studies'. Along with Peggy McIntosh, (1990), who produced a list of fifty privileges that Whites are entitled to by virtue of their skin colour, in Bell's book *Faces at the Bottom of the Well: The Permanence of Racism* (Bell 1992), the chapter called 'The Rules of Racial Standing' is celebrated as seminal scholarship that exposes the normalised racial hierarchy where Whites are the beneficiaries of advantage by virtue of their skin colour rather than merit.

Despite writing specifically about law in the US, according to CRT scholars, Bell's five rules of racial standing are fundamental to understanding overt and covert White supremacy in all contexts (Taylor 2000; Leonardo 2004). Here are the rules of racial standing:

1. Black people's expertise and suffering are ignored.
2. Black people cannot be objective, and are purposefully kept from juries and recording cases involving 'race'.
3. All Blacks are bound by these 'rules' except those who gain 'enhanced status'.
4. Blacks who are 'recruited' by Whites to 'condemn' the rules are given 'superstanding status'. Those who refuse will face recriminations.
5. Once you know the rules, you start to see them everyday.

Through these 'rules' and the associated central tenet of White supremacy, CRT scholars have established an internal mechanism that disqualifies and delegitimises critical analysis of CRT. This mechanism operates in two ways.

Firstly, if a White person challenges CRT, they are accused of using the privilege of *whiteness* to reject threats to *that* very privilege. Using 'the rules', CRT scholars can reject any criticism of CRT from a White person by simply accusing that White person of attempting to sustain the White supremacy *status quo*. Put another way, when a White person challenges the notion of White supremacy, CRT scholars can accuse that challenge of displaying precisely the White superiority that is being exposed by CRT. In these instances, CRT is adopting ad hominem attacks to sidestep fundamental challenges to its theoretical coherence and value. Simply being White renders illegitimate the basic act of questioning the efficacy of CRTs proposals. It means that the fundamentals, logic and coherence of the challenge to CRT are not taken seriously because the retort rests on attacking the critic's White skin colour. The attack is obliterated without engaging with the virtues of the argument.

Secondly, and on par with the first point, if a Black person attempts to critically analyse CRT, then they are accused of being 'recruited' by Whites (rule 4) and acquiring the property of whiteness and privileges that go with it. According to 'the rules', if criticism of CRT has come from a Black person, they are bestowed with the privileges that go with White supremacy because that person is rewarded with 'enhanced status' (rule 3) for attacking CRT and the threat it poses to White supremacy. Bell (1992, 114) claims:

> [T]he usual exception to this rule [of White supremacy] is the black person who publicly disparages or criticizes other blacks who are speaking or acting in ways that upsets whites. Instantly such statements are granted "enhanced standing" even when the speaker has no special expertise or experience.

As a CRT advocate, Gillborn (2009b, 11) uses the idea of 'enhanced standing' by claiming that as the Black chair of the British Equality and Human Rights Commission (EHRC), Trevor Phillips's 'interventions . . . carry so much weight . . . because he and certain other commentators, from a minorities position, can say the things that White racists want to say. And they will be called courageous and brave as a result of that'. Here, Phillips is being accused of being rewarded with the privilege of being granted a voice by Whites because he challenges the assertion of White supremacy, and this in turn grants Phillips a louder voice from which he gains superstanding status (rule 4). The fundamental point here is that whilst Phillips, and other Black people, will of course be embraced by racists as people of good sense, I would argue that CRT scholars ought to be engaging *directly* with the strengths or otherwise of the arguments made by Phillips first and foremost, rather than engaging in ad hominem as the principal response.

'The rules of racial standing' are illustrated by Bell in his famous parable 'Space Traders' (Bell 1992), which was made into a short film. In the films narrative, Earth is invaded by aliens, who offer to solve the planet's economic and ecological problems in exchange for all Black people. The White people in power met this proposal with dismay, which instigated political wrangling as the prize was salvation of planet Earth and preservation of human life. During ensuing discussion a Black professor became the key decision-maker and broker. Eventually, the professor was given 'superstanding status' after he agreed to sell out and convince his fellow

African Americans that they should leave with the aliens. The point being made here is that Black people are given access to the properties of whiteness, but only if they sacrifice the Black 'race' and support the White supremacy project.

'The rules' provide CRT with a mechanism that is preemptive of criticism and is self-defensive. Examination of CRT is rejected through ad hominem attack on its critics. 'The rules' potentially allow CRT scholars to undermine all challenges by attacking the author and sidestepping the argument of the author. The upshot is that it is impossible to attack CRT without being accused of subscribing to White supremacy. There are two contradictions here. Firstly, and as discussed above, CRT advocates providing Black people with special access to voice, over and above White people. However, if the Black person uses this privilege to criticise CRT, then they are silenced by claims that they have gained properties of whiteness. It seems that CRT scholars deploy voice in a nominal fashion, and only when it is convenient to their propositions. In this way, voice is available to Black people only with the qualification that it is used to advocate CRT; this way, any criticism is foreclosed.

The second contradiction is that if CRT scholars are serious about developing CRT conceptually and methodologically to work intersectionally, as Crenshaw (1988) suggests, then criticism like the type offered here should be a welcomed as part of a dialectal developmental process. It may be suggested that it is especially important to heed critical fire from Marxists and feminists in a bid to work more intersectionally and across different analytical lenses to strive towards an intellectual formation and solidarity movement fighting against *all* forms of injustice. However, as David Harvey (2005, 41) suggests, this is some way off: 'It has long proved extremely difficult . . . to forge the collective discipline required for political action to achieve social justice.'

CONCLUSION: THE FUTURE FOR
CRT AND INTERSECTIONALITY

In this chapter I have sought to provide a critical examination of CRT. I began by introducing CRT and its historical roots in legal studies. I then went on to outline the basic tenets of CRT, which are attracting interest from a more diverse wave of scholars beyond legal studies in the US. This section provided the platform to begin a critique of the crucial relationship between 'race' and CRT in section 2. Here, it was argued that a more complete conceptualisation of the concept of 'race' was necessary to strengthen the role that 'race' played in CRT analyses. The third and fourth sections provided an outline of 'voice' and 'White supremacy'. After laying out the general claims of both, they were treated to critical examination. The argument was that, whilst both tenets may have potential benefits and the goals may be to advocate social justice, the way they are conceptualised and practiced needs further clarification and development.

Despite the criticisms contained within these sections, this chapter should not be seen as a rejection of CRT in toto, rather an exposé of absences and limitations in CRT scholarship as it stands. For example, one of the issues that I have tried to draw out is that, whereas some of the CRT scholarly claims may be valuable, far more scholarship within CRT is too sectarian and superficial. Of course I am not suggesting that this problem is exclusive to CRT scholarship; however, the fact that it is prohibits a sensible debate between CRT scholars and its critics.

The difficult task is to build a complex and nuanced theory of 'race' that goes beyond ideal abstraction to provide a nonradically inductive and realistic account of *all* those who are served injustice within the *status quo*. For example, whilst the building of Black solidarity alone could be potentially empowering, it is way off from *understanding* and mobilising transformation of the multifaceted dynamics of oppression. To gain this understanding, sophistication is needed in analyses. This involves building critiques that are multidimensional, and subscribing to what can be called horizontal intersectionality and vertical intersectionality.

Horizontal intersectionality is crossing the traditional sociological boundaries of identity politics—most commonly the holy trinity of 'race', social class and gender, where scholars argue for the prominence of one without acknowledging the dialectical relationship between all three. Going beyond a 'single-axis framework' (Crenshaw 2003) allows for intersectionality by working more closely with scholars from various ideological positions, though it has to be noted that in the US there does exist a substantial body of work that does engage with feminism and Latino/Latina and Chicano/Chicana struggles (e.g., Crenshaw 2003). However, such a body of work engaging with contemporary Marxism, for example, the kind that may be termed cultural/phenomenological/Western/neo-Marxism, appears to be a blind spot in research. There is scope to address this; for example, both Marxists and CRT scholars would agree that racism is pervasive (see, for example, the debate between Dave Hill and David Gillborn in the UK [Hill 2009]). However, the discussion around how 'race' and class work dialectically in different moments and spaces is something that needs further regard. This is the last-instance argument that needs to be reinvigorated through the Marxian-inspired works of, inter alia, Georg Lukács, Antonio Gramsci, Louis Althusser and Pierre Bourdieu.

In addition, vertical intersectionality is about acknowledging the strata within the intersections. These are taxonomies of people stratified within the larger categories of 'race', social class and gender. For example, these taxonomies refer to opportunities and outcomes relating to White/Black, working class/ruling class, men/women. This kind of scholarship is crucial, given that important recent studies indicate that the White working class are the very much at the tail end of oppression in Britain. Rather than dismiss these finding by branding the White working-class plight as undeserving of recognition and relegating these finding as an act of White supremacy, it would be beneficial to do two things. Firstly, to deal with these empirical findings in the context of the White supremacy thesis; and secondly, to side with all those involved in the quest for fairness and justice, to build solidarity. It is evident that people power and working within alliances are key to facilitate change. This is exemplified by the epochal emancipatory moments in social human history (for example, during the battle against apartheid in South Africa the Cuban Communists supported the cause); the result demonstrates that major shifts in the political and social world can occur through working in alliances for the greater good.

Building a theory for the contemporaneous moment that builds on historical development and one that feeds action, and vice versa, is what working dialectically is about. After all, discrimination is co-created amongst the nexus of identities in time and space, both CRT scholars and Marxists would probably agree. For Marxists, this entails responding to the criticism that issues other than class are relegated to something to be dealt with after the revolution. This can only be done with an application of an argument that is dialectical. In the same vein, CRT scholars must go beyond essentialising 'race', especially in an abstract empiricist way. These are the challenges for those working within Marxist and CRT perspectives to fundamentally embrace, to move towards an integrated theory that nourishes practical action.

In sum, with the ambition of contributing to the development of an alignment between Marxist-based analyses and CRT (cf. Cole 2009), in this chapter I have aimed to raise questions to help address Darder and Torres's (2004, 100) crucial question:

> How do we launch a truly universal emancipatory political project anchored primarily upon a theory of 'race'? Where is a critique of capitalism or an explicit anticapitalist vision in a critical theory of 'race'?

REFERENCES

Abrams, Kathryn. 1991. Hearing the call of stories. *California Law Review* 79 (4): 971–1052.

Banton, Michael. 2010. The vertical and horizontal dimensions of the word race. *Ethnicities* 10: 127–140.

Bell, Derrick. 1987. *And we are not saved: The elusive quest for racial justice.* New York: Basic Books.

———. 1992. *Faces at the bottom of the well: The permanence of racism.* New York: Basic Books.

Bernasconi, Robert, and Tommy Lott. 2000. *The idea of race.* Indianapolis: Hackett.

Chitty, Clyde. 2001. IQ, racism and the eugenics movement. *FORUM* 43 (3): 115–120.

————. 2009. *Eugenics, race and intelligence in education*. London: Continuum.

Cole, Mike. 2009. *Critical Race Theory and education: A Marxist response*. New York: Palgrave.

Cole, Mike, and Alpesh Maisuria. 2007. 'Shut the f*** up', 'you have no rights here': Critical Race Theory and racialisation in post-7/7 racist Britain. *Journal for Critical Education Policy Studies* 5 (1).

————. 2010. Racism and Islamophobia in post-7/7 Britain: Critical Race Theory, (xeno-) racialisation, empire and education: A Marxist analysis. In *Class in education: Knowledge, pedagogy, subjectivity*, ed Debra Kelsh, Dave Hill and Sheila Macrine. New York: Routledge.

Crenshaw, Kimberlé. 1988. Race, reform and retrenchment: Transformation and legitimation in antidiscrimination law. *Harvard Law Review* 101: 1331–1387.

————. 2003. Demarginalizing the intersection of race and sex: A Black feminist critique of antidiscrimination doctrine, feminist theory and antiracist politics. In *Critical race feminism*, ed. Adrien Wing. New York: New York University Press.

Darder, Antonia, and Rudolfo Torres. 2004. *After race: Racism after multiculturalism*. New York: New York University Press.

DeCuir, Jessica, and Adrienne Dixson. 2004. 'So when it comes out, they aren't that surprised that it is there': Using Critical Race Theory as a tool of analysis of race and racism in education. *Educational Researcher* 33 (5): 26–31.

Delgado, Richard. 1989. Storytelling for oppositionists and others: A plea for narrative. *Michigan Law Review* 87: 2411–2441.

————. 1990. Mindset and metaphor. *Harvard Law Review* 103 (8): 1872–1877.

————. 1991. Brewer's plea: Critical thoughts on common cause. *Vanderbilt Law Review* 44 (1): 1–14.

————. 1993. On telling stories in school: A reply to Farber and Sherry. In *Foundations of Critical Race Theory in education*, ed. Edward Taylor, David Gillborn and Gloria Ladson-Billings. New York: Routledge.

————. 1995. *Critical Race Theory: The cutting edge*. Philadelphia: Temple University Press.

Delgado, Richard, and Jean Stefancic. 2000. *Critical Race Theory: The cutting edge*. 2nd ed. Philadelphia: Temple University Press.

Dixson, Adrienne, and Cellia Rousseau. 2005. And we are still not saved: Critical Race Theory in education ten years later. *Race, Ethnicity and Education* 8 (1): 7–27.

Farber, Daniel, and Suzanna Sherry. 1993. Telling stories out of school: An essay on legal narratives. In *Foundations of Critical Race Theory in education*, ed. Edward Taylor, David Gillborn and Gloria Ladson-Billings. New York: Routledge.

Gillborn, David. 2002. 'So when it comes out, they aren't that surprised that it is there": Using Critical Race Theory as a tool of analysis of race and racism in education. *Educational Researcher* 33 (5): 26–31.

————. 2005. Education policy as an act of white supremacy: Whiteness, Critical Race Theory and education reform. *Journal of Education Policy* 20 (4): 485–505.

————. 2006a. Critical Race Theory and education: Racism and antiracism in educational theory and praxis. *Discourse: Studies in the Cultural Politics of Education* 27 (1): 11–32.

————. 2006b. Rethinking white supremacy: Who counts in 'WhiteWorld'. *Ethnicities* 6 (3): 318–340.

————. 2008a. *Racism and education: Coincidence or conspiracy?* London: Routledge.

————. 2008b. Race, class and exclusion. In *Marxism 2008—a festival of resistance*. London: Socialist Workers Party.

————. 2009a. Who's afraid of Critical Race Theory in education? *Power and Education* 1 (1): 125–131.

————. 2009b. Whatever happened to institutional racism? How the 'white working class' were made into the new race victims. In *What now for widening participation in the arts?* National Arts Learning Network Annual Conference 2009.

————. 2010a. The white working class, racism and respectability: Victims, degenerates and interest-convergence. *British Journal of Educational Studies* 58 (1): 3–25.

————. 2010b. Full of sound and fury, signifying nothing? A reply to Dave Hill's 'Race and class in Britain: A critique of the statistical basis for Critical Race Theory in Britain'. *Journal for Critical Education Policy Studies* 8 (2).

Hanley-Lopez, Ian. 1994. The social construction of race: Some observations on illusion, fabrication and choice. *Harvard Civil Rights-Civil Liberties Law Review* 29.

Harvey, David. 2005. *A brief history of neoliberalism*. Oxford: Oxford University Press.

Hill, Dave. 2009. Culturalist and materialist explanations of class and 'race': Critical Race Theory, equivalence/parallelist theory, and Marxist theory. *Cultural Logic: Journal of Marxist Theory and Practice*, http://clogic.eserver. org/2009/2009.html.

Hylton, Kevin. 2009. *Race and sport: Critical Race Theory*. London: Routledge.

Ladson-Billings, Gloria. 1998. Just what is Critical Race Theory and what's it doing in a nice field like education? *International Journal of Qualitative Studies in Education* 11 (1): 7–24.

Ladson-Billings, Gloria. 2009. Fighting for our lives: Preparing teachers to teach African-American students. *Journal of Teacher Education* 51 (3): 206–219.

Leonardo, Zeus. 2004. The colour of supremacy: Beyond the discourse of 'white privilege'. *Education Philosophy and Theory* 36 (2): 137–152.

————. 2009. *Race whiteness and education*. London: Routledge.

Lukács, Georg. 1919 [1967]. History and class consciousness. Merlin Press and Marxist Internet Archive.

Maisuria, Alpesh. 2011. Ten years of New Labour education policy and racial inequality: An Act of whiteness or neo-liberal practice?. In *Blair's educational legacy and prospects: Ten years of New Labour*, ed. Anthony Green. London: Palgrave.

Matsuda, Mari. 1989. Public response to racist speech: Considering the victim's story. *Michigan Law Review* 87 (1): 2320–2381.

McIntosh, Peggy. 1990. White privilege : Unpacking the invisible knapsack *Independent School* 49 (2): 31–36.

McLaren, Peter, and Valerie Scatamburlo-D'Annibale. 2010. Classifying race: The compassionate racism of the right and why class still matters. In *Handbook of cultural politics and education*, ed. Zeus Leonardo. Rotterdam: Sense Publishers.

Miles, Robert. 2009. Apropos the idea of 'race' . . . again. In *Theories of race and racism*, ed. Les Back and John Solomos. London: Routledge.

Mills, Charles. 2003. *From class to race: Essays in white Marxism and black radicalism*. New York: Rowman and Littlefield.

Preston, John. 2007. *Whiteness and class in education*. Dordrecht, Netherlands: Springer.

————. 2009. The rediscovery of the white working class in education: From 'concrete' to 'abstract' racial domination. In *CeCeps seminar series 'Social class and inequalities in the policy frame'*. London: Institute of Education, University of London.

Taylor, Edward. 2000. Critical Race Theory and interest convergence in the back-lash against affirmative action: Washington State and Initiative 200. In *Foundations of Critical Race Theory in education*, ed. Edward Taylor, David Gillborn and Gloria Ladson-Billings. New York: Routledge.

UNESCO. 1952. *The race question in modern science: The race concept—results of an inquiry.* Paris: United Nations Educational, Scientific and Cultural Organisation.

Warmington, Paul. 2009. Taking race out of scare quotes: Race-conscious social analysis in an ostensibly post-racial world. *Race Ethnicity and Education* 12 (3): 281–296.

Williams, Patricia. 1991. *The alchemy of race and rights: Diary of a law professor.* Harvard, MA: Harvard University Press.

5 Race Slash Class
Mixed-Heritage Youth in a London School

Indra Dewan

ABSTRACT

This chapter draws on qualitative research conducted with mixed heritage teenagers attending a gender and ethnically mixed London comprehensive school. It presents the students' perspectives in relation to themes such as multiculturalism, friendship, appearance and the police tactic of 'stop and search' to explore their diverse experiences and how these are constituted primarily along class lines. Whilst mixed-race girls from middle-class backgrounds were most likely to reap the benefits of a society which promotes equality of opportunity, meritocracy and cultural diversity, mixed-race boys from working-class backgrounds most often experienced life through the lens of race, class and gender prejudice. An intersectional antiracist feminist approach is drawn upon to critically interrogate the imbrications of race, class and gender in students' everyday and educational lives, and to engage in transformative pedagogy within the school setting. The findings challenge the dominant popular and public discourses of cosmopolitanism and individualism, and highlight the importance of developing an intersectional understanding of mixed-race difference to be better able to respond to the social and educational needs of young mixed-race people.

INHABITING DIFFERENT WORLDS

This chapter draws on qualitative research conducted with young mixed-heritage people attending a London comprehensive school. It reveals how race, class and gender are imbricated in their everyday and educational lives, and highlights the heterogeneity of their experience. Mixed-heritage identity has been relatively well-researched within contexts such as education, ethnic monitoring and classification, children in care, families and religion (Parker and Song 2001; Mahtani and Moreno 2001; Olumide 2002; Ali 2003; DfES 2004; Ifekwunigwe 2004; Okitikpi 2005; Barn and Harman 2006; Aspinall et al. 2006; Caballero et al. 2008; Dewan 2008; Aspinall 2010; Caballero and Edwards 2010). However, whilst the dimensions of race and gender have often been included in these studies, little published work to date has explored the issue of class nor, significantly, how the inter-sections between class, race and gender impact differentially on people of mixed heritage. This chapter, which presents a preliminary analysis of the research findings, begins to redress this gap in the literature.

Initial findings destabilise popular and political UK discourse which promotes the idea that we are moving towards a more cosmopolitan, egalitarian and meritocratic society in which race, class and gender are no longer socially or politically relevant issues. This dominant perspective is sustained by the overarching discourse of individualism which fosters the notion that through their own efforts people can be the makers of their own destinies (Rose 1998; Savage 2000; Beck and Beck-Gernsheim 2001; Furlong and Cartmel 2008). Discussed in greater depth later in this chap-ter, the cosmopolitan discourse promotes the idea that mixed-race identi-ties presage an enlightened race-free society in which people of all races and cultures are fully recognised and affirmatively embraced. The teenag-ers in my study, regardless of gender and class, advocated this discourse in their talk. They said that mixed-race identity encouraged understand-ing between cultures and heralded a progressive stance towards issues of race and equality. There were, however, marked differences in how this discourse actually played out in students' lives. Middle class youth—es-pecially girls—regarded mixedness as an unreservedly desirable identity, and believed that their racial heritage had no bearing on the opportuni-ties available to them. Those from working-class backgrounds—especially boys—expressed what I would call a 'thwarted cosmopolitanism' in that they embraced the values of cosmopolitanism but often struggled with the negative effects of race, class and gender. In this sense, these boys carried a 'triple burden' of oppression. A loose typology—subject to change and somewhat unsophisticated given that my analysis is incomplete, and race and class are ambiguous and porous concepts—may help to illustrate and frame the relative success of young mixed-heritage teenagers in negotiating this dominant cosmopolitan discourse:

a) middle-class girls: most successful—tended to identify with, and ben-efit from, middle-class cosmopolitan culture.
b) middle-class boys: middling successful—identified with middle-class and/or Black culture, and were often regarded by others as Black.
c) working-class girls: middling successful—often identified with Black culture and had high, or relatively high, educational aspirations.
d) working-class boys: least successful—tended to identify with Black culture and believed in cosmopolitan values which were frequently frustrated by experiences of prejudice and discrimination.

I am less concerned in this chapter with trying to find causes for these divergent identities and experiences than with demonstrating how race, class and gender intersect to produce them. The chapter considers themes such as multiculturalism, relationships with peers, appearance and the effects of racial profiling to exemplify some of the striking and subtle contrasts between the experiences of mixed-heritage youth from middle-class and working-class backgrounds. In the next section I discuss my conceptual framework.

THEORISING RACE, CLASS AND GENDER— AN INTERSECTIONAL APPROACH

Poststructuralism underpinned the development of Black feminist and post-colonial theory, out of which intersectionality theory arose in the 1990s (Crenshaw 1989, 1995; McCall 2005). With reference to their marginalisation within the feminist movement, which was spearheaded by White middle-class women, Black feminists first highlighted the interlocking systems of racial, class, sexual and heterosexual oppression (Carby 1982; Childers and hooks 1990; Mirza 1997), the different values and experiences of Black and ethnic minority women and the limitations of gender as a single and primary unit of analysis.

My research findings contest any critical social theory which is mono-dimensional in its approach—not just feminism, but also Critical Race Theory and Marxism, whose protagonists continue to argue about the relative status of patriarchy, race and class in the hierarchy of systems of oppression (see Gillborn 2008; Cole 2009). Intersectionality theory is premised upon the idea that we cannot 'privileg[e] a single dimension of experience', nor separate social experiences into 'discrete and pure strands' (Brah and Phoenix 2004, 76–78), and is usefully applied to my study as it can reveal how the intersections between class, race and gender constitute the teenagers' very different experiences of identity. I underpin intersectionality theory with a feminist antiracist poststructuralist approach: This enables insights into the composite and multifaceted dimensions of the participants' lives, and how their racialized identities intersect with gender and class to (re) produce different social locations, self-perceptions and experiences. Such an approach also allows us to focus on questions of power and injustice: it promulgates the idea that identities and knowledge are provisional, relative and socially constructed within plural contexts whilst simultaneously holding on to the truth claim that inequality is wrong, unacceptable and needs to be challenged.

NOTES ON RACE AND CLASS

In this section I briefly explain how I use the concepts of race and class in this chapter. The terms 'mixed race' and 'mixed heritage' are applied interchangeably to describe young people who self-identify as mixed race and have parents (and in some cases grandparents) of different racial backgrounds. These terms are not trouble-free: The implicit assumption is that mixed-race identity has a biological basis and arises from two or more distinct races. Although there have been attempts to use alternative expressions, the term 'mixed race' is widely understood and has never been seriously challenged in Britain. The research participants invariably used the term 'mixed race' to describe themselves and others; none used expressions common in academic research such as 'mixed heritage', 'dual parentage', or 'bi-racial', etc., and some second-generation students used the term 'quarter-caste'. Today, few people in social science and education arenas refute the idea that race—and gender, class, identity, inequality, etc.—are socially constructed phenomena which nevertheless have demonstrable personal and political consequences. We cannot challenge raced practice—both ideological and material—if race is seen as a purely abstract concept. In order to deconstruct and revoke the negative historical and structural effects of reified categories such as race, gender and class, it is imperative that we do not skirt around them (for example, by putting 'race' in inverted commas), but place them firmly on the academic, policy, curriculum and practice agenda.

In terms of class, eligibility for free school meals is still commonly used as the main indicator of socioeconomic background, especially in large-scale studies. I take the view that economic circumstances reveal only one aspect of class (Reay 1998) and therefore draw on students' own 'class talk' to classify students as middle or working class. Because of the sensitive nature of this subject, only participants who brought up the issue of class themselves were specifically asked about their class identifications. Information about parents' occupations and where they lived (postcode and type of housing), as well as implicit references to class in talk about their everyday lives and social relations, were also used to ascertain the class background of students.

My study shows that students whose parents did not have 'traditional' middle-class jobs but were financially secure and/or valued education highly were frequently unclear about their class location. Clover (Scottish-English-Danish/Bajan, 14), whose mother worked as a play therapist in schools and whose father was a self-employed fitness teacher, said: 'I wouldn't say I was really middle class, I'm kind of in-between. Like my mum's not working really hard and we get by easily, we have enough money for luxuries, like we're not struggling.' A prevalent view, too, was that middle-classness could be acquired despite being born into a working-class family. Simon (Antiguan/Irish, 15), for example, said, 'My parents have gone and moved up and stuff but their families were very much working class . . . they [his parents] did a degree and are now professionals and stuff.' Jas (Indian/English, 14) grapples with the question of whether class is determined by inherited wealth or can be procured later in life by association. Jas said:

My mum always says she's middle class, but her family never had any money, and her sister always says we're working class, they always argue about it, so I don't think there's any clear barrier between the two anymore. And my dad kind of defies class, now he's quite middle class—his girlfriend's middle class—but when he was born and in his childhood he wasn't and it seems your class is kind of defined by how you grew up, so I don't know if he switched classes or what.

My suspicion is that a small number of students from middle-class backgrounds performed Black working-class identities, and vice versa. Although relevant to this study, much more research is required to unravel the complexities of such identifications.

THE SCHOOL CONTEXT

The research, which began in April 2008, is being conducted in a gender-mixed ethnically diverse school with a liberal multicultural ethos and an international focus, and one which has a substantial mixed-heritage population. I have worked part-time at the school as an art and supply teacher for six years, and have continuously observed and conversed with students and staff on issues around race, identity and education. This has given me considerable insight into the school's habitus, which provides the context for the research. I have conducted qualitative interviews with fifty-four students aged eleven to eighteen so far, and this chapter draws specifically on interviews with twenty-two students aged fourteen and fifteen. The research process has brought home to me just how little opportunity young mixed-heritage people have for talking about their experiences of being mixed race; consequently, one of the wider aims of the research has been to encourage students to speak about, and engage constructively with, their own identities and experiences.

Talk about race, colour and culture is commonplace amongst the Black, ethnic minority and mixed-race students at the school, and a way of categorising and positioning themselves and others. In conversations during art lessons, for example, they chat about whether particular people are Black or mixed race. Their views on what mixed race means reflect common understandings of mixed-race identity that are anchored in ideas about race biological difference (phenotype, skin colour, etc.), to which specific meanings are attached in popular and public discourse. At the same time, and perhaps paradoxically, notions about who is and who is not mixed race are very much influenced by a multiculturalist 'anything goes' discourse of mixed race. This interest in a person's racial and cultural background has frequently been extended to me, and many students over the years have asked me quite openly, 'Where are you from, miss?' Their talk reveals how ideas around birthplace, nationality, race, culture and parental heritage become intertwined and conflated with notions about racial background. A typical conversation goes something like this:

> 'Where are you from, miss?'
>
> 'What do you mean?' I ask innocently.
>
> 'Like where are you *from?* Where was you born?'
>
> 'I was born in London.'
>
> 'Yeah, but what's your country?'
>
> 'I don't have a country, but I grew up in Scotland.' (I know full well what they are getting at.)
>
> 'M-i-i-i-ss', my questioner is beginning to get exasperated, 'where's your mum and dad from?'
>
> 'Ah, now I see what you mean, why didn't you ask that in the first place? My mum's German and my dad was from India.'
>
> 'Oh, so you're mixed race. I'm mixed race as well. . . . '

When asked the 'where are you from?' question by White adults within five minutes of meeting me, I often sense they are trying to place me according to some spurious categorical notions they have about race and personhood. With school students, however, my pedagogic self swings into play, and I seize the opportunity, sometimes somewhat mischievously, to continue the conversation. For many of these young people race is real, and talks such as these are important on a personal emotional level and a sociopolitical level; they are an opportunity to illuminate the links between biological and sociological depictions of race, and to interrogate the meanings and false assumptions behind raced concepts, discourses and practices.

The student database was initially used to locate people of mixed heritage, and I then approached students directly about whether they self-identified as mixed race and wanted to be involved in the project. The ethnicity data were not always correct, and some students came to the project through hearing about it from peers. Standard procedures around parental consent were followed for all participants involved. Some students have shown a keen interest in the project and have asked to be interviewed again, giving reasons like 'It [the interview] made me think about things' and 'Things have changed, I have a lot more to say' and 'It's like therapy for me.'

As a sociologist and supply teacher, I believe that I was positioned by students as an 'outsider' or as a marginal member of the school. As an art teacher I was seen as an 'insider', known to most of the students, and probably regarded by some as part of the system they struggled against. The few participants with whom I spoke about how it felt to be interviewed by me saw me as an 'insider' on account of my colour and insider knowledge about what it means to be mixed race. This raises epistemological, representational and ethical issues about who can legitimately and effectively research whom, and within the context of this research, about how students understood embodied race differences—as expressing or representing 'interpretations of the social world that needs explaining' (Mirza and Joseph, 2010, 5), or as essentialist differences which privilege a certain epistemic knowledge. This subject is discussed in a forthcoming article.

In the next part of the chapter I briefly examine some of the contemporary popular discourses around mixed-race identity in Britain. These discourses reveal how intersections between race, gender and class position mixed-heritage people in different ways, and provide the context for a discussion of the interview data which follow.

CONTEMPORARY DISCOURSES AROUND THE 'MIXED-RACE' SUBJECT

Contemporary discourses around mixed-race identity in Britain are paradoxical in their depictions of mixed-race identity. On the one hand, mixed-race people, boys especially, are seen as Black (and therefore working class) and portrayed in the media as knife-wielding yobs who reject education and live in a moral-free world of instant gratification. This discourse is underscored by statistics which reveal that mixed-race boys have low educational attainment levels (Gillborn and Mirza 2001), high school-expulsion rates (DfES 2004) and that mixed-heritage children are overrepresented in the care system (Okitikpi 2005).

On the other hand, popular understandings of mixed-race identity are upheld by a cosmopolitan perspective which combines the ideologies of multiculturalism and political equality, embraces internationalism and different cultural outlooks and values and conveys an openness to the world. I neither engage with the growing body of academic literature on cosmopolitanism nor discuss its theoretical merits (see Beck 2006), but draw on the concept as a layperson would. Within this discourse, mixed-heritage people are celebrated as symbols of a culturally rich society which has successfully overcome its race -relations problems: As not 'too Black, too different, too dangerous' (Smith 2006), they have become the acceptable face of diversity—the embodiments of a cosmopolitan progressive society, and 'exemplars of contemporary cultural creativity' (Parker and Song 2001, 4). They are, effectively, the living proof that equality and meritocracy do exist.

This cosmopolitan discourse also frames the phenomenon of young mixed-race people increasingly becoming the exotic subjects/objects of the media, advertising and modelling gaze, as can be seen in, for example, Benetton and Levi's adverts. Not surprisingly, the 'UK's first mixed-race model competition' was recently held in Manchester (Mix-d: Face 2010). One explanation for the demand in mixed-race actresses is that they carry the 'seductive' appeal of the 'ethnically ambiguous' (Arlidge 2004). A recent study on mixed race, moreover, has drawn on scientific research to show that mixed-race people have the greatest health and attractiveness.

A bemused Oona King, former Labour MP and London mayoral nominee, responds to these findings—'White supremacy is so last century. These days it's on-trend to be a mixed race supremacist . . . now it seems that mixed race genes are being hailed as the latest Darwinian "must have" accessory' (King 2010). These pro-mixed-race observations are reflected in my everyday conversations with young people who often particularise their racial and cultural ancestries by going back several generations in descriptions of themselves. Multiethnicity is viewed as interesting, worldly and sophisticated, and a way of asserting how unique you are. One difficult aspect of the celebratory discourse is that cultural difference defined as benign variation results in 'harmonious, empty pluralism' (Mohanty 2003, 191) and masks the racist, sexist and classist assumptions embedded within this discourse, and their adverse effects on mixed-race people.

COSMOPOLITAN LIVES

I now turn to the findings and look at how race, class and gender are imbricated in the young people's lives and articulations. I examine the findings within the context of the popular cosmopolitan and race-centred discourses around mixed-heritage identity discussed above, and the theory of intersectionality.

Students, regardless of class background, tended to endorse a cosmopolitan view of the world in their articulations. However, only middle-class teenagers seemed to benefit from the benign affirmative effects of the cosmopolitan discourse. They perceived mixed-heritage identity as unproblematic, positive and even sought-after, and none said they had ever experienced unequal chances in education on account of being mixed race. They usually did well at school, and a few were involved in high-profile political activities such as standing as candidates for the Youth Parliament and successfully competing in annual Model UN conferences in London. Race, it seemed, was not a negative issue for them. Their middle-class identity, one could argue, diminished the significance of race in their lives; thus class can to some extent be seen as an equaliser of race difference.

Notions of 'multitude' and 'diversity' were also talked about by middle-class students especially. They enjoyed living in an area and attending a school which was culturally very mixed. Holidays abroad were the norm, and many had travelled to distant places including their countries of heritage. The heritages of grandparents and sometimes great-grandparents were often included in self-descriptions, which is perhaps not surprising when understood within the context of a society that espouses cultural multiplicity, individualism and personal competition. Interest was also expressed in different religions, languages, music and international foods.

Friendships, too, were initially described as culturally and racially diverse—which is in keeping with the multicultural ethos of London society and the school—although more in-depth interviewing often revealed that they were rather mono-cultural. This was corroborated by my postpran-dial perusals in the playground and canteen. I found that class was a stark divider in terms of the alliances mixed-race students made: They mixed *across* race/culture lines and *along* class lines.

The aspect of the cosmopolitan discourse which fetishises young mixed-race women's appearance resonated with many of the girls' articulations: mixed-race girls had a clear advantage over other girls in terms of their skin colour, which was moreover particularly good for getting a tan in the summer. Although skin tanning is intentional and seen as distinct from bio-logical skin colour, the two were clearly linked in some girls' talk, momen-tarily transforming the meaning of race. Alise's (Ghanaian-English/Irish, 14) comments were typical and test Ahmed's (1998) claim that skin is the 'unstable *border* between the body and its others' (45, original italics). She demystifies the race = colour link by playing with the idea that a tan—as a construction which is politically harmless—can darken, and therefore enhance, skin that is already brown. She thus draws on ideas of 'ethnic ambiguity' and mixed-race 'exoticism' in which race ceases to *necessarily* be a marker of otherness:

Indra: What are the positive things about being mixed race?
Alise: I tan easily! I don't burn. Yeah, I love getting tans. That's the positive. I think the negative is that I have to moisturise a lot cos my skin goes really dry easily. That's the only negative thing really.
Indra: So you like to be darker?
Alise: Yeah, have you ever noticed when you get a tan you kind of look like you've got smoother skin? And it's not just about being darker, I think, it's like they say in the adverts, the sun kissed you, it looks really nice. And dark skin I think is gorgeous, and I love dark skinned children as well, they're so cute!

Dress was a clear marker of class background in the school. The data sug-gest that students were acutely aware of the class differences between them, which were easily discernible by dress style, accent, postcode and how much money a person has. Clothes determined who was seen as a 'chav' (generally White working-class people), 'skater' (generally White middle-class people) and 'rude' (usually Black/mixed-race boys). Middle-class teenagers looked down on 'chavs'. Alise's observation is an example of how dress can be a cul-tural marker that is 'read onto bodies as personal dispositions' (Skeggs 2004, 1): 'Skaters think that chavs are lower class like in the ghetto kind of thing—they think they're stupid, most of them.' Girls in particular were at pains to dissociate themselves from the 'chavvy look', and talked about the constant punitive pressure exerted on them by other girls to conform to the 'perfect look' in terms of dress, body shape and complexion. Despite their frustra-tion, resistance to this pressure was perceived to carry high personal costs.

Drawing on cosmopolitan notions which downplay the significance of race and skin colour, Alexandra (Zambian/English, 15) claimed that people nowadays looked more at how others dressed than at their skin colour, yet also inadvertently draws on a skin colour/fashion link in declaring that she does not dress like Black girls. So Alexandra distances herself from the idea that skin colour (and culture and class) is important but also from the way that specifically Black girls dress, thereby essentialising Black girls. Indeed, she recognises the social construction of racial dress codes whilst suggesting that Black girls have a fixed idea of what Black girls, and therefore Alexandra too, should wear. She said:

> I don't really dress like the typical sort of black girl or mixed race girl, like usually you don't see black girls in like skinny jeans and stuff, which is more like what I wear. . . . People look more at what you're wearing, like what kind of music you might listen to, so I think that's what people see first, not really what your skin colour is, or like your culture or class . . . I could probably imagine that if someone maybe saw me—I think it would be more like black girls who'd think that— they'd be more kind of 'oh she dresses kind of different', but that's just because they've got the perception of black girls dress like them, whereas I don't really think I dress like them personally.

RACE TALK

In this section I look in particular at the experiences of mixed-race students, often from working-class backgrounds, for whom race was a salient aspect of life. As we have seen, middle-class students tended to fit comfortably into the school habitus and seemed relatively untouched by the effects of race. Young people from working-class backgrounds, on the other hand, often had difficulties with the social and educational demands of school, and especially outside school experienced life through the lens of race. Having said that, the school has accomplished a great deal in terms of identity-specific provision for marginalised Black and mixed-race students, and has introduced a successful peer mentoring scheme which recently won an award.

As a child, Taylor (Ghanaian/English, 14) had questioned her skin colour difference to her mother: 'I wanted to be white and used to ask my mum why are you black and I'm light, and she told me and I don't really think of colour anymore . . . to be honest colour doesn't really come to my mind, I just see myself as Taylor, not a black girl or a white girl or a mixed race, just Taylor.' Nevertheless, Taylor identifies with Black culture and has mostly Black friends. Like many students, she talks about shared interests in music, pastimes, fashion and humour as forming the basis of her friendships, where these interests seem to clearly express race and class identifications. I ask Taylor what draws her more to Black people, and she replies:

Maybe the way they act, the things they like is similar to me, and maybe it could be like music as well. Like mostly white people like rock and that, I like hip hop so maybe it's that. And some of my white friends they're more like, they have to go out every night and get drunk and all of that, like go to a party, and most of my black friends they just go out during the day, not like night-time and they don't get drunk—most of my white friends they think what we do is boring and getting drunk is better. And the way they dress as well . . . Most of my black friends they just wear whatever, not like what white people wear, like it's different.

Taylor negotiates her identity through her own understanding of herself as mixed, and the expectations of others to define herself as Black. Portraying Black and White people as belonging to two distinct camps, as her Black friends do, she defends her whiteness and makes clear that she is Black *and* White. Taylor, however, was sometimes excluded from her Black friendship group because she was 'not Black enough' (Dewan 2008). She claimed that this type of rejection was typical of girls, and that boys' interracial friendships were less troubled.

Indra: Do other people ever make you think about your colour?

Taylor: Yeah, my friends do. I do have mixed friends, like white, black, Somalian, Indian, all that, but most of my friends are black, and they say 'I don't see you as white you're black, you're black, and your second name proves it' [surname Black]. I do find it annoying sometimes that they ignore my white side. It's as if white people are not good enough, black people are better, that's how they make it out. Most of my black friends they don't really mix with white, they think they're boring or whatever, or they're too white—it's stupid when they say that. . . . Something happened and I felt a bit left out—I was like with my black friends and I think I was the only mixed race person there and they done things and just went 'oh you won't understand cos you're not black'.

Indra: Was it girls or boys?

Taylor: Girls. The boys they don't really, it's mostly girls who say 'oh you're not black, bla-bla-bla', it's not boys, they just see you as who you are, not, oh that black girl that white girl.

Indra: Does that make it easier to be with boys?

Taylor: Yeah, they're comfortable to be around. They don't judge you and yeah, they wouldn't like make them stupid remarks either. Boys, they'll be with their boys, and if you're a mixed race boy, they won't get pressured by their friends saying 'oh you're too white, you're too black' all of that, but if it's a girl they would cos some girls are silly and bitchy.

Alongside dress, accent was a marker of a person's social class at the school. A few teenagers from working-class backgrounds pointed out that their mothers had taught them to 'speak properly', and how this affected them in terms of their credibility with Black girls. Lauren (Jamaican/French-English, 15) said her Black friends teased her for 'speak[ing] quite posh compared to them apparently' and that this signified that she was 'acting white'. Lauren explains further:

> Sometimes with people, quite a few of my friends are black, like they don't mean it in like a negative way, but sometimes they're like 'oh she acts so white', sort of like a joke, and I'm just like 'okay, but I'm not black I'm mixed race, I can act however I want to'. But they don't mean it in a bad way to be offensive, it's just like a joke sort of thing.

In dismissing her friends' remarks as unimportant, Lauren draws attention to the increasing normalisation of a subtle form of discrimination which slyly mocks ethnic minority people on account of their facial features, skin colour, hair or cultural habits. Such discrimination is intended to hurt and simultaneously go unnoticed. When I was supply teaching at the school recently, for example, I confiscated a drawing a boy had done of his friend's parents who were both African, depicting them as caricatures with large lips and accentuated noses. He said that his friend had also found the drawing funny. We see here the flip side of the cosmopolitan discourse, in which cultural difference becomes the source of racial ridicule. This kind of interaction occurs between boys especially and is negated as 'just joking' (see Frosh et al. 2002), where not laughing alongside the others sets the injured party up for further derision and exclusion. Talking with mixed-race students about the prejudice they experienced in school elicited comments like 'I just try and ignore it', 'I can't do anything about it anyway', and as one boy who was constantly teased about his dreadlocks put it, 'I've just got so used to it I don't care. It's their problem, their business.'

On the periphery of a renowned gang in North London, Cheyenne (English-Italian/Jamaican-Brazilian, 14) believed that a lack of money induces those who already feel excluded because of their race into criminal activity more. She focused on the dimension of class in her analysis of the inequalities she observed in school and talked about her own experiences of exclusion by middle-class students because of the 'poor' way she dressed. Cheyenne suggests that race discrimination arises out of class discrimination:

> I don't think it's a race thing. The people who've got quite a lot of money hang around together in a large group cos they've got the clothes and stuff, and I know when I'm in my music class basically everyone thinks they're better than me cos they're able to have private tuition and stuff. I think it's to do with money more than race. If I grew up in a rich area and had like more money and stuff I think I'd be less pushed out by

them [white people], but because of the area I live in and the people I socialise with people get pushed out. Even if I wanted to I couldn't just start hanging out with skaters because of the way I dress and stuff.

Boys from working-class backgrounds and/or who identified strongly with Black culture were most likely to experience the 'thwarted cosmopolitanism' I talked about at the start of this chapter. Although they had mostly Black friends and were drawn mainly to Black culture, they were also interested in diverse lifestyles and felt that being mixed race gave them insights into different ways of thinking. Simon (Antiguan/Irish, 15), for example, said: 'I'll read about China from the 18th or 19th Century. Also I'll read Japanese stuff and African stories, listen to African music and so on . . . I feel like I understand how different people see different things in the world.' Students also frequently mentioned a vision of society in which they wished 'cultures could come together more' (James, Irish-English/Monserratian, 14).

At the same time, boys from working-class backgrounds were likely to have negative experiences outside school because of their 'triple burden' of race, class and gender which placed them in a testing position vis-à-vis gangs who were looking for trouble, and police trying to prevent trouble. None of the boys I spoke with felt safe being out after dark without the 'protection' of a group of friends, and most were regularly stopped and searched by the police—'I am constantly frisked, cos black boys always are' (Simon). More in-depth research and analysis needs to be done to fully appreciate the sociological, ethical and emotional impact of experiences such as these on young racialized teenagers. In the next section I focus in particular on what a small number of participants said about their everyday experiences 'stop and search'.

RACIAL PROFILING: STOP AND SEARCH

The Metropolitan Police on their Web site (www.met.police.uk) state that stop-and-search powers allow the police to tackle crime and antisocial behaviour, and to stop more serious crimes occurring. Police officers can use stop-and-search tactics 'If they think you're carrying a weapon, drugs or stolen property; if there has been serious violence or disorder in the vicinity; if they are looking for a suspect who fits your description; as part of anti-terrorism efforts'. Evidence shows that although people from Black and ethnic minority backgrounds are not more likely to offend than people from the majority group, they are significantly overrepresented in all stages of the criminal justice process; the lack of confidence in the criminal justice system and the police is therefore unsurprising (see Criminal Justice Unit 2005). The use of stop-and-search methods without 'reasonable suspicion' has recently come under heavy criticism for being divisive and counterproductive to community relations. James (Irish-English/Monser-ratian, 14) talked about his experience of being stopped and searched at the annual steam fair, one of the local community highlights of the year and a lovely occasion for all the family.

Indra: Have you ever been stopped and searched?
James: Yeah, just patrol like. Like at the steam fair over there.
Indra: What did they do?
James: They just stopped and searched, they done it for like everyone really, just to check if they had any knives, they heard like gangs were coming or something like that.
Indra: What did you think of that?
James: It annoyed me, but I can't do anything about it. I don't think I look that suspicious [we both laugh—no, he certainly does not look suspicious].
Indra: Did they check everybody?
James: Yeah. Everybody that looked suspicious. Like people in their little groups or something.
Indra: Was it mostly boys?
James: Yeah, it wasn't really girls, they don't suspect anything from the girls.
Indra: Was it mostly black boys?
James: [Laughs] Yeah. Like they don't really go up to skater guys, if you see what I mean, they don't really come up to like a guy with a hat on or something.

Similar to James, Cheyenne (Jamaican-Brazilian/English-Italian, 14) talked about the race, class and gender stereotyping of the police. Mixed-race girls were usually only stopped and searched when they became 'masculinised' by association with a group of Black boys. Neither James nor Cheyenne questioned the legitimacy of stop-and-search practices, nor assumptions about the supposed deviance of groups of Black boys. For Cheyenne it was not discrimination per se which was the main problem—indeed, like James, her talk suggests that stop-and-search methods are perhaps necessary to combat the problem of knife crime on London streets—but the unfair treat-ment of Black and mixed-race students in comparison with White middle-class youth. Cheyenne said:

Like when I'm just walking by myself or with my friends who are girls I would never get stop and searched but when I'm walking around with like two or three black boys I've been stopped and searched so many times, like basically every time we go out and police pass by they say 'I'm stop and searching you for bla bla, bla' and I think it's a stereotype they need to sort out. Like a lot of the skater people they tend to do a lot of drugs and stuff and I think the police need to understand that as well, be searching for that as well as searching for knives and phones.

The students in my study generally recognised the sway of the media in fuelling racial stereotypes, and how the word 'gang' is meted out to Black and ethnic minority people on the basis of their colour, class and gender (Alexander 2008). Jordan (Congolese-Belgian/Congolese, 15) believed he was stopped and searched often because police (and many teachers) assumed that 'the way you look is the way you behave', referring to the notion that 'most black males are associated with guns, like crime and gangs and stuff like that.' He is initially reserved and simply says: 'I think that I am being treated unfairly, that's it really, that's all I can say about it', but then goes on to talk about his experiences, slowly and thoughtfully.

Indra: And being treated unfairly, what does that then make you feel?
Jordan: It makes me feel kind of a bit upset, but makes me think, makes me think of why I'm being treated unfairly.
Indra: And what conclusion do you come to?
Jordan: Prejudice, people being prejudiced.
Indra: About you, how people see you?
Jordan: Ah-hm.
Indra: What is their prejudice?
Jordan: Probably I'm young.
Indra: Young.
Jordan: Yeah. Black. Yeah. Probably involved in a gang.
Indra: In your experience is there any truth in it?
Jordan: There is some truth, but I feel that because there's a minority doing that, that the majority are being mistreated unfairly because of the minority, and that's quite annoying yeah.

Jordan describes an incident which took place in the mainly middle-class multicultural area in which the school is situated.

Jordan: We were in KFC (Kentucky Fried Chicken) in [names location], there was just like three of us, and then the police just came in and told us that someone was in possession of sharp objects so we got stopped and searched and we didn't have a clue what they were talking about.
Indra: With people sitting there, watching?
Jordan: Yeah. And I felt that they took advantage of their power kind of. Hmm. Like in the way they were treating us, like standing up there in the corner, grabbed us, searched our bags, yeah.
Indra: They said to everybody or just you?
Jordan: Just to us, out of the blue . . . they just grabbed us, put us against the wall, said 'stand still', and started searching us. And then they

gave us like a little receipt. Apparently after that you have to get a receipt thing just in case you want to get any complaints, but even if I did complain, I don't think anything would happen.

Indra: Do you talk to your parents about it?

Jordan: Not really, cos it doesn't really bother me that much, I just take it on the chin and move on, yeah.

Jordan and other students who had similar experiences seemed to have normalised their experiences and appeared on the surface to be unmoved by these events—as Jordan points out, he 'takes it on the chin'. Only a few students expressed frustration about the ingrained negative misconceptions that they believed police and members of the public hold about mixed-race and Black youth. This supports research which has found that the vulnerability of masculine identities means they have to be constantly asserted, thus camouflaging the fears and stresses which underlie them (Mac an Ghaill 1994; Sewell 1997, 2009). Although most students, like Jordan, appear nonchalant, their sense of injustice is palpable.

Indra: Do you feel that when you're in a situation like that, how do you come to terms with it?

Jordan: I just say that's how it is.

Indra: Do you feel that you've got any power at all?

Jordan: No. The police is the law and you can't go against the law.

Indra: So it's a kind of *dis*empowering thing I imagine.

Jordan: Yeah.

Indra: Can you imagine if it kept happening, would you and your friends get angry about it?

Jordan: I wouldn't say we'd get angry, I would just say we try to avoid it more. So if we see like a police officer we just move away, or start talking on the phone. That's why I think, that's one of the main reasons why youth nowadays don't really like police officers, yeah.

Their feeling of powerlessness should not be surprising. As Furlong and Cartmel (2008) have pointed out, 'situations which would once have led to a call for political action are now interpreted as something which can only be solved on an individual level by personal action' (p. 6). Thus, within the context of the omnipresent discourse of individualism, private troubles—even discrimination—fall back on the individual and become seen as personal failings instead of the consequences of enduring social structures which shape people's lives in unjust and unequal ways. This study underscores the necessity of undertaking more in-depth research to understand the social and psychological costs of government methods such as stop and search on young people.

CONCLUSION

An intersectional approach underpinned by antiracist feminist thought has been applied to my research to draw attention to how interlocking aspects of race, class and gender impact upon and constitute young mixed-heritage people's identities, social locations, experiences and aspirations. Class, especially, is the 'silent player', and has profound implications for how successfully mixed-heritage students are able to negotiate the dominant individualist and cosmopolitan discourses. Whereas the middle-class mixed-race girls in the study most often reaped the benefits of a liberal cosmopolitan culture which (cl)aims to promote diversity, equality of opportunity and individual responsibility, mixed-race boys from working-class backgrounds tended to encounter a 'thwarted cosmopolitanism' in which their positive experiences of equality, meritocracy and fair treatment remained limited.

The research contributes to the growing body of work which critiques the notion that people are wholly responsible for their own 'failure' or 'success'; it emphasises the incongruity between the discourses of individualism and cosmopolitanism which hold fast to the dictum that we *can* be the authors of our own destinies regardless of race, class and gender status, and the social processes and structures which continue to configure some people's lives in exigent ways. It also highlights the pressing need for an intersectional understanding of mixed-race experience, and suggests that critical feminist antiracist emancipatory work with young racialized people of both genders is crucial to be able to identify, discuss and challenge in constructive ways the dominant negative assumptions and practices which are sustained by neoliberal discourse. Darian is aware of how race, colour, gender and class have impacted harmfully on his life so far, and began the process of attempting to overcome the impediments in his path by putting what he called 'black negativity' behind him when his father went to prison. I end with a quote from Darian: The vision may be quixotic, but it is a timely and simple reminder that we are not yet in that place where race, colour, culture, nationality, class and gender are no longer issues, and that we need to continue our efforts to rise above prejudice.

> Just like Obama is a mixed race president but everyone's saying he's black, and that shouldn't be cos if mixed race people are seen as black then everyone's going to think that there's black and there's white but there's no in-between, so you're either on one side or the other and that's going to make people stick to their like 'I'm black, I'm white, I'm Chinese, I'm Indian, I'm Pakistani', and I think there needs to be a time when everyone should understand that those cultures can all come together and be one.

REFERENCES

Ahmed, Sarah. 1998. Animated bodies: Skin, colour and tanning. In *Vital signs: Feminist reconfiguration of the bio/logical body*, eds. Magrit Shildrick and Janet Price. Edinburgh: Edinburgh University Press.

Alexander, Claire. 2008. *(Re)thinking 'gangs'*. London: Runnymede Trust.

Ali, Suki. 2003. *Mixed-race, post-race: Gender, new ethnicities and cultural practices*. London: Berg.

Arlidge, John. 2004. Forget black, forget white. EA is what's hot. *The Observer*, 4 January. Accessed July 2010.

Aspinall, Peter. 2010. Concepts, terminology and classifications for the 'mixed' ethnic or racial group in the United Kingdom. *Journal of Epidemiology and Community Health* 64 (6): 557–560.

Aspinall, Peter, Miri Song and Ferhana Hashem. 2006. Mixed race in Britain: A survey of the preference of mixed race people for terminology and classifications. *The Inheritance Project*. Canterbury: University of Kent.

Barn, Ravinder, and Vicki Harman. 2006. A contested identity: An exploration of the competing social and political discourse concerning the identification and positioning of young people of inter-racial parentage. *British Journal of Social Work* 36 (8): 1309–1324.

Beck, Ulrich. 2006. *The cosmopolitan vision*. Cambridge: Polity Press.

Beck, Ulrich, and Elizabeth Beck-Gernsheim. 2001. *Individualisation: Institutionalised individualism and its social and political consequences*. London: Sage.

Brah, Avtar, and Ann Phoenix. 2004. Ain't I a woman? Revisiting intersectionality. *Journal of International Women's Studies* 5 (3): 75–86.

Caballero, Chamion, and Rosalind Edwards. 2010. *Lone mothers of mixed racial and ethnic children: Then and now*. London: Runnymede.

Caballero, Chamion, Rosalind Edwards and Shuby Puthussery. 2008. *Parenting 'mixed' children: Difference and belonging in mixed race and faith families*. London: Joseph Rowntree Foundation.

Carby, Hazel. 1982. White women listen! Black feminism and the boundaries of sisterhood. In The Centre for Contemporary Cultural Studies, eds. *The Empire strikes back: Race and racism in 70s Britain*. London: Hutchinson.

Childers, Mary, and bell hooks. 1990. A conversation about race and class. In Marianne Hirsch and Evelyn Fox Keller, eds. ,*Conflicts in feminism*. New York: Routledge.

Cole, Mike. 2009. *Critical race theory and education: A Marxist response*. New York: Palgrave Macmillan.

Crenshaw, Kimberlé. 1989. Demarginalizing the intersection of race and sex: A black feminist critique of antidiscrimination doctrine, feminist theory, and antiracist politics. *University of Chicago Legal Forum* 1989: 139–167.

———. 1995. Mapping the margins: Intersectionality, identity politics, and violence against women of color. In *Critical race theory: The key writings that formed the movement*, ed. Kimberlé Crenshaw. New York: The New Press.

Criminal Justice Race Unit and Victims and Confidence Unit. 2005. *The experiences of young black men as victims of crime*. Criminal Justice System, www.cjsonline.gov.uk. Accessed July 2010.

Dewan, Indra Angeli. 2008. *Recasting race: Women of mixed heritage in further education*. Stoke-on-Trent, UK: Trentham Books.

DfES. 2004. *Understanding the educational needs of mixed heritage pupils*. RR549. London: DfES.

Frosh, Stephen, Ann Phoenix and Rob Pattman. 2002. *Young masculinities: Understanding boys in contemporary society*. London: Palgrave Macmillan.

Furlong, Andy, and Fred Cartmel. 2008. *Young people and social change: New perspectives*. Berkshire: Open University Press.

Gillborn, David. 2008. *Racism and education: Coincidence or conspiracy*. London: Routledge.

Gillborn, David, and Heidi Mirza. 2001. *Educational inequality: Mapping race, class and gender*. London: HMI.

Ifekwunigwe, Jayne O., ed. 2004. *'Mixed race' studies: A reader*. London and New York: Routledge.

King, Oona. 2010. At last! It's cool to be mixed race, 25 April, www.dailymail. co.uk/debate/article-1268580/At-Its-cool-mixed-race-handy-Im-African-American-Jewish-Geordie-Irish-Scottish-Hungarian.html. Accessed July 2010.

Mac an Ghaill, Mairtin. 1994. *The making of men: Masculinities, sexualities and schooling*. Buckinghamshire, UK: Open University Press.

Mahtani, Minelle, and April Moreno. 2001. Towards a more unified discourse in 'mixed race' theory. In *Rethinking 'mixed race'*, eds. David Parker and Miri Song. London: Pluto Press.

McCall, Leslie. 2005. The complexity of intersectionality. *Signs: Journal of Women in Culture and Society* 30, (3): 1771–1800.

Metropolitan Police. www.met.police.uk/stopandsearch. Accessed July 2010.

Mirza, Heidi Safia. 1997. *Young, female and black*. London: Routledge.

Mirza, Heidi Safia, and Cynthia Joseph. 2010. *Black and postcolonial feminisms in new times: Researching educational inequalities*. London: Routledge.

Mix-d Face. 2010. www.mix-d.org/face/competition. Accessed February 2011.

Mohanty, Chandra Talpade. 2003. *Feminism without borders: Decolonizing theory, practicing solidarity*. London: Duke University Press.

Okitikpi, Toyin. 2005. *Working with children of mixed parentage*. Lyme Regis, UK: Russell House Publishing.

Olumide, Jill. 2002. *Raiding the gene pool: The social construction of mixed race*. Sterling, VA: Pluto Press.

Parker, David, and Miri Song, eds. 2001. *Rethinking 'mixed race'*. London: Pluto Press.

Reay, Diane. 1998. Rethinking social class: Qualitative perspectives on class and gender. *Sociology* 32 (2): 259–275.

Rose, Nikolas. 1998. *Inventing our selves: Psychology, power and personhood*. Cambridge: Cambridge University Press.

Savage, Mike. 2000. *Class analysis and social transformation*. Buckingham, UK: Open University Press.

Sewell, Tony. 1997. *Black masculinities and schooling: How black boys survive modern schooling*. Stoke-on-Trent, UK: Trentham Books.

———. 2009. *Generating genius: Black boys in search of love, ritual and schooling*. Stoke-on-Trent, UK: Trentham Books.

Skeggs, Beverley. 2004. *Class, self, culture*. London and New York: Routledge.

Smith, Laura. 2006. Absent voices. Society, *The Guardian*, 6 September. Accessed August 2007.

6 'If You're Holding a Degree in This Country No-One's Gonna Ask No Questions'

Intracategorical Intersectionality and BAME Youth Postcompulsory Educational Achievement in the UK

Andrew Morrison

ABSTRACT

This chapter examines Black, Asian and minority ethnic (BAME) youth achievement and aspiration within further and higher education in the United Kingdom. The author applies an intracategorical, intersectionalist, model of 'race', class and gender, complemented by a Bourdieusian theoretical framework, to the in-depth individual case studies of three young people of different South Asian backgrounds. It is argued that this approach to intersectionality offers the potential to go beyond a simplistic BAME category to consider how class and gender interact with 'race' in the development of some minority youth educational identities.

INTRODUCTION

Dominant postcompulsory educational policy discourses in the UK have tended to focus upon youth 'underachievement' among Black, Asian and minority ethnic groups (or BAME—the preferred term of the Equality and Human Rights Commission and other official bodies in the UK and so used within this chapter). By contrast, this chapter seeks to examine BAME youth achievement and aspiration within further and higher education (FHE) and to propose an adequate theoretical framework through which we may address it. The paper begins by considering BAME youth participation and achievement within the FHE sector. Following this, an intracategorical intersectionalist model of 'race', class and gender is proposed as a theoretical basis upon which we may develop a nuanced understanding of the ways in which these social categories articulate with each other in the development of educational identities. In support of this model, data drawn from a recent investigation into the educational and occupational decision making of a group of full-time students on an Advanced Vocational Certificate in Education (AVCE) in travel and tourism at a large college of further and higher education (FHE) in the West Midlands of the UK are then analysed.

BAME YOUTH ACHIEVEMENT
WITHIN HIGHER EDUCATION

Headline figures on BAME participation within higher education (HE) in the UK make for optimistic reading. In the 2007–08 academic year, minority ethnic students comprised 17.2 per cent of all students within the sector (ECU 2009, 43), a proportion which exceeds their share of the 18–24 year old population in the UK, which stands at 14.2 per cent (RfO 2010, 6). A broadly comparable picture emerges from US data. Whereas minority ethnic groups comprised just over 20 per cent of the US population at the last census (U.S. Census Bureau 2010), they were awarded 28 per cent of all BA degrees (Snyder and Dillow 2010, 4).

In both countries, however, such headline statistics hide considerable differences in participation between and within groups. In the UK, the British Indian group had the highest rate of representation in 2007–08 (at 3.3%), closely followed by the Black or Black British African group (3.2%) (RfO 2010, 6). The most underrepresented groups—in terms of their proportions within the wider population—were the British Bangladeshi group (at 0.6% against 1.1% in the UK population) and the British Pakistani group (at 1.9% against 2.2% in the UK population) (RfO 2010, 6). However, figures for particular groups themselves mask considerable intragroup differences. Among Black Caribbean groups, participation rates for women are considerably higher (at 52%) than for males (at 33%); this situation is reversed within the Bangladeshi group in which male participation stands at 43 per cent whereas for females it is 33 per cent (Connor et al. 2004, 43). In addition, although figures for BAME representation across the HE sector as a whole are encouraging, it is apparent that BAME students are clustered within less prestigious 'new' (i.e., post-1992) universities. They represent 22 per cent of all undergraduates at post-1992 universities compared with only 15 per cent at pre-1992 institutions (Connor et al. 2004, 44), although patterns vary considerably across BAME groups. Moreover, evidence suggests that relative disadvantage within the UK's hierarchy of HE institutions plays into later labour market disadvantage, with consequent negative implications for future earning power (Chevalier and Conlon 2003).

Figures for the United States also reveal very uneven patterns of participation among minority ethnic groups. Both Black groups and Hispanic groups are underrepresented relative to their numbers within the wider population. Thus, whereas Black groups comprised 12.9 per cent of the population in the last census (US Census Bureau 2010), only 10 per cent of BA degrees were awarded to Black students; the disparity is even more marked with regard to Hispanic groups, who comprise 15.8 per cent of the US population but gained only 8 per cent of all BA degrees (Snyder and Dillow 2010, 4). By contrast, although Asian groups (including Pacific Islanders) comprise only 4.8 per cent of the overall population, they earned 7 per cent of all BA degrees (Snyder and Dillow 2010, 4).

Returning to the UK context, we can see there are three important aspects to BAME participation within HE. Firstly, aggregate numbers would appear to be generally positive in relation to their proportions within the wider UK population. Secondly, the relatively higher rates of participation compared to White students have been achieved from a relatively disadvantaged class position. As Connor et al. (2004, 35) observe, BAME students in HE are more likely to be children of parents from lower socioeconomic classes compared with all students. Thirdly, there are sharp gender differences within BAME groups.

The description given above of BAME representation in higher education in the UK is thus a complex one in which class, 'race' and gender all feature, making for complex patterns of access and attainment within the sector. Such a description raises two closely linked questions. Firstly, how are we to understand the ways in which these social categories might affect the postcompulsory educational ambitions and opportunities of young people of minority ethnic backgrounds in the UK? Secondly, how are we to address the complex interactions between these social categories in the formation of educational experiences and identities? In the following section I shall outline an intracategorical intersectionalist framework which addresses these two questions.

SOCIAL CATEGORIES AND INTERSECTIONALITY

McCall (2005, 1771) notes that intersectionality—' . . . the relationships among multiple dimensions and modalities of social relations and subject formations'—has itself become a central category of analysis within social science generally, and within feminist research in particular. McCall (2005) then goes on to offer a threefold typology of approaches to intersectionality. I will discuss types one and two as being most relevant to this present research.

The first approach is termed 'anticategorical complexity' and is based upon a methodology which aims to deconstruct analytical categories themselves (McCall 2005, 1773). The ontological premise of this approach derives from a Foucauldian postmodernist focus upon the power of discourse to create social reality: Language (in the broadest sense) creates categories rather than the other way round (McCall 2005, 1777). Because discourse itself is fluid, unstable and socially specific, traditional structural designations such as 'man' or 'woman' are themselves understood to be fractured and fluid and open to a wide range of constructions. As a result, it is argued that 'race', class or gender, as general explanatory categories, homogenise and essentialise important internal difference *within* categories. The methodological consequence of this approach is to challenge the completeness of any set of groups and to further fraction them. Thus, a normative binary gender divide may multiply to incorporate various forms of sexuality and so become a complex multiple divide; similarly, the social groups that comprise the category of 'race' may be rendered ultimately indefinable due to multiracialism (McCall 2005, 1778).

The second approach identified by McCall (2005) is that of 'intracategorical complexity'. This form of intersectionality shares the caution of the first type towards master social categories, but is prepared to provisionally accept them in order to attempt to capture people's lived experiences at underresearched points of intersection. The basis of this type of research is not upon dimensions *within* categories (as with type one) but *across* them, as embodied within individuals. Thus, to use the example given by McCall (2005, 1781), an Arab American, middle-class, heterosexual woman is located at the intersection of multiple categories ('race', class, gender and sexuality). This approach to intersectionality will, therefore, accept categories as units of analysis as a means to focus on the processes by which they are (re)produced, experienced and resisted (McCall 2005, 1783)

The anticategorical approach has much to say about the socially and historically specific character of our knowledge of the world. It serves as a caution against the dangers of glossing over internal difference and thus of reifying structural categories. Nevertheless, I believe that the intracategorical approach to intersectionality offers greater potential for critical educational research. Whereas social groupings of 'race', class and gender do not represent fixed and homogenous realities, they nevertheless produce very real *effects* in individuals' lives. Moreover, both material and cultural relations are implicated. Class (in the restricted sense of employment relations) derives ultimately from material social relations, but can engender cultural subjectivities that may then go on to develop an autonomous power of their own (Fraser 1999, 32). By contrast, 'race' and gender are culturally constructed categories that ultimately depend for their existence upon social actors' belief in them. However, they too are strongly implicated in material social relations. For example, as Fraser (1999, 31) notes, gender structures the fundamental economic division between paid 'productive' labour and unpaid 'reproductive' and domestic labour. Similarly, 'race' also has a historical and continuing function in the division of labour (Young 1999). For these reasons, therefore, I accept Fraser's (1999, 31) argument for viewing 'race', class and gender as 'bivalent', that is, based both in the economic structure and in the cultural status order of society The complex and mutually constitutive relationships between these axes of difference suggest that although we may draw what Archer et al. (2001) term strategic 'provisional boundaries' around particular groups, we must nevertheless be cognizant of the artificiality of the exercise and of the simultaneity of identity within individuals' lived experiences. Thus, I concur with Archer's (2003a, 21) suggestion that

> social identities might be conceptualized as integrally inter-meshed and inter-related—such that axes of 'race', ethnicity, social class and gender cannot easily be separated out from one another because they are combined in such a way that they 'flavour' and give meaning to each other.

This, in turn, raises the question of how we are to understand, for example, how gender is always classed or class racialized. In short, how are we to address the complex interplay between material and cultural social relations in the ongoing formation of the educational aspirations of minority ethnic young people? How are we to link their microlevel perspectives to wider macrolevel structures such as 'race', class and gender? Here I turn to the work of Pierre Bourdieu.

THE BOURDIEUSIAN SCHEMA

Through his three key concepts of the habitus, field and capital, the French sociologist Pierre Bourdieu offers us a theory of culture that connects individual subjectivities with objective structure through a continual dialectic in which the individual is both a product and producer of social relations. The habitus is Bourdieu's attempt to represent the microlevel subjective side of the dialectical relationship. It is a set of deeply embedded dispositions produced through socialisation by which individuals orient themselves to the social world on a more or less subconscious level. The material conditions and social relations of the individual's position form a structure of dispositions that tend to anticipate the objective conditions of their position. Thus, on the basis of these dispositions, social practices tend to reproduce the objective structures from which they are derived.

If habitus represents the subjective side of the dialectical relationship, field is the objective part. Individuals, institutions and collectivities all exist in social space in some form of structured social relation to one another. An example of a field would be the field of education, which we may then further divide into subfields, for example, the field of postcompulsory education. An individual's habitus will encounter and adjust itself to the demands of the field through what Bourdieu (1990, 66) terms a 'feel for the game', that is, through socialisation. The levels of investment which individuals and classes of individuals are able to bring into the field will depend upon the overall volume and distribution of the different kinds of capital to which they have access. Bourdieu employs the term 'capital' in its widely understood economistic sense. For the purposes of this chapter, I shall discuss his most widely known and applied type of capital: cultural capital. Cultural capital refers to often intangible, but socially crucial, embodied cultural attributes: a sense of social self-confidence, a 'cultivated' outlook, a particular style of bodily comportment. We can 'spend' this capital in the field to gain cultural and, ultimately, material advantage over others with lesser resources.

If we apply Bourdieu's concepts together as a coherent whole, we arrive at a 'concrete' concept of social class, that is, one which attempts to combine varied forms of differentiation within a single term (Sayer 2005, 73). This offers advantages to an intracategorical intersectional approach. Firstly, by combining economic capital with different forms of cultural capital (e.g., educational and linguistic capital amongst others), and by showing the interrelationship between them, Bourdieu is able to show that differentiation lies not along one axis but along several, depending upon both the volume *and* the composition of the different forms of capital to which an individual has access. This makes Bourdieu's definition of class a flexible one (Sayer 2005, 77). Secondly, Bourdieu's concept of class offers a means of understanding the ways in which inequalities can be produced and reproduced through cultural processes as well as material ones.

THE LIMITS OF THE BOURDIEUSIAN FRAMEWORK: ETHNICITY AND GENDER

Bourdieu's work offers much, therefore, to an intracategorical approach to intersectionality. Nevertheless, it must also be recognised that the Bourdieusian schema has relatively little to say regarding the place of gender and ethnicity within social processes. As Anthias (2001, 842) notes, for Bourdieu the central determining component of an individual's class is their employment relations under which their gender and ethnicity are subsumed. The result is that gender is not treated as a form of capital or 'constitutive of material positionality' in its own right, whereas 'race' does not feature in his theory of culture (Anthias 2001, 842). However, whereas these caveats should be noted, they are by no means insuperable to researchers and, indeed, Bourdieu's theoretical schema continues to enjoy a central place within sociological analysis (Skeggs 2004). Two recent studies show how two of Bourdieu's key concepts—capital and habitus—may be reworked to address the question of minority ethnic youth ambitions within post-16 education in the UK.

ETHNIC CAPITAL AND THE DIASPORIC HABITUS

The studies of Modood (2004) and Archer and Francis (2007) are an attempt to locate and to analyse a particular 'ethnic effect' as a means to explain the educational aspirations and achievements of some BAME groups. Both studies are based in, but also develop on, a Bourdieusian conceptual framework. Modood (2004, 95) argues for the existence of a 'triadic motor' to explain the success of certain BAME groups, particularly Chinese and Asian groups. The triadic motor consists of familial adult-child relationships; transmission of aspirations and attitudes; and norms enforcement (Modood 2004, 100). Where Modood (2004) claims to depart from Bourdieu is in his elision of cultural and social capital, whereby, for example, the most significant adult-child relationships may not be those between a child and parent. The emphasis in his analysis lies in the power of a form of ethnic group social capital (or 'ethnic capital') to form identity and social expectations:

> The transmission of a normative identity will be more important than, say, parental–child 'quality time', talking together about schoolwork or friendships, or any specific skills and knowledge transfer. (Modood, 2004, 100)

For Modood (2004) it is the acquisition of this form of capital that helps to explain how Asian migrant working-class parents with relatively little levels of 'appropriate' cultural capital and 'know-how' are successfully able to motivate their children towards HE study in greater proportions than their White social class peers. In their study of British-Chinese academic success, Archer and Francis (2007) appear to have arrived at a similar conclusion, although they are much more cautious than Modood (2004) about abandoning the concept of cultural capital altogether as an explanatory factor in BAME achievement. The authors noted that within their study sample, parents of all classes appeared to share the same high-level aspirations for their children (Archer and Francis 2007, 142). Furthermore, like Modood (2004), they went on to observe that many of the parents of working class and/or migrant background lacked the dominant forms of cultural capital associated with knowledge of the HE sector. British-Chinese aspirations and success were therefore attributed to two key factors: firstly, the role of social capital, particularly the effects of social competition between and within 'British-Chinese families; secondly, the existence of a specifically British-Chinese 'diasporic habitus' (Archer and Francis 2007, 140).

British-Chinese social competition was seen to promote educational aspirations through a concern for the maintenance of a 'collective Chinese family honour' (Archer and Francis 2007, 138). Individual 'failure' was seen not simply as a personal or even familial stigma, but a collective ethnic one, to the extent that the discourse of social competition acted as a form of discursive boundary marker for a particular racialized identity (Archer and Francis 2007, 139). Underlying the social competition was the workings of a diasporic habitus. This 'specifically aspirational habitus' (Archer and Francis 2007, 140) transcended the experiences of individual parents and was, instead, expressed as a discourse of ambition rooted in a collective history of poverty and migration.

These two studies demonstrate how Bourdieu's concepts of habitus and capital may be adapted to foreground racialized social processes within classed relations. In so doing, they employ Bourdieu's concepts within an intersectional approach. In the remainder of this chapter, I will apply Bourdieu's concepts of habitus, capital and field, and also other relevant 'class culturalist' analyses, to address the educational aspirations of three young people of different Asian-British backgrounds. My focus is upon the intersectional relations between the 'race', class and gender of the students. Of course, it must be acknowledged that an intersectional approach is not limited simply to analysis of the trio of 'race', class and gender. Society is stratified by other axes of differentiation such as nationality, disability and sexuality. Nevertheless, following the arguments that I have outlined above, I have chosen to focus upon 'race', class and gender on the basis that these three ' . . . constitute both central classificatory elements in society and systems for allocating social value and positionality' (Anthias 2001, 843). They are, thus, the primary divisions under which other (important) divisions will be subsumed.

The next section of this chapter will give details of the author's study of youth post-16 educational experiences and decision making. This is followed by the accounts of the three students—'Samira', 'Satnam' and 'Mohammed'. These were drawn from the wider research sample for discussion within this article to illustrate the value of an intracategorical intersectionalist approach to an understanding of BAME youth achievement within FHE.

THE RESEARCH STUDY

The aim of the wider study was to evaluate the relationships between the 'race', class and gender of young people within full-time vocational further education, and their educational and occupational decision making. The research was conducted at a large further and higher education (FHE) college in a major, ethnically mixed city in the West Midlands of England. The population for the study was the students and staff of the Advanced Vocational Certificate of Education (AVCE) in Travel and Tourism.

THE ADVANCED VOCATIONAL CERTIFICATE OF EDUCATION (AVCE) IN TRAVEL AND TOURISM

The AVCE is a two-year postcompulsory qualification at level three within the UK's National Qualifications Framework, or International Standard Classification of Education (ISCED) Level 3. AVCEs were introduced as part of the UK government's *Curriculum 2000* reforms to postcompulsory provision. The purpose of the AVCE was to offer a 'broad vocational' alternative to the traditional 'academic' 'A' level qualification, with the aim of forming an alternative route into higher education or of preparing students for employment. As such, the AVCE represented an attempt to bridge the UK's historic academic-vocational divide in postcompulsory education, and to achieve for vocational education the elusive 'parity of esteem' with the more established academic route.

SAMPLING METHODOLOGY

The research adopted a case-study approach involving:

- a questionnaire survey of a sample of seventy-two first- and second-year students;
- three focus group interviews with second-year students;
- eleven individual interviews and one double interview with second-year students;
- nine individual interviews with members of the AVCE teaching staff.

'Samira', 'Satnam' and 'Mohammed'

The data discussed within this chapter derives from interviews conducted with three students, 'Samira', 'Satnam' and 'Mohammed', who were all eighteen years old and in the second year of the AVCE at the time of the research. 'Samira' and 'Satnam' were interviewed twice—once in a focus group and once in an individual interview. 'Mohammed' was interviewed once in an individual interview. All interviews were tape-recorded with the participants' permission and then transcribed. All three students are the children of first-generation immigrants to the UK, whereas 'Samira' and 'Mohammed' were themselves born outside of the UK. When asked to identify their religious background, if any, 'Samira' and 'Mohammed' described themselves as Muslim whereas 'Satnam' described herself as Hindu. The fathers of two of the students were employed in routine manual work, whereas the mothers of all three were homemakers (see table below).

Table 6.1   Details of Interviewees

Name	Gender	Father's Occupation	Mother's Occupation	Ethnic Group
'Samira'	Female	Factory production line worker	Homemaker	'Other Asian Background'
'Satnam'	Female	Foodpacker	Homemaker	'British Indian'
'Mohammed'	Male	n/a	Homemaker	'Other Asian Background'

From the interviewees' accounts, all of their parents had had little formal education in their countries of origin and their knowledge of the UK postcompulsory sector was very limited. Levels of familial cultural capital in relation to the field of FHE are therefore relatively low and would appear to place the students and their parents within the 'unskilled' chooser category (Ball et al. 1996) of educational decision makers. Despite this, all three students indicated clear aspirations to progress on to a higher education course; indeed, in the course of the interviews, it soon became clear that educational credentials were viewed as important markers of success by each of the students. Their narratives are, in fact, empirical examples of the ways in which ethnicity, gender and class interlock with each other to produce particular discursive constructions of education, and of success based upon educational achievement.

RESEARCH POWER DYNAMICS

At the time of the research, I was a lecturer at the case study institution. However, I did not actually teach the students and this was a deliberate methodological choice. I felt that by researching students within the same institution, but whom I did not actually teach, I would benefit from relative ease of access whilst retaining some 'distance' between my roles as lecturer and researcher. I was keenly aware of the asymmetrical power relations between me and the students, and I felt that this was a way of attenuating them somewhat. Access to the students was gained initially through their specialist travel and tourism lecturers, to whom the aims of the project were explained. Following permission from the lecturers, the students themselves were approached directly. Again, the aims of the project were explained. It was made clear that the project was entirely separate from my role as a lecturer and that participation was completely voluntary. Guarantees of confidentiality and anonymity were also made.

It is evident that a researcher engaged in examining the interlocking effects of the 'race', class and gender of research participants must consider the ways in which their own 'race', class and gender interact with those of the participants. Indeed, the resultant power dynamics which occur during the social interaction of an interview are particularly sensitive and contentious. Brar (1992, 195) claims that shared religious, cultural and linguistic characteristics bring us more valid data, whereas Archer (2002, 129) argues that this is not necessarily the case.

Clearly, it may be assumed that in an interview between a thirty-six-year-old White, middle-class male lecturer and three working-class young people from different British-Asian backgrounds, researcher and participants will be divided, to some extent, in terms of cultural and linguistic characteristics. Because this present research involves a single researcher, however, I believe that the effects of this upon my findings are essentially unknowable. Thus, whereas Archer (2002), for example, was able to draw inferences regarding the effects of her own positionality upon her British Muslim participants by comparing data gained by her (as a White female researcher) compared with that gained by two Asian female colleagues, I clearly have not been able to do so. This does not, of course, absolve the researcher of any responsibility to be sensitive to issues of power and representation—indeed, quite the opposite. In contemporary UK society there is a silence around whiteness as a racialized identity to the extent that 'White' is seen simply as normative and thus remains unquestioned (Mason 2000; Bhavnani et al. 2005). In consequence, as Archer (2002, 129) notes, for White researchers, their 'race' remains an absent presence which may actually function to silence certain discourses or accounts.

STUDENT NARRATIVES

i) 'Mohammed'

'Mohammed's' account offers some evidence for the workings of a diasporic habitus (Archer and Francis 2007), that is, a specifically aspirational habitus in which education is highly valued for its potential for social mobility. 'Mohammed' came to the UK from Dubai at 'an early age'. His mother is a lone parent with a very limited income from social security benefits. From Mohammed's account, in Dubai she had had very little opportunity for formal education. Since settling in the UK she has taken a number of part-time classes and acts as a key influence upon 'Mohammed':

> My mum is the one that, like, studied. She's the one that tells me to do my studying. 'Studying, studying, studying—that's the key for you'. At first when we come up here [i.e., UK] she's learnt to speak English and that. So, she done that, she knows her English and everything now. She's taking, like extra . . . like knitting and all that, so she's doing them courses as well. But, she's thinking of doing teaching as well.

For Archer and Francis (2007, 140), this habitus is related to a collective immigrant experience of poverty and hardship which continues to motivate present behaviour and values, and through which educational aspirations are framed in particularly racialized terms. 'Mohammed' does not frame educational ambition in such terms, and neither did the other two interviewees. Nevertheless, it is reasonable to infer that 'Mohammed's' mother's experience of immigration and the wish to protect 'Mohammed' from such difficult experiences were a contextual factor.

Indeed, the application of another of Bourdieu's concepts—field—adds much to our understanding of possible contextual factors surrounding 'Mohammed's' orientation towards education. Although racism was never explicitly mentioned by 'Mohammed' or the other two participants, we know that the field of the labour market in the UK is characterised by deep racialized inequalities (Savage 2000, 135). An implicit (and often explicit) awareness of racism in the labour market will condition the attitudes of young minority ethnic people towards education, as Archer and Francis (2007, 135) found in their research with British-Chinese pupils and their parents. Indeed, other research among young people of South Asian origin (see, e.g., Bhatti 1999; Ahmad 2001; Bagguley and Hussain 2007) offers significant evidence that Asian students and their parents are also concerned with racism and see post-16 qualifications as a form of protection against it.

Whereas 'Mohammed's' account of the influence of his mother upon his education points to a desire for social mobility borne of the experiences of immigration, other aspects of his motivations can be located within wider working-class discourses surrounding the perceived value of post-16 education. For 'Mohammed', as a working-class student, participation in further and higher education is seen as a way of setting down a marker of success in a competitive, individualistic world—a way of 'becoming somebody' (Ball et al. 2000). In particular, further education (FE) credentials means avoiding manual work in factories, a fate which would have strongly displeased his parents:

Interviewer: Did you ever think of leaving school and looking for a job?
'Mohammed': No, not really. Cos I had a part-time job as well and that kept me going. But sometimes I was thinking, what's the point of education? I might as well move on to a job, a full-time job. But then I was thinking, say if I go on to a job and I don't really enjoy it and I leave, then, like, I won't have nothing on my CV apart from, you know, 'the ex-employee'. It's better to have like a certificate saying that I've worked hard, pushed myself and achieving something . . . so that's what I thought I'd do instead.
Interviewer: And what do you think your parents would have thought if you'd left school at 16 to get a job?
'Mohammed': Depends what job it is. They didn't like want to see me working in a factory or anything like that. They wanted, like, a nice decent job with good pay and with, like, later on in life move up, not stay in the one position.

The desire to avoid manual work and to gain a 'nice decent job' with the potential for social mobility is a common motivation for FE and HE study among young working-class people according to Archer (2003b). Whereas FE and HE offered 'Mohammed' the opportunity to avoid a working-class 'fate' in manual labour, the material underpinnings of 'Mohammed's' ambitions were apparent in his tendency to emphasise the personal economic value of post-16 credentials. 'Mohammed' was initially disappointed that the AVCE would not lead to a well-paid job but then saw a degree in tourism business management as a more reliable route:

'Mohammed': When, like, I started it [AVCE course] I was really interested in it, on the course, and then we got in the second year teachers are saying 'the pay's not all that' and they got, like, doubts in my head that I don't want to do it. But they should have told us this before at interview but they never mentioned nothing about it. It wasn't just me, it was the majority of the students as well.

Interviewer: If you did do a degree, what would you hope to get out of it?

'Mohammed': Someone told me like with this degree they give you . . . like after your degree they put you on a placement for a week, like working in an organisation. If they're impressed with what you have to offer them, they take you on. So, if they do take you on you'll start with £26,000 basic. So, if they do do that at this college . . . but I heard that they do it at another college. That's why I have to go to Open Day and ask them what I will get. So, I'll take it on.

In Bourdieusian terms, 'Mohammed' is seeking to convert cultural capital in its 'institutionalised state', that is, educational qualifications (Bourdieu 1986), into economic capital. Such a focus upon the instrumental value of post-16 qualifications may also, to an extent, be seen as a gendered discourse. His emphasis upon the economic returns to HE was absent from the narratives of 'Satnam' and 'Samira' (discussed below). Moreover, other research into working-class young people and higher education (see Archer 2003b) has also found that working-class men are more likely than women to highlight the instrumental and financial value of HE participation.

ii) 'Satnam'

'Satnam's' narrative also points to the workings of a diasporic habitus, whereby education is seen as a 'way out' of difficult past and present circumstances. 'Satnam' was born in the UK; her parents left India for the UK as teenagers. 'Satnam' believes that both her parents left formal education at twelve or possibly earlier. As with 'Mohammed', according to 'Satnam' there was a very strong parental expectation that she would continue on to further education:

Interviewer: What do you think your parents would have said if you'd wanted to leave school at 16 and get a job?

'Satnam': I don't think they would have agreed with that at all cos my parents have always expected me to do education. If I went straight into a job . . . I wouldn't really know cos I really wanted to do education myself . . . but I don't think my parents would really

agree with it, me going straight into work, cos obviously if you do go straight into work at age 16 your pay's really low isn't it? It's like £3.61 and also I don't think it's worth it really. I think you should do your education and then go and [inaudible] cos you're not qualified or anything like that.

As with 'Mohammed', there are aspects of 'Satnam's' narrative that resonate with broader working-class constructions of the value of post-16 study and which may be seen to reflect 'Satnam's' class location. Unlike 'Mohammed', however, class-based attitudes to career choices expressed themselves more in the need for a level of material security through stable employment than in the need for economic returns per se:

Interviewer: Why do you want to do a degree in retail management?
'*Satnam*': I think retail management is a kind of a business that never ends. Cos retail's always in business no matter where you go. I mean, like, the [local shopping centre] is open now. That's all like retail isn't it, most of the stuff? I think retail is always in business, like tourism one day . . . cos of what happened on the 11th, 12th of 11th [sic]. It does affect travel and tourism in a way. I think it's always dropping its profits and going up and I don't want to be in a sort of job where you get bankrupt or something. I wanna be in a job where it's, like, always in business, for example retail.
Interviewer: So you think that's more secure than travel and tourism?
'*Satnam*': Yeah. Cos then you've got a job haven't you? If you lose that job in, like, a retail shop or whatever you know you can always move on but with travel if you go into one airline, all airlines are affected by it. And it's a bit hard, that's what I think.

The desire for stable employment, and the assumption of a direct correspondence between HE credentials and occupational success is characteristic of what Brown and Scase (1994, 94) have identified as the 'traditional bureaucratic' orientation to work and careers, a trait which they found to be most common among working-class, minority ethnic and female students. Thus, 'Satnam's' desire for a degree and a stable career illustrates the complex interlocking of 'race' with class, and the ways in which these in turn connect with prevalent discourses on the value of post-16 credentials. That is, a degree and relatively secure professional employment are viewed by 'Satnam' as a form of defence against the interlocking limitations of racism and the material constraints of class.

iii) 'Samira'

Of the three interviewees, 'Samira's' account of her motivations for FE and HE study perhaps offers the fullest insight into the complex interplay of 'race', class and gender in the formation of educational identities and aspirations. As with 'Mohammed' and 'Satnam', there is evidence for the workings of a diasporic habitus. 'Samira' left Sri Lanka with her parents when she was fifteen. Parental experience of hardship and foreclosed opportunities has clearly made an impression upon her and, like 'Mohammed', her mother is a particular influence:

Interviewer: What have your parents said about you going on to uni?

'Samira': My mum's really forcing me to go on to uni. She's like, 'You have to go to uni'. I'm like, 'Mum, I don't know yet'. She says, 'No, don't say that cos if you're holding a degree in this country no-one's gonna ask no questions'. Even if you go to an employment interview and they ask, 'What have you done for an education?' and you say you went to college and finished college and that's it, they'll probably say, 'Oh well, you finished college, you didn't do a degree'. That's gonna put you down, isn't it?' So, she ['Samira's' mother] loves to study, she goes, 'If I was your . . . if I came [to the UK] your age I'd have been like all over the place studying everywhere'. That makes me, you know, in a way it motivates me as well because she's so talented so I got to be talented as well. It's no point being around and doing nothing. I've got to do something.

The account given by 'Samira' thus chimes closely with those of 'Mohammed' and 'Satnam' in the way in which it points to the influence of immigrant parents. The aspirations that 'Samira's' mother holds for her daughter are clearly functioning as a form of capital that 'Samira' is able to draw upon in the construction of her own educational identity—'she's so talented so I got to be talented as well. It's no point being around and doing nothing'. In addition, however, 'Samira's' narrative also offers hints of how gender articulates with ethnicity (and also social class) to produce a particular orientation towards post-16 participation. According to 'Samira', her mother was anxious that she should pursue education after 16 and avoid the 'early' marriage that she herself had had:

Cos my mum's educated as well. She goes, 'education's very important'. Because she got married in the early years as well and she left education because of marriage. She doesn't want the same thing to happen to me.

'Samira' herself also seemed anxious to avoid 'early' marriage and disapprovingly cited the example of other female family members who had not been 'allowed' to go to university due to marriage:

Most of my side relatives, some of them, they don't let their girls go to uni 'cos they get married early at this stage. It's like, get married, go and settle your life, go, your husband's gonna work for you, get back. It's just like they gotta go and live their life with their husbands. So, sometimes I think it's crazy. You gotta stand up for your own thing. You can't just tell your husband everything, 'come on, do this for me, post my letter, go to the mailbox.' You can't tell them everything. You gotta know what you're doing as well. You gotta have your own reputation.

For 'Samira', education is functioning as a site for the contestation of accepted familial gender roles. In Bourdieusian terms, 'Samira's' developing habitus has become somewhat divided against itself. As an individual's habitus is the evolving product of a range of different relations within different social fields, and as these fields will intersect in ways that are not always compatible (in this case, home life and education), so an individual is confronted with contradictions and ambivalences.

It is a contestation in which 'Samira's' mother is clearly playing a crucial role. Previous research into the post-16 educational careers of young South Asian women offers a varied picture of the role of mothers. For example, Bhatti (1999, 138) reports that in families where the mother may have had little opportunity for education herself, she acted as an 'agent of change' in strongly encouraging her daughter to make use of educational opportunities that she herself did not have. Research by Ahmad (2001, 144) among Muslim South Asian families also identified a broad appeal of HE that cut across levels of class and parental education. However, she also found that where a mother had had few educational opportunities, it was the father who was more determined to promote their daughter's education (Ahmad 2001, 145). In contrast, Abbas (2003) found that parental *class*, rather than gender, was the determining factor in the levels of support and freedom accorded to the young South Asian Muslim women of his study, with working-class Muslim women experiencing ' . . . the operationalisation of certain negative religio-cultural norms and values that inhibits the progression of a certain few' (Abbas 2003, 424). Nevertheless, a later study by Ijaz and Abbas (2010) into the attitudes of first- and second-generation Muslim parents towards their daughters' higher education found that both parents of all social classes were very positive towards their daughters' educational ambitions.

Clearly, therefore, ethnicity, class and gender all cross cut each other in complex ways. This makes any broad generalisations about either the role of mothers in the post-16 educational careers of young women of South Asian background, or about the role of the young women themselves, very difficult. Nevertheless, Ahmad's (2001) discussion of the 'modern tradition'—whereby there is a familial expectation of female progression to HE—enables us to locate the case of 'Samira' within a wider canvas of shifting gender relations. Ahmad (2001) identified two important motivations, among others, for parental encouragement of their daughters' ambitions. Firstly, she found evidence that mothers wanted their daughters to gain qualifications in order to achieve a position of independence from future husbands and in-laws (Ahmad 2001, 145), a discourse of female empowerment also encountered by Abbas (2003, 321). The first interview extract above from 'Samira' offers clear hints of such maternal desires. Secondly, Ahmad (2001, 145) also argues that in gaining a degree, a daughter may confer a level of cultural capital upon her family thus enabling the parents to ' . . . distance themselves from the stereotype of the patriarchal and "non-educated" family'. There are strong hints of these pressures for 'respectability' in 'Samira's' comments about her mother's encouragement for her to continue her education:

> She ['Samira's' mother] goes, 'Education is something important where you can just learn more and you know the situations every day in life. Then you go to college [inaudible] you get to know the world, how it is. If someone's talking about some topics you won't be able to interact with them, you'll be like, "yeah I think so." You don't know what you're gonna say. If you go to college you have the knowledge of talking, you know, having a proper relationship with a subject.'

Whereas postcompulsory education is functioning as a site for the contestation of accepted familial gender roles for 'Samira', it also holds out the promise of a more secure material future. Like 'Mohammed' and 'Satnam', 'Samira' perceived a direct correlation between H.E credentials and her occupational future:

> I'm hoping to get something what I can go further with. If I get a degree then obviously I'm gonna start my own business. Because obviously I should know by the time I finish what I'm doing. If I don't know what I'm doing I might as well not join the course

Personal social 'improvement' is one of the benefits typically ascribed to higher education among working-class HE aspirants. For example, the idea of 'bettering oneself' occupationally, through the acquisition of a degree, was also a very important motivation for HE study among the working-class interviewees researched by Archer and Hutchings (2000). This finding contrasts strongly with evidence from research with middle-class students who are much more likely to cite a personal interest in a subject as their motivation (Archer 2003b, 127). Nevertheless, although 'Samira' (like 'Mohammed' and 'Satnam') placed emphasis upon the instrumental value of a degree, like 'Satnam' (but unlike 'Mohammed') she also focused upon its potential for conversion into relatively 'safe' employment. This certainly appears to be her uppermost concern in her choice of a Retail Management degree:

Interviewer: What appeals to you about retail management?

'*Samira*': It's like a never-ending part retail is. Clothes trends just change, people are loving it, visualise it. They see something and think, 'Oh, I gotta get that'. So, you probably never end cos everyone's gotta be trendy everyday . . . and it's never gonna end I think, retail management. So, you go back to things, buy it and make money from that, repeat business everyday.

Again, previous research (see Archer 2003b) has found evidence for a gendered division, with working-class female students tending to place more value on employment security than their male peers. 'Samira's' desire for 'safe' employment and her belief that HE credentials can ensure it may thus reflect a particular gendered orientation towards education and careers, which interlocks with other aspects of 'Samira's' classed and racialized educational identity.

Having presented the accounts of the three young people, I shall now turn to a consideration of the value of the theoretical model that I have applied to analyse their narratives.

'RACE', CLASS AND GENDER, AND THE INTRACATEGORICAL MODEL OF INTERSECTIONALITY

To consider the value of the intracategorical approach to intersectionality employed within this study, we first need to return to the dilemma with which all critical research is faced: the simultaneous indispensability and impossibility of a foundational reference to an epistemic or political subject (Gressgard 2008, under 'The epistemic status of difference'). Or, whereas social categories are also social constructs, they may be the necessary starting point for critical social research. As we have seen, there are two broad approaches which should be seen as points along a continuum: a deconstructionist approach, which radically questions identitarian categorisations, and a realist approach, whereby identity is framed in terms of multiplicity. This research has adopted the latter approach.

Following this form of intersectionality, 'race', class and gender are provisionally accepted as concepts that may serve a useful purpose in relation to the description and analysis of individuals within social groupings. This has been complemented by a Bourdieusian analytical framework as a means of considering the complex interrelationships between these social categories as they are embodied within the young people discussed in this chapter. I believe that the theoretical framework employed has offered this study two important insights. Firstly, the Bourdieusian theoretical schema has allowed for a linking of the micro and macro levels of analysis. Secondly, Bourdieu's concept of capital, which shifts our notion of class from macroeconomic relations to that of resources possessed by individuals (Savage et al. 2005), illuminates the mutually constitutive relationship between economic and cultural relations and offers a clear application with regard to 'race' and gender. Both of these points are borne out by reference to the findings of this research, as I shall now discuss.

In this chapter I have made claims for evidence of a diasporic habitus (Archer and Francis 2007) and an ethnic capital effect (Modood 2004). Following a Bourdieusian framework, we may see the parents' high expectations of their children as a form of cultural resource which the students are able to draw upon in the construction of their own educational identities. It is crucial, however, that we link habitus and capital to another of Bourdieu's concepts, that of field, as he himself insisted (Bourdieu and Wacquant 1992). The students' (and their parents') aspirations thus need to be viewed in the light of the field of the UK labour market with its deep racialized inequalities. By linking microlevel perspectives to macrolevel structural conditions in this way, we can see that the students' aspirations are not an expression of some fixed, essential, ethnic 'quality'. Rather, they are an adaptive response to racialized material inequalities.

Indeed, as Bourdieu shows us, cultural and material relations are inextricably intertwined. Or, to put it another way, the 'race' of each student within this study is simultaneously classed and cannot be seen out of this context. In fact, material social relations run through the students' accounts as a leitmotif. Their desire for stable, secure employment thus needs to be seen in the context of the field of higher education in the UK which represents a riskier investment for working-class students, and of the field of the graduate labour market in which they can expect to earn notably less on average than their middle-class peers (Pollard et al. 2004).

Of course, neither 'race' nor class can be decontextualised from the third in the trio of axes of difference discussed within this chapter: gender. Here, the data have offered hints of distinct gendered differences in the students' aspirations—whereas 'Mohammed' placed emphasis upon qualifications as a tool for economic advancement, the two female students foregrounded the need for a level of material security. Again, following a Bourdieusian framework, these subtle but important differences need to be seen in the context of the field of a UK graduate labour market in which women typically earn 10 per cent less than their male counterparts (Purcell and Elias 2004, 12). Finally, the case of 'Samira' has been used to illustrate the complex simultaneity of an individual's identity: educational aspirations are acting as a site of contestation within the context of shifting gendered and racialized social relations.

Thus, by retaining 'race', class and gender as concepts, the intracategorical model has been able to link the students' narratives to broader social processes. By contrast, in moving away from such general explanatory categories and, instead, focusing on the local level, the postmodernism of the anticategorical model brackets out the possibility of wider structural explanations for individuals' experiences. As Robert Young notes, however, experience is not 'self-intelligible'; instead, 'It is a highly mediated frame of understanding, which only *seems* to be local. Like all cultural and political practices, it is interrelated with other practices and experiences, and as such its explanation comes from its outside' (Young 1999, 7–8, emphasis in the original). The implication therefore, as Brah (1994, 152) writes, is that microlevel analysis ' . . . must be framed against wider economic, political and cultural processes in non-reductive ways . . . structure, culture and agency are conceptualized as inextricably linked, mutually inscribing formations'.

A concept-based, intracategorical approach thus opens up the possibility of an examination of individuals' social *positions* (their 'race', class and gender), and also related processes of social *positioning*, that is, how individuals come to be 'raced', 'classed' and 'gendered' in relation to such processes (Anthias 2005, 36). Nevertheless, an intracategorical approach also raises its own questions. How researchers draw boundaries around individuals' social categories—what differences get noticed and why—is itself an act of power on the part of the researcher. As Gressgard (2008, under 'Deconstructionism as ideology critique') notes, we may view this from two perspectives: the imposition by the researcher of theoretical categories upon empirical complexity or the founding of analytical categories based on the self-representations of research participants. Neither approach is wholly satisfactory or without its problems. Ultimately, therefore, I would concur with Archer et al. (2001) in their observation that researchers must acknowledge the power relations at play in the drawing of boundaries and their own position in producing theorisations.

REFERENCES

Abbas, Tahir. 2003. The impact of religio-cultural norms and values on the education of young South Asian women. *British Journal of Sociology of Education* 24 (4): 411–428.

Ahmad, Fauzia. 2001. Modern traditions? British Muslim women and academic achievement. *Gender and Education* 13 (2): 137–152.

Anthias, Floya. 2001. The concept of 'social division' and theorising social stratification: Looking at ethnicity and class. *Sociology* 35 (4): 835–854.

———. 2005. Social stratification and social inequality: Models of intersectionality and identity. In *Rethinking class*, ed. Fiona Devine, Mike Savage, John Scott and R. Crompton, 24–45. Basingstoke, UK: Palgrave Macmillan.

Archer, Louise. 2002. 'It's easier that you're a girl and that you're Asian': Interactions of 'race', and gender between researchers and participants. *Feminist Review* 72: 108–132.

———. 2003a. *Race, masculinity and schooling*. Maidenhead, UK: Open University Press

———. 2003b. The 'value' of higher education. In *Higher education and social class*, ed. Louise Archer, Merryn Hutchings and Alistair Ross, 119–136. London and New York: RoutledgeFalmer.

Archer, Louise, and Becky Francis. 2007. *Understanding minority ethnic achievement*. London and New York: Routledge.

Archer, Louise, and Merryn Hutchings. 2000. 'Bettering yourself'? Discourses of risk, cost and benefit in ethnically diverse, young working-class non-participants' constructions of higher education. *British Journal of Sociology of Education* 21 (4): 555–574.

Archer, Louise, Merryn Hutchings and Carole Leathwood. 2001. Engaging in commonality and difference: Theoretical tensions in the analysis of working-class women's educational discourses. *International Studies in Sociology of Education* 11 (1): 41–62.

Bagguley, Paul, and Yasmin Hussain. 2007. *The role of higher education in providing opportunities for South Asian women.* Bristol, UK: The Policy Press.

Ball, Stephen J., Richard Bowe and Sharon Gewirtz. 1996. School choice, social class and distinction: The realization of social advantage in education. *Journal of Education Policy* 11 (1): 89–112.

Ball, Stephen J., Sheila Macrae and Meg Maguire. 2000. *Choice, pathways and transitions post-16: New youth, new economies in the global city.* London and New York: RoutledgeFalmer.

Bhatti, Ghazala. 1999. *Asian children at home and at school.* London and New York: Routledge.

Bhavnani, Reena, Heidi Safia Mirza and Veena Meetoo. 2005. *Tackling the roots of racism.* Bristol, UK: The Policy Press.

Bourdieu, Pierre. 1986. The forms of capital. In *Education, culture, economy and society*, ed. Albert H. Halsey, Hugh Lauder, Phillip Brown and Amy Stuart Wells, 46–58. Oxford: Oxford University Press.

———. 1990. *The logic of practice.* Trans. Richard Nice. Cambridge: Polity Press.

Bourdieu, Pierre, and Loic J. D. Wacquant. 1992. *An invitation to reflexive sociology.* Cambridge: The Polity Press.

Brah, Avtar. 1994. 'Race' and 'culture' in the gendering of labour markets: South Asian young Muslim women and the labour market. In *The dynamics of 'race' and gender: Some feminist interventions*, ed. Haleh Afshar and Mary Maynard, 151–171. London and Bristol, PA: Taylor & Francis.

Brar, Harbhajan Singh. 1992. Unasked questions, impossible answers: The ethical problems of researching race and education. In *Ethics, ethnicity and education*, ed. Mal Leicester and Monica J. Taylor, 188–202. London: Kogan Page.

Brown, Phillip, and Richard Scase. 1994. *Higher education and corporate realities: Class, culture and the decline of graduate careers.* London: UCL Press.

Chevalier, Arnaud, and Gavan Conlon. 2003. *Does it pay to attend a prestigious university?* London: Centre for the Economics of Education.

Connor, Helen, Claire Tyers, Tariq Modood and Jim Hillage. 2004. *Why the difference? A closer look at higher education minority ethnic students and graduates.* London: DfES Research Report No. 552.

Equality Challenge Unit (ECU). 2009. *Equality in higher education statistical report 2009*, http://www.ecu.ac.uk/publications/equality-in-he-stats-09.

Fraser, Nancy. 1999. Social justice in the age of identity politics: Redistribution, recognition and participation. In *Culture and economy after the cultural turn*, ed. Larry Ray and Andrew Sayer, 25–52. London, Thousand Oaks and New Delhi: Sage.

Gressgard, Randi. 2008. Mind the gap: Intersectionality, complexity and 'the event'. *Theory and Science* 10 (1), http://theoryandscience.icaap.org/content/vol10.1/Gressgard.html.

Ijaz, Aisha, and Tahir Abbas. 2010. The impact of inter-generational change on the attitudes of working-class South Asian Muslim parents on the education of their daughters. *Gender and Education* 22 (3): 313–326.

Mason, David. 2000. *Race and ethnicity in modern Britain*. 2nd ed. Oxford: Oxford University Press.

McCall, Leslie. 2005. The complexity of intersectionality. *Signs: Journal of Women in Culture and Society* 30 (3): 1771–1800.

Modood, Tariq. 2004. Capitals, ethnic identity and educational qualifications. *Cultural Trends* 13 (2): 87–105.

Pollard, Emma, Richard Pearson and Rebecca Willison. 2004. *Next choices: Career choices beyond university*. Brighton, UK: Institute for Employment Studies (IES) 405.

Purcell, Kate, and Peter Elias. 2004. *Higher education and gendered career development*. Warwick, UK: Institute for Employment Research (IER).

Race for Opportunity (RfO). 2009. *Race into higher education*, http://www.bitc.org.uk/workplace/diversity_and_inclusion/race/hesa_report.html.

Savage, Mike. 2000. *Class analysis and social transformation*. Buckingham, UK: Open University Press.

Savage, Mike, Alan Warde and Fiona Devine. 2005. Capitals, assets, and resources: Some critical issues. *The British Journal of Sociology* 56 (1): 31–47.

Sayer, Andrew. 2005. *The moral significance of class*. Cambridge: Cambridge University Press.

Skeggs, Beverley. 2004. Context and background: Pierre Bourdieu's analysis of class, gender and sexuality. *The Sociological Review* 52 (2): 19–33.

Snyder, Thomas D., and Sally A. Dillow. 2010. *Digest of education statistics 2009* (NCES 2008–022). National Center for Education Statistics, Institute of Education Sciences, U.S. Department of Education: Washington, DC.

United States Census Bureau 2010, http://quickfacts.census.gov/qfd/states/00000.html.

Young, Robert. 1999. The linguistic turn, materialism and 'race': Towards an 'aesthetics of crisis'. *Alethia* 2 (1): 6–11.

7 Intersections of 'Race', Class and Gender in the Social and Political Identifications of Young Muslims in England

Farzana Shain

ABSTRACT

This chapter draws on a qualitative study of Muslim boys' educational experiences in England, to focus on their social and political identifications in a post 9/11 context. It offers an alternative reading of the boys' identifications to dominant policy and academic accounts that focus on 'radicalization'. The discussion emphasises intersections of 'race', religion, gender and class in the boys' strategic take-up of identities in the context of their schooling and neighbourhood experiences.

INTRODUCTION

This chapter focuses on the impact of racism on the lives and schooling of Muslim youth against the backcloth of debates about the politicisation of Muslim identities. Since the mid- to late 1980s, economic and social changes at a global level have resulted in an increased focus on religious identities. In the UK, the Rushdie affair[1] sparked fierce debate about the (in)compatibility of Muslim cultures with Western values and about the extent to which Muslims could be integrated into British society. Such debates spiralled out of control when the July 2005 London bombings were connected to 'homegrown' terrorism. Since then, Muslim youth, especially Muslim boys and young men, have come under unprecedented scrutiny and surveillance, with discussions about Islamic radicalization and 'extremism' dominating media, policy and academic debates. A group that was once regarded as passive and law-abiding, especially when compared with their African-Caribbean counterparts, has, since the late 1980s, been firmly recast in the public imagination as violent, dangerous and a threat to the social order. Whereas statistics (DfES 2007) show them to be among the 'losers' in the achievement game, Pakistani and Bangladeshi boys have not been the focus of concerns about underachievement in the same way that boys in general have. Instead, discourses of 'self-segregation' (Cantle 2001; Ousley 2001; Denham 2002) and global (in)security posed by the 'war on terror' currently position them as 'at risk' of either violent criminality (drugs and/or gangs and rioting) or terrorism and extremism. These dominant representations are also gendered, with boys and men constructed as violent oppressors and girls and young women, the victims or symbols of that oppression. Not only do such representations deny agency to Muslim youth, who are assumed to be too readily and easily brainwashed into violent ideologies, but they also contribute to an overemphasis on religious and cultural factors in relation to Muslim youth's experiences and identities. This is despite the wealth of critical sociological research emphasising complexity in the identity, work and 'lived' experiences of young people from ethnic minority communities.

This chapter draws on wider research (Shain 2011) exploring the impact of the 'war on terror' on the educational identities of Muslim boys to offer an alternative reading of their social and political identifications. The first section contains a brief review of recent policy and academic debate focusing on the apparent radicalization of Muslim youth. The second section locates my theoretical framework for analysing Muslim boys' experiences in the context of recent theorising on youth identities. The third section reports on data drawn from my wider study to challenge dominant cultural and religious readings of Muslim youth's experiences. I focus on intersections of 'race', religion, gender and class in the boys' strategic take-up of identities in the context of their local schooling and neighbourhood experiences.

BACKGROUND: ANALYSING THE 'TURN TO RELIGION'

Since the 1990s, empirical research on second- and third-generation British South Asians has noted an increasing tendency among British Pakistanis and Bangladeshis to assert Muslim identities (Eade 1990, 1994; Werbner 1996; Samad 1998; Saeed, Blain and Forbes 1999; Archer 2003; Ramji 2007). The Rushdie affair was a major turning point for British Muslims. Not only did it invoke the recategorisations of various ethnic (Mirpuri, Bangladeshi, Pakistani) groups as religious (Muslim) ones, but it also occurred around the same time as other protests involving Muslim youth in Europe's inner cities.[2] Such protests were interpreted as signalling the emergence of the radicalization of Muslim youth across the landscape of Europe and beyond, representing a generalised threat to Western democratic ideals.

Sociological accounts focusing on the political mobilisations linked to the Rushdie affair tied this 'turn to religion' to class factors rather than an increase in religiosity. Samad (1992) observes that the anti-Rushdie protests, which brought young Muslim men in Bradford to the fore, centred on rights claims in the face of ongoing material disadvantage and aggravated racialized tensions. Modood (1992) asserts that the demonstrations symbolised working-class anger and hurt pride. His explanation for this anger taking a religious outlet focuses on the abandonment of young people by a secular intelligentsia which did not understand or feel responsible for its own working class. Glynn (2002, 977) argues, however, that 'there is certainly a vacuum and a lack of secular leadership but that vacuum is not due to the absence of a middle-class which would hardly be expected to breach the gap of class experience'. Like Yuval-Davies (1992), she identifies the 'turn to religion' as a consequence of the demise of socialism linked with the collapse of the former Eastern bloc. She argues that when people no longer see socialism as being able to offer a way out, working-class anger will turn to other movements. Yuval Davis argues that 'in the third world, and among third world minorities in the west, the rise of fundamentalism is intimately linked with the failure of nationalist and socialist movements to bring successful liberation from oppression, exploitation and poverty' (Yuval-Davies 1992, 280).

Since the July 2005 bombings, policy and academic debate have intensified around a focus on Islamic radicalization (Glees and Pope 2005; Leppard and Fielding 2005; Buijs, Demant and Hamdy 2006; Spalek 2007; Abbas 2007; Choudhury 2007). Whereas structural factors such as the economic interests underpinning Western governments' foreign policy have been acknowledged in academic accounts (Buijs, Demant and Hamdy 2006; Spalek 2007; Abbas 2007; Choudhury 2007), policy and media attention have focused most intensely on cultural and religious factors to explain the apparent radicalization of Muslim youth. In the immediate aftermath of the London bombings, the former prime minister, Tony Blair, made explicit links between the bombings and attendance at madrasas, avoiding the issue of British foreign policy. Elsewhere, debate and discussion have focused on the lure of 'mad mullahs' and radical Islamist groups to politically and socially alienated young Muslims (Leppard and Fielding 2005; Glees and Pope 2005). Academic research on radicalization (Glees and Pope 2005; Buijs, Demant and Hamdy 2006; Choudhury 2007) has focused on themes such as identity crisis, suggesting, at times, a linear progression from individual experiences and perceptions of blocked opportunities and identity crises to full-scale radicalization (see Choudhury 2007 for a review).

THEORISING IDENTITIES: 'RACE', CLASS AND GENDER IN ARTICULATION

As Peach (2005) notes, British discourse on minorities has shifted from 'race' in the 1960s, to ethnicity in the 1970s and, since the 1990s, to religion. However, policy and academic literature have continued to promote pathological accounts that position ethnic minority cultures as problematic, backward or inherently inferior when compared with 'Western' family structures and cultural practices. Since the 1980s, sociologists of youth and education (Mirza 1992; Haw 1994; Basit 1997; Connolly 1998; Dwyer 1999; Archer 2003; Shain 2003) have challenged the fixed and static conceptions of culture found in culture-clash frameworks that positioned ethnic minorities as passive victims, caught between two cultures (Watson 1977). Alternative theoretical frameworks, drawn from neo-Marxist, postcolonial and poststructuralist theorising (Hall 1980, 1992, 1996; Bhavnani and Phoenix 1995; Brah 1996) have been applied by feminist researchers to argue for a focus on the complex reality of the 'lived' experiences of young people. In these alternative accounts, young people's identities are read as multiple, constantly negotiated and always in process (Hall 1992, 1996).

In education, feminist theorising on 'race' has emphasised the significance of intersecting structures of 'race', gender and class in shaping, for example, Eurocentric formulations of curriculum. Such formulations have historically positioned Black students, especially girls, as underachievers who 'lack' self-esteem (Mirza 1992). Mirza challenges such culturalist explanations, suggesting that the Black girls in her study were not lacking in self-esteem. She found that the families of the girls she studied played a significant role in compensating for Eurocentric and racist assumptions embedded in education and the labour markets. Contrary to dominant stereotypes of Black youth as underachievers, the girls in her study were academically successful. However, racism in the labour market was a significant factor in reproducing their disadvantaged social situations.

Research on Muslim and Asian girls (Dwyer 1999; Archer 2003; Shain 2003; Bhopal 2010) has also focused on the more active role played by British-born Asian and Muslim youth in negotiating identities drawn from both residual 'home' cultures and the local cultures they currently inhabit.

Claire Dwyer (1999) challenges dominant representations of Muslim girls as oppressed victims of backward Muslim cultures. She focuses instead on the active roles played by Muslim women in negotiating their identities in relation to a complex network of peer, teacher, family and neighbourhood relations. Her research suggests ongoing contestations over identities, set against the backcloth of structural limits posed by 'race', class and gender relations which define the boundaries of acceptable and appropriate forms of Muslim femininity.

The theoretical approach drawn on in my analysis of Muslim boys' identities (Shain 2011) continues within this framework, identifying structures of 'race', gender and class as crosscutting and produced in articulation, that is, in the intersection of people's everyday lives with relations of domination and subordination (Rutherford 1990). Brah and Phoenix (2004, 76) define the concept of intersectionality as:

> Signifying the complex, irreducible varied and variable effects which ensue when multiple axis of differentiation—economic, political, cultural, psychic, subjective and experiential—intersect in historically specific contexts. The concept emphasises that different dimensions of social life cannot be separated out into discrete and pure strands.

This theoretical approach recognises that people are located in material contexts which provide constraints and structure the limits of possibilities for agency and action. In relation to Muslim boys, this entails recognition of the historical forces of colonialism and imperialism in shaping the classed locations and settlement patterns of Muslim communities in areas of England that have subsequently suffered the most from economic decline. These settlement patterns have had a lasting legacy in terms of the types of schooling and educational and employment opportunities available. By most economic measures, Muslims, especially Pakistani and Bangladeshi communities, are the poorest and most disadvantaged of the ethnic minority communities living in England. For example, Pakistani men are twice as likely and Bangladeshi men are three times more likely to be unemployed compared to White men. Pakistani and Bangladeshi women are four times more likely than White women to be jobless (ONS 2006). Seventy per cent of Bangladeshi pupils and 60 per cent of Pakistani pupils live in wards that are ranked as being among the 20 per cent most deprived areas of England (DfES 2009) and this contributes to continued material disadvantage as they enter into and progress through schooling.

These poor and disadvantaged working-class Muslim communities have also been subject to dominant racialized and classed cultural definitions of them as 'lacking', 'deficient' and as responsible for their own marginality (Alexander 2004). Discourses of integration emerging out of the official responses to the 2001 inner-city disturbances positioned Muslim communities as 'insular' and isolationist. The Bradford Ousely Report, for example, warned of 'the growing threat of self-segregation' of the city's diverse ethnic communities (Ousley 2001), implying that residential segregation was a matter of choice. Such propositions ignore racism in housing policies and the material disadvantage and racialized tensions that may lead to ethnic minorities' decisions to live closely together, to avoid racist harassment.

In the aftermath of the inner-city disturbances in Bradford, political statements such as those made by former Home Secretary David Blunkett (2001) powerfully depicted Muslim communities as insular and 'refusing to integrate'. Blunkett asserted that Muslim Pakistani and Bangladeshi communities were responsible for their own marginality: mothers by not learning English, and the family and elders, once commended for strong discipline, were now condemned for not being able to control boys. Yet, if stories of forced veiling and forced marriages are to be believed, these communities are, at the same time, apparently overcontrolling girls (Shain 2003).

In the aftermath of 9/11, arguments about (lack of) integration have intersected with discourses of the 'war on terror' to position Muslim boys as dangerous, suspect, vulnerable (to extremism) and a threat to a mythical 'British way of life'. Boys and young men have been constructed by these policy discourses as 'politically alienated', which Alexander (2004) suggests is a code for 'at risk' of radicalization. Girls and women have been constructed as the symbols of this radicalization (see, for example, media coverage of the veil controversy in England in 2006).

However, these dominant cultural readings of Muslim boys are hegemonic (Gramsci 1971): dominant, but constantly being challenged in and through schooling and local contexts, sometimes in ways that may reinforce dominant stereotypes of violent masculinity as they were in the so-called riots in 2001. Schooling is the major pubic site where dominant cultural definitions may be reinforced and contested on a daily basis.

Drawing on the Gramscian concept of articulation developed by postcolonial readings of identities, I see Muslim boys' identities as produced through an ongoing negotiation between internal and external definitions of identities or 'modes of being' (Brah 1996).

External or objective definitions derive from complex interrelationships between various structural factors (race, religion, class and gender) and, in particular, local, social and historical contexts. Internal definitions relate to young people's subjective experiences of these situations. Adopting this approach to identities means that different boys may subjectively experience their current locations in different ways, depending on the ways in which they are positioned and position (Davies and Harre 1991) themselves in relation to dominant discourses.

PERFORMING MUSLIM MASCULINITIES

In contrast to dominant representations of Muslim boys as 'disaffected' or 'at risk' of radicalization, recent sociological research suggests that Muslim boys and young men may strategically take up (Archer 2003) or reject (Hopkins 2006, 2007) Muslim identities to challenge dominant stereotypes of weak Asian passivity (Archer 2003). At the same time, they may make investments in Islamic cultural capital to support bids for patriarchal power in the face of declining economic capital (Dwyer 1999; Hopkins 2006; Ramji 2007). Such research draws on the concept of multiple and relational masculinities (Connell 1987, 1995) that are embedded in institutional practices and also embodied in gender practices (Swain 2002). Masculinity is conceptualised as multiple, constantly repositioned and contested in ongoing performances. The hegemonic form of masculinity (Connell, 1995) is often underwritten by violence, though it may not always be the most common type on view. The fact that many boys are enticed into fitting into and conforming to the demands of idealised, culturally exalted forms of masculinity suggests that hegemony works by consent (Swain 2002). Thus, masculinities are simultaneously constructed in relation to boys' classed locations (prospect of unemployment), patriarchy (dominance over women) and racism (Islamophobia in policy and media discourses and anti-Muslim racism on the ground).

Louise Archer (2003) draws on discussion-group interviews with thirty-one Muslim boys aged fourteen and fifteen in a northern mill town in England. Drawing on feminist poststructuralism and a discourse-analytic approach, she argues that the boys take up a range of masculinities in different contexts. For example, Muslim identities were drawn on to resist notions of 'weak' Asian masculinity. However, patriarchal Asian identities were drawn on in relation to gender and the boys' assertions of their privilege. In the context of local identities, the boys in Archer's study drew on popular Black cultural forms represented through 'gangsta' masculinities. Archer (2003, 50) argues, for example, that

> The boys' construction of a 'strong' Muslim brotherhood might be more usefully read in terms of an intertwining of racial and patriarchal themes, through which boys resist popular stereotypes of 'weak' and 'passive' Asian masculinity. The boys' identifications could be seen as straightforwardly challenging this stereotype, replacing it with an alternative association of Muslim masculinity with strength. The boys' association between Muslim identity, unity and strength challenge contemporary western ideals of individualistic white masculinity and elsewhere the boys differentiated between 'strong' collective Muslim families and unstable, highly individualistic dualistic western/white family structures.

Hopkins (2006, 2007) conducted focus-group discussions and individual interviews with fifty-five young Muslim men aged sixteen to twenty-five in Scotland. Like Archer, he found that his respondents took up a range of identity positions, moving between different intersecting scales, sometimes asserting their identities as 'local' through neighbourhood relations and at other times as 'nationalists' through a strong appeal to Scottish nationalism. The young men drew on, but in some cases also rejected, global Muslim identities through spiritual connections to the *umma*, (a global Muslim brotherhood). Hopkins suggests that the young men's identifications were contradictory in that they simultaneously argued that men and women are equal in Islam, whilst advocating sexist stereotypes about their expectations of Muslim women. Hopkins refers to this as 'sexist equality' and sees it as supporting Linda McDowell's (2002, 115) argument that young men's masculinities are constructed around a belief in 'domestic conformity' whereby young men focus on earning wages and reproducing sexist and heterosexual familial situations.

Dwyer (1999, 479) and Ramji (2007) note that this policing by young men appeared to be a means by which their own adolescent masculine, ethnic and religious identity could be maintained. Ramji (2007), drawing on Bourdieu's concepts of capital and field, argues, in relation to her study of Muslim men and women, that religion was a particularly important source of gaining status especially when access to other forms of capital, for example, economic, was limited because of racism and prejudice. She argues that young men's investments in Islamic cultural capital were a reaction to the growing educational divide between themselves and Muslim women. Class seemed to influence how this was voiced. Working-class Muslim men in her study had less access to economic capital and so relied on religion to give them access to a cultural capital, which could then be converted to other capital such as social, or indeed economic if it created a situation where only men are allowed to work.

The complex catalogue of shifting and strategic identifications suggested by these studies of young Muslim men suggests a need to move beyond prevailing discourses of Asian gangs (Alexander 2000) as well as popular and academic theorisations of radicalization which position Muslim boys as disaffected from their local cultures and processes of local democracy.

In the next section I explore some of the ways in which the boys in my research were able to take up and position themselves in relation to dominant discourses of schooling and cultural definitions of them as newly dangerous and suspect in the context of the 'war on terror'.

THE STUDY

The research was conducted between May 2002 and October 2003 in Oldwych (all names are pseudonyms) in the West Midlands and consisted of group and individual interviews with twenty-four working-class Muslim boys aged between twelve and eighteen. At the time of the research, Oldwych had a population of around 250,000. The proportion of ethnic minorities, including Irish, was around 6 per cent but around 8 per cent for those under the age of sixteen. Ethnic minorities were overwhelmingly concentrated in two wards: Newtown and Belstone, where they accounted for almost 50 per cent of the population. Like many of the wards in the northern towns, these areas were also severely economically deprived, with higher than average numbers of children in them claiming free school meals, and high rates of unemployment. Newtown also had a significant concentration of asylum seekers, which had been a focal concern of British National Party organisation in the wider city.

Fieldwork was conducted across two sites. The first was a youth group located in Newtown, where boys met once a week. The second was a mixed comprehensive secondary school, Leyton High, which was located near Newtown, serving young people aged eleven to sixteen. Of the twenty-four boys who took part in the research, seventeen were Pakistani, including one who described himself as mixed-race White English and Pakistani; four were Bengali; two were Afghani; and one was Turkish. Yacoub, a Newtown youth worker, described himself as British Pakistani.

Global Politics

The interviews with the boys focused on a range of themes, including their experiences of family, neighbourhood and schooling. However, because of the timing of the research, global politics emerged as a strong theme. Across the interviews, 9/11 and the ensuing 'war on terror' had significantly affected both school and community life. The following comments were typical of many expressed:

> They started being more sickening in their attitudes towards Asian people they look at every other Asian as a terrorist . . . they judge the whole crowd by . . . they judge the majority by the minority. [Before 9/11], it was bad but not that bad. That just triggered it. They didn't used to call us terrorists then they used to call us Pakis. (Shahid, Leyton)

***

> People are really sceptical about this whole thing thinking there's justification for them to kill Muslims if they suspect that . . . they can suspect what they want . . . it's like a different day, a different era. And, as much as the people have been discussing 9/11, it has had a massive impact on the community. We've had a lot of how can you put it . . . from the white community . . . some really ignorant comments. . . . Like, oh I wonder what it would be like, you couldn't really go on holiday now could you? Because we look like terrorists [to them] . . . That's the sort of stupid thing they're saying. Whatever they've been fed by the press that's what they've been repeating. Because they're white they class themselves as being the same culture as the Europeans and the Americans. I don't see any belonging . . . Growing up, Asian people have got this togetherness . . . white people don't have in their

own families let alone in their communities. (Yacoub, youth worker,
Newtown youth group)

***

As we used to walk home it's like mainly a white area, we used to
get called racist abuse, like, you terrorist and all this . . . go back
to Afghanistan and all this. And we aren't even from Afghanistan.
(Hamid, Leyton)

A range of themes is suggested by the above comments. First, at the local
level of schooling and in their local environments, the boys reported a
significant increase in anti-Muslim racism, whether experienced through
name-calling, dissociation or physical attack. However, the boys suggested
that the events of 9/11 and the ensuing 'war on terror' had not produced
any significant new experience—rather, it had aggravated and intensified
existing tensions and re-racialized them. As Shahid's account suggests,
before 9/11 'it was bad, but not that bad'. The main new factor was the
intensity of name-calling. Whereas in the past, boys had routinely been
called 'Paki', they reported that terms such as *Afghani*, *terrorist*, and *sui-
cide bomber* had been added to the usual repertoire of racist insults. In
addition to name-calling, boys expressed an increased sense of stigmatisation as a result of being judged to be associated with Islamic terrorism. Such
accounts revealed strong external positioning through racist discourse of
Muslim boys as problematic.

A second theme related to the construction of polarised 'us and them'
identities. That is, the boys drew specifically on Muslim 'we' identities that
were constructed in relation to a collective 'they' composed of 'whites',
'Europeans' and 'Americans', sometimes collapsed into a single entity and
at other times referenced interchangeably. This concurs with the findings
of recent empirical studies on second- and third-generation British South
Asians, which note an increasing tendency among British Pakistanis and
Bangladeshis to assert Muslim identities (Eade 1990, 1994; Werbner 1996;
Samad 1998; Saeed, Blain and Forbes 1999, Archer 2003; Ramji 2007).
Collectively 'they', at one level, were imbued with the power to judge
Muslims in collusion with a powerful and highly partial media that also
represented imperial interests. However, drawing on notions of community and family, the boys subverted these dominant readings by suggesting that Muslim and Asian families were stronger and less individualistic
than White family structures. Yacoub drew on a culturalist argument after
recounting a catalogue of direct and indirect abuse that had been thrown
at him in the months following 9/11. Zahid also suggested that White/
English/European families lack the solidarity that he sees as characteristic
of Muslim and Asian families:

> To mix in with the English you need to be very different, like in our culture we don't move from our parents' house until we're married and we've got kids of our own but they move out when they're eighteen. But then we're not like that because we respect our parents much more than these people. We take care of them. English parents are always in homes and you never see an Asian Pakistani or an Indian [in a home]. Everybody just likes their parents to live with them. (Zahid, Leyton)

In Zahid's account, superior family and cultural forms are inclusive of Indians, though elsewhere some of the boys were keen to draw out distinctions between Indians, and Pakistani and Bangladeshis. Archer (2003) also found the boys in her study sometimes constructed themselves and their family norms as superior to Western and White family forms and cultural practices.

Thirdly, as in young people's recounts of the Paris Banlieus' disturbances in 2005 (Cesari 2007), scathing references were made to the role of the media in the perpetuation of racist discourses about Muslims and in the engineering of moral panics about Muslims. The Communities and Local Government Department (2009) also found that most Muslim communities in Britain share this perception of the media as 'anti-Muslim'. In my own research, an all-powerful media were constructed as strongly aligned to American, British and European imperial interests. This reading of imperialist media practice was also influenced by their local media experiences in Oldwych. In the local newspaper, stories about Muslims often began with sentences such as 'here we go again, Muslims have managed to . . . ', implying that Muslims received favouritism from the local council and sometimes suggesting that Muslims were attempting to impose *sharia* law in the local area.

> Media is bad news, you know because at the end of the day who's running the media? Americans and all the British and they're the ones that hate Muslims. And at the end of the day, Muslims are going to take over one time and they ain't gonna like it. They'll come in numbers. (Arshad, Newtown)

***

> It was just like all everything was going bonkers basically. Like everyone was talking about it and taking the wrong idea because it was not the English people's fault, it was the media's fault because they give the wrong idea to the public. (Zahid)

The above accounts reveal strong racialized and classed suggestions that White people, mainly working-class residents, are the cultural dupes of the media who believe 'whatever they're fed by the press', Yacoub said earlier. Zahid talked about pitying English people because they lack the ability to distinguish propaganda from reality. Arshad invoked a 'clash of civilisations' (Huntingdon 1996), suggesting irreconcilable tensions between Muslims and the West. Assertions of a strong Muslim identity ('Muslims will come in numbers') represent a strategic response to counter and resist the widespread stigmatisation and anti-Muslim racism that the boys encountered through schooling and in their local environment post-9/11. These assertions served to position the local White working class as 'weak' and lacking in political literacy and therefore to subvert dominant discourses which positioned Muslims as a fundamental threat to the Britishness of the nation.

These strong assertions of Muslim collectivity suggest a take-up of global Islamic identities in the context of talk about international politics and in particular the 'war on terror'. However, contrary to dominant policy and media representations, these religious identifications were not fixed and elsewhere the boys reverted to categorisations of themselves and others as Asians, for example, in the context of talk about national and local polices of cohesion and integration.

Defending Territory

In the context of schooling, a strong collective Asian masculinity cohered around an Asian male peer group that was inclusive of others, including other Muslims (namely Turkish and Afghani students) and also White boys and girls. The peer group was constructed through a collective experience of stigmatisation (as Newtowners, ethnic minorities, gang members and sometimes simply as Muslims). Internally, a range of strategies was employed to gain or refuse membership, including the need to demonstrate toughness and machismo but also to show a community ethos revolving around support and backup of fellow members.

Racism was a central factor in the formation of the Asian boys' peer group. It was also central to local neighbourhood identities and experiences that involved protection of local areas from racist attack. However, at the same time as this racialized defence of neighbourhood and school peer group existed, the boys also invested heavily in their local neighbourhood identities in ways that cut across ethnic and religious ties. Mudasser's comment that one of his friends 'comes from Newtown but he moved out to Ryton but he's a bit of an outcast . . . ' was fairly typical of the ways in which differences were often exaggerated in routine struggles over difference and commonality within and across ethnic and religious groupings.

Avtar Brah's observations about the local cultures inhabited by Muslim youth are particularly useful to refer to here:

> The lived cultures than young Muslim[s] . . . inhabit are highly differentiated according to such factors as country of origin, rural/urban background prior to migration, regional and linguistic background in the subcontinent, class position in the subcontinent as well as in Britain, and regional location in Britain. British Asian cultures are not simply a carry over from the (country of origin) . . . Hence Asian cultures of London may be distinguished from their counterparts in Birmingham. Similarly, east London cultures have distinctive features as compared with those from west London. (Brah 1993, 448–449)

One aspect of this related to the boys' location in Newtown, which, like neighbouring Belstone, hosted the majority of the ethnic minority population. Historically there had been rivalries between White working-class youth in Belstone and Newtown that were carried over and racialized as minority (mainly Muslim) youth took up residence in those White working-class areas. As the excerpt below illustrates, this involves struggles over territory not only with White youth but also with other Muslim Asian boys:

> The only common factor was that we're Muslim . . . But the differences [in perception between the youth of both neighbourhoods] were . . . Right, from Belstone . . . 'The thing about Newtown is that they all dress like niggers'. Newtown, 'The thing about Belstone is that they're all well-behind . . . proper typical Pakis' so this is what these are labelling theories that come from the European side . . . We call it area-ism. (Yacoub: youth worker, Newtown)

The boys from Newtown drew a distinction between their own brand of street culture (which borrowed and adapted commercialised 'Black' or African-Caribbean styles of dress and musical affiliations). Other Asian and Muslim boys were negated for displaying what the Newtown boys regarded as a more provincial or 'towny' masculinity. Bollywood consumption was explicitly rejected by many boys as feminine or 'teppy'—a contested label referring to (stereo)typical Pakistani behaviour (Qureshi 2004), which also varies across regional and geographical contexts.

Masculine rivalries between Asian boys took on many forms but were most commonly contested through football.

> We play five a side in tournaments but we the thing is you know what the problem is with the . . . it's a territorial thing. Newtown v Belstone . . . (Arshad, Newtown)

Girls and Struggles Over Masculinity

Girls played a significant role in these masculine rivalries with White girls, most commonly referenced in relation to struggle and competition with White boys:

> When we went [to another youth group], they [white boys] weren't better than us in table tennis, they weren't better than us in pool and when we played football against them they thought they were better than us but then we proved 'em wrong. And we beat 'em at that. That just topped it off that just put the cherry on the cake. (Arshad, Newtown)

***

> We would talk to the girls but the boys wouldn't talk to us and they didn't like it that we were talking to their girls and Tariq was doing something naughty with one of 'em so [FS: So, what happened?]. It all kicked off didn't it? (Nadim, Newtown)

Ramji (2007) argued that the Muslim young men in her study saw White girls as 'easy' and relationships with them were pursued as a way of 'getting one over' on White boys. Dating a Sikh or Hindu girl was seen as the ultimate way of 'getting one over on an old adversary'.

There were few Sikh and Hindu girls in Newtown but White girls were commonly cited as symbols of masculinity in competitive racialized fight talk. In group interviews boys were more likely to construct girls in highly sexualised terms, again as part of group bonding, but in individual interviews boys often talked in less objectivised ways about White girls as part of their friendship groups, as long-term girlfriends and even as part of their imagined futures as potential partners. In the context of local intermasculine rivalries, it seemed, if Yacoub's account is to be believed, that Asian boys had become the 'new Black' (Alexander 2000).

> The young kids are treated as foreigners so they're seen as different. So they're seen as something else. The young girls then are looking for their kicks and so they're heading for the Asian lads and white lads don't like stuff like that because they've again become European and territorial about *their* girls and suddenly they care about them. So it causes a whole range of everyday realities for the Asian lads. (Yacoub, Newtown)

Yacoub asserts here that one of the consequences of being stigmatised as 'bad boys' is that a newfound sense of danger is also highly attractive to some White girls. This account also suggests White girls' collusion in the production of this hegemonic form of racialized masculinity (Connell 2005). Yacoub positions White girls as agentic if predatory (they head for the boys), but denies agency to the boys at the same time (who are targeted and have no choice but to consent). At the same time he positions girls as symbols of masculinity or as markers of racialized boundaries (Anthias and Yuval-Davies 1992) in masculine struggles over territory and turf.

Yacoub's account also invokes colonial fears about interracial mixing due to a desire to preserve ethnic purity (Ware 1992). These fears were reworked in the context of the Notting Hill and Nottingham riots in the 1960s when newspaper reports mentioned, as a cause of the violence, the sight of a White woman walking with a Black man. Such fears resurfaced in recent political and media representations of rape crimes involving young Pakistani men in England. Political figures such as Jack Straw and Ann Cryer have been at the forefront of claims suggesting that cultural requirements around arranged marriages lead to the unavailability of young Pakistani women, which in turn leads Pakistani men to target vulnerable White girls. In Germany too, ex-banker and finance senator Thilo Sarazzin made similarly tenuous connections between Islamic cultural restrictions and the apparent tendency for Turkish Muslim youth in Germany to target White girls (Kreikenbaum 2010).

At the same time as White girls were constructed by boys in my own study as 'available', Asian girls were relationally constructed as 'out of bounds', as Sajid suggests here:

Sajid: My mate Hussein there he might go out with a girl [laughs].
FS: Would you?
Sajid: I've *been* out a few girls.
FS: Are they English or Pakistani?
Sajid: English, and I won't go with Pakistanis because end of the day you know the brothers . . . [laughs] you get beat up. It's not worth it [laughs]. (Leyton)

However, White girls were not constructed as 'easy meat' in the sense that Straw and Sarrazin implied. Sajid defended his long-term relationship with his White girlfriend. A significant number of the boys also saw White girls as part of their imagined futures—as future wives (Shain 2011).

Asian girls were commonly referenced through a discourse of protection. For example, certain areas were considered 'too dangerous' for them to be in—though it could be suggested that such discourses also helped to legitimate the boys' occupation of the public and the discursive construction of the home as a safe space, that is, to defend patriarchal privilege. They were also referenced as in need of male protection.

I stick up for anybody . . . white, Asian, I've got a lot of white friends . . . I stick up for them. My friends are white boys and Asian boys but if someone cusses my sisters' friends or Asian girls then I get a bit offended they're like my sisters init? I get offended . . . (Aziz, Leyton)

Through such referencing, boys like Aziz constructed themselves as protectors of Asian femininity, but by appropriating the discourse of protection the boys denied agency to Asian girls. These constructions are interesting when compared with the views of Asian and Muslim girls (Shain 2003). In this earlier research, Asian girls often castigated Asian boys for their relationships with White girls, suggesting it was part of their incorporation into dominant White culture. Asian girls were not passive, but extremely willing and able to fight their own battles (ibid.).

What these accounts suggest are ongoing negotiations and struggles over youthful masculinities, not simply a take-up of religious and cultural identifications with Islam. In the context of schooling and neighbourhood struggles, structural factors such as racism (both cultural—in the form of Islamophobia and anti-Muslim racism—as well as continuing forms of biological racism) and local classed geographies and histories played a significant role in shaping the boys' experiences and identities. As Amin (2002) suggests, it is at the very local level that commonalities and differences are worked out in everyday struggles over belonging and inclusion/exclusion.

CONCLUSIONS

I have argued that, contrary to dominant policy and political debates, which read Muslim youth exclusively through the lens of culture and religion, their experiences, are shaped by complex intersections of 'race', class and gender in articulation with local geographies and histories.

It is this articulation that underpins and influences the varied nature of the contemporary forms of racism that shape the experiences of Muslim youth in England. The current focus on the supposed radicalization of Muslim youth is significant for understanding the ways in which Muslim youth are currently positioned as the victims of 'backward' Muslim cultures, with boys being assumed to be constantly in danger of being brainwashed into radicalism and girls being both the victims and symbols of these repressive cultures. The accounts of Muslim boys referred to in this chapter challenge these dominant discourses on Muslim masculinity and illustrate the range of intersecting factors that shape their experiences of schooling and their social and political identifications. Whereas it is undoubtedly true that the politicisation of religion has had an impact in terms of bringing Muslim identities to the fore in certain contexts, in the local struggles engaged in by Muslim youth a range of other preoccupations is also significant in shaping identities. These include various struggles over schooling, masculinity and femininity, and over territory that is played out in the context of their local class cultures.

KEY FOR INTERVIEW ANALYSIS

[ ]   word(s) replaced to clarify meaning
. . . .   extraneous material removed
. . .   short pause
***   different interview
—   another excerpt from the same interview
(Newtown/Leyton) location of interview

NOTES

1. *The Satanic Verses* controversy began in 1988 with the publication of a novel in which the author Salman Rushdie explored themes of cultural alienation, racism and the role of religion. Rushdie cast doubts on the authenticity of the *Quran*, implying that parts of it were the work of the devil. It was in England, and particularly in Bradford, that the strongest reaction to the book was manifest. Although the first book burning was held in Bolton in December 1988, when 7,000 people staged a demonstration, the greatest publicity and condemnation was directed at the famous book burning in Bradford in January 1989. On February 14, 1989, a *fatwa* was issued by Ayatollah Khomeini in Iran. Demonstrations were staged in many parts of the world but the participation of young Asian men in Bradford grabbed the attention of observers and social analysts.
2. This research is reported more fully in Shain (2011).
3. For example, the headscarf controversy in France in 1989, when three schoolgirls were sent home from school for wearing the *hijab*, sparking a major controversy about the relationship between Islam and the secular values institutionalised in the French state.

REFERENCES

Abbas, Tahir, ed. 2007. *Islamic political radicalism*. Edinburgh: Edinburgh University Press.
Alexander, Claire, E. 2000. *The Asian gang*. Oxford: Berg.
———. 2004. Imagining the Asian gang: Ethnicity, masculinity, and youth after 'the riots'. *Critical Social Policy* 24 (4): 526–549.
Amin, Ash. 2002. Ethnicity and the multicultural city: Living with diversity. *Environment and Planning* 34 (6): 959–980.
Anthias, Floya, and Nira Yuval-Davies. 1992. *Racialized Boundaries: Race, nation, gender, colour and class and the anti-racist struggle*. London: Routledge.
Archer, Louise. 2003. *Race, masculinity and schooling*. Buckingham, UK: Open University Press.

Basit, Tehmina. 1997 *Eastern values, Western milieu: Identities and aspirations of adolescent British Muslim girls*. Aldershot, UK: Ashgate.

Bhavnani, Kum Kum, and Ann Phoenix. 1995. Identities and racisms: Differences and commonalities'. *Feminism Psychology* 5 (2): 294–298.

Bhopal, Kalwant. 2010. *Asian women and higher education: Communities of practice*. Stoke-on-Trent, UK: Trentham.

Blunkett, David. 2001. Blunkett's 'British test' for immigrants. *Independent*, December 9, http://www.independent.co.uk/news/uk/politics/blunketts-british-test-for-immigrants-619629.html.

Brah, Avtar. 1996. *Cartogrophies of Diaspora*. London: Routledge.

Brah, Avtar, and Rehana Minhas. 1985. Structural racism or cultural difference. In *Just a bunch of girls*, ed. Gaby Weiner, 14–25. Buckingham, UK: Open University Press.

Brah, Avtar, and Ann Phoenix. 2004. Ain't I a woman? Revisiting intersectionality. *Journal of International Women's Studies* 5 (3): 75–84.

Buijs, Frank J., Froukje Demant and Atef Hamdy. 2006. *Strijders van eigen bodem. Radicale en democratische moslims in Nederland*. Amsterdam: University Press.

Cantle, Ted. 2001. *Community cohesion*. London: Home Office.

Cesari, Jocelyn. 2007. Ethnicity, Islam, and les Banlieues: Confusing the issues. Social Science Research Council, http://riotsfrance.ssrc.org/Cesari/.

Choudhury, Tufail. 2007. *The role of Muslim identity politics in radicalization (a study in progress)*. London: Communities and Local Government Department, http://www.communities.gov.uk/documents/communities/pdf/452628.pdf.

Communities and Local Government Department. 2009. *The Afghan Muslim community in England: Understanding Muslim ethnic communities*. London: Communities and Local Government Department.

Connell, Robert W. 1987. *Gender and power*. Stanford, CA: Stanford University Press.

———. 1995. *Masculinities*. Berkeley: University of California Press.

———. 2005. Growing up masculine: Rethinking the significance of adolescence in the making of masculinities. *Irish Journal of Sociology* 14 (2): 11–28.

Connolly, Paul. 1998. *Racism, gender identities and schooling*. London: Routledge.

Davies, Bronwyn, and Rom Harre. 1991. Positioning: The discursive production of selves. *Journal for the Theory of Behaviour* 20 (1): 44–63.

Denham, John. 2002. Building cohesive communities: A report of the Ministerial Group on Public Order and Community Cohesion. London: Home Office.

Department for Education and Skills. 2007. *Gender and education: The evidence on pupils in England*. London: Department for Education and Skills.

———. 2009. *Deprivation and education: The evidence on pupils in England, foundation stage to key stage 4*. London: Department for Education and Skills.

Dwyer, Claire. 1999. Veiled meanings: British Muslim women and the negotiation of differences. *Gender, Place and Culture* 6 (1): 5–26.

Eade, John. 1990. Nationalism and the quest for authenticity: The Bangladeshis in Tower Hamlets. *New Community* 16 (4): 493–503.

———. 1994. Identity, nation and religion: Educated young Bangladeshi Muslims in London. *International Sociology* 9 (3): 77–94.

Glees, Anthony, and Chris Pope. 2005. *When students turn to terror: Terrorist and extremist activity on British campuses*. London: The Social Affairs Unit.

Glynn, Sarah. 2002. Bengali Muslims: The new East End radicals? *Ethnic and Racial Studies* 25 (6): 969–988.

Gramsci, Antonio. 1971. *The prison notebooks*. London: Lawrence and Wishart.

Hall, Stuart. 1980. Race, articulation and societies structured in dominance. In *Sociological trends: Race and colonialism*, ed. UNESCO, 305–365. Paris: UNESCO.

———. 1990. Culture, identity and diaspora. In *Identity, culture, community, difference*, ed. Jonathon Rutherford, 222–237. London: Lawrence and Wishart.

———. 1992. New ethnicities. In *Race, culture, difference*, ed. James Donald and Ali Rattansi, 252–259. London: Sage in association with the Open University.

———. 1996. Who needs identity? In *Questions of cultural identity*, ed. Stuart Hall and Paul Du Gay, 1–17. London: Sage.

Haw, Kay. 1994. 'Muslim girls' schools: A conflict of interests? *Gender and Education* 6 (1): 63–76.

Hopkins, Peter. 2006. Youthful Muslim masculinities: Gender and generational relations. *Transactions of the Institute of British Geographers* 31 (3): 337–352.

———. 2007. Global events, national politics, local lives: Young Muslim men. *Environment and Planning* 39: 1119–1133.

Huntingdon, Samuel. 1996. *The clash of civilizations and the remaking of world order.* New York: Simon and Schuster

Kreikenbaum, Martin. 2010. *The lies of Thilo Sarrazin.* World Socialist Website, September 28, http://wsws.org/articles/2010/sep2010/sarr-s28.shtml.

Leppard, David, and Nick Fielding. 2005. The hate. *Sunday Times*, July 10.

McDowell, Linda. 2002. Masculine discourses and dissonances: Strutting 'lads', protest masculinity and domestic respectability. *Environment and Planning D: Society and Space* 20: 97–119.

Mirza, Heidi. 1992. *Young, female and black.* London: Routledge.

Modood, Tariq. 1992. British Asian Muslims and the Rushdie affair. In *Race, culture, difference*, ed. James Donald and Ali Rattansi, 260–267 . London: Open University.

Office for National Statistics. 2006. *Social trends.* London: Office for National Statistics.

Ousley, Herman. 2001. *Community pride not prejudice: Making diversity work in Bradford.* Bradford, UK: Bradford Vision.

Peach, Ceri. 2005. Muslims in the UK. In *Muslim Britain: Communities under pressure*, ed. Tahir Abbas, 18–30. London: Zed Books.

Qureshi, Karen. 2004. Respected and respectable: The centrality of performance and 'audiences' in the (re)production and potential revision of gendered ethnicities. *Participations*, 1 (2), http://www.participations.org/volume%201/issue%202/1_02_qureshi_article.htm.

Ramji, Hashmita. 2007. Dynamics of religion and gender amongst young British Muslims. *Sociology* 41 (12): 1171–1189.

Rutherford, Jonathon, ed. 1990. *Identity, community, culture, difference.* London: Lawrence and Wishart.

Saeed, Amir, Ned Blain and Douglas Forbes. 1999. New ethnic and national questions in Scotland: Post-British identities among Glasgow Pakistani teenagers. *Ethnic and Racial Studies* 22 (5): 821–844.

Samad, Yunas. 1998. Media and Muslim identity: Intersections of generation and gender. *Innovation: European Journal of Social Science* 10 (4): 281–282.

———. 1992. Book burning and race relations: Political mobilization of Bradford Muslims. *New Community* 18 (4): 507–519.

Shain, Farzana. 2003. *The schooling and identity of Asian Girls.* Stoke-on-Trent, UK: Trentham Books.

———. 2011. *New folk devils: Muslim boys and education in England.* Stoke-on-Trent, UK: Trentham.

Siddiqui, Hanna. 1991. Winning freedoms. *Feminist Review* 37: 18–20.

Spalek, Basia. 2007. Disconnection and exclusion: Pathways to radicalization? In *Islamic political radicalism: A European perspective*, ed. Tahir Abbas, 192–206. Edinburgh: Edinburgh University Press.

Swain, Jon. 2002. The resources and strategies boys use to establish status in a junior school without competitive sport. *Discourse: Studies in the Cultural Politics of Education* 23 (1): 91–107.

Ware, Vron. 1992. *Beyond the pale: White women, racism and history*. London: Verso.

Watson, James, ed. 1977. *Between two cultures: Migrants and minorities in Britain,*. Oxford: Basil Blackwell.

Werbner, Pnina. 1996. Fun spaces: On identity and social empowerment among British Pakistanis. *Theory, Culture and Society* 13 (4): 53–79.

Yuval-Davies, Nira. 1992. Fundamentalism, multiculturalism and women in Britain. In *Race, culture, and difference*, ed. James Donald and Ali Rattansi, 278–291. London: Sage in association with the Open University.

8   Understanding Class Anxiety and 'Race' Certainty in Changing Times

Moments of Home, School, Body and Identity Configuration in 'New Migrant' Dublin

Karl Kitching

ABSTRACT

Using ethnographic interview 'moments', I examine how *anxiety about class* and *certainty about 'race'* become articulated through staff and students' constructions of place (e.g., the neutral school or the 'at risk' household) and identity (e.g., mixing 'us' and Others) in a changing Dublin school. There is critical, local and international relevance to examining certainty about 'race' and class defensiveness through the lens of place and identity. Privileged and excluded groups' defence of and uncertainties about change and continuity in 'their' places mutually make and are made by globally racialized, classed and gendered power relations (Nayak 2003). Analyses of maintained, changed, elided and disrupted discourses of 'race' and class in an *Irish* school locale offer important lessons to critical antiracists in other countries, given Ireland's fluctuating fortunes as a 'global hub', and its previous imagining as a discretely White-Irish, Catholic territory (Lentin and McVeigh 2006). The interview data provide examples of how definitive, fixed constructions of the 'racial Other', often previously imagined/assured to be geographically foreign, are afforded new fixity and certainty through talk about peers, youth cultures, neighbourhoods, school, homes and households. The data analyses invariably highlight how already formed, maintained and defended discourses of class in this school setting may be used to 'deracialize' the politics of peer, school and social relations (Gillborn 1995), to strengthen constructions made about 'race' or to avoid talk about 'race' altogether.

INTRODUCTION

The contemporary concept of intersectionality is often credited to the extensive and often interweaving work of contemporary Black feminism, critical legal studies, and postcolonial studies (Crenshaw 1991; Brah and Phoenix

2004). It provides a resource for analyses of identity constellations emergent in particular school moments transnationally (Youdell 2006), and simultaneously informs analysis of overt policy texts (e.g., Irish interculturalism) and their underpinning subtexts (e.g., Irish nationalism; Bryan 2008). In this chapter, my aim is to critically explore schooled identities in a context of rapid mass immigration to Ireland, using poststructural, intersectional perspectives. My broad critical objective, in common with many texts that use similar tools, is to show that racism can be interrupted by dynamically contextualizing and unravelling what types of subjectivities are made possible, privileged and excluded in different contexts, and by interrogating the multifaceted, continuous ways in which subjects construct Self and Other in these contexts (Fanon, 2000; Youdell 2006).

An intersectional perspective is a particularly useful tool in uncovering the shifting interplay of inequalities facing new migrant and White-Irish working-class students at subcultural, peer and institutional level (Devine and Kelly 2006; Kitching 2010a, forthcoming). Before beginning the ethnographic interview analysis, I briefly discuss the contribution of intersectional tools and politics to understanding and deconstructing racialized subjectivation. A short account of some of the contemporary and embedded characteristics of inequalities in the Irish social context is provided subsequently. I then discuss the methodological and ethical underpinnings of this particular research project.

DECENTRING SUBJECTS AND COMPLICATING ANTIRACISM: IDENTITY AS A MAINTAINED, SITUATED PERFORMANCE

Perhaps key to understanding intersectionality is the decentring of the 'normative subject' of feminism' (Brah and Phoenix 2004, 78). The decentring of White feminist normativity was fuelled by the work of a variety of subaltern social movements, which generated Black feminist and postcolonial questioning of a unified, a priori and self-referential subject of struggle. Normalising feminist projects are also famously 'troubled' by Butler's (1990) political philosophy. Following Brah and Phoenix (2004), intersectionality can be regarded as referring to:

> The complex, irreducible, varied, and variable effects which ensue when multiple axis [*sic*] of differentiation—economic, political, cultural, psychic, subjective and experiential—intersect in historically specific contexts. The concept emphasizes that different dimensions of social life cannot be separated out into discrete and pure strands (2004, 76).

Brah and Phoenix (2004) demonstrate how rooted the principles of intersectionality are in historical struggles, such as the *Ain't I a Woman?*

words of Sojourner Truth, and many subsequent feminist coalitions. These movements questioned the idea that subjects are entirely free of the modern conditions of their emergence (particularly deeply embedded colonizer-colonized, male-female power relations; Brah and Phoenix 2004). Gendered, classed and/or racialized identity, particularly from poststructural perspectives, can be considered nonstable, as it is an actively reiterated *performance*, made possible through the sociohistorically embedded meanings and subjectivities available in/constituting each moment (Butler 1990). Given that these interweaving perspectives require an understanding of 'Self' as actively, socially maintained across changing places through available norms, languages and knowledges, identity performance can be considered a maintenance of *intelligibility as a possible subject* at the ontological level (Rose 2000; Youdell 2006), which may produce, embed or repress certain fears and certainties about place, Self and Other on a conscious, emotional level. For example, 'going home', 'spiritual homes' and having 'two homes' may take on complex psychological meanings for contemporary migrant, diasporic and mixed-'race' students (Ali 2003). Family and student *respectability* (Skeggs 1997) is a hard-won, constantly exchanged and contested form of cultural capital distributed through encodings of good neighbourhoods, mothers, and school sites. The active defence of respectability is discernable in accounts of class strategies and the education market (Ball 2003), intrasubjective conflict, gender and social mobility (Walkerdine et al. 2001), and White flight, 'urban' schools and 'ghettoisation' (Leonardo 2007).

An important example of how simultaneous 'race', class and gender readings can unravel the complex maintenance of identity is Nayak's (1999, 2003) analyses of the 'defence' of local, regional and national landscapes by White working-class males in different parts of England. Such work shows how inequality is situated and experienced dynamically, rather than returning us to apolitical 'resistant White-working-class = the origins of racism' equations. The contradictory borrowing of the racialized Other's styles by (White) youth, and the simultaneous, racist rejection of the Other's existence, is one example of how fraught the relationship between (often working-class) White subjectivities and the liberal antiracism espoused by class-stratified institutions can be (Yousman 2003). Such perspectives complement the wider critical antiracist field in arguing that *anti*racist discourses need to be vigilantly monitored in praxis: official antiracism can be deployed in ways that may not fundamentally challenge the multiple inequalities sustained by institutions (Ahmed 2004; Gillborn 2008). Ahmed (2004) shows how institutional antiracist policy statements can be nonperformative (i.e., they cannot be seen as synonymous with antiracist action) in their often ahistorical reductionism, for example, where 'White guilt' and 'Black marginalisation' are uncritically cast and recast on to tacitly re-hierarchised, 'informed' institutional actors. Bryan (2010) has voiced critique over the Irish state's recent deployment of a form of middle-class, corporate multiculturalism, where institutions were antiracist insofar as they overtly welcomed certain migrants positively as contributors to the boom economy. Whereas politicians spoke of 'not making the mistakes of other countries' (e.g., Britain, the Netherlands) with respect to racism and 'ghettoisation', Irish education policies glossed over the deep implications of statements against institutional racism (and religious exclusion), and rendered migrant students desirable if they could learn to speak English and make individual successes of themselves (Devine 2005; Bryan 2010; Kitching 2010a).

In the wider public sphere, despite the fact that new migrant communities have developed something of a media presence in Ireland (Kenny 2010), gendered, racialized discourses on migrant mothers were manipulated within mainstream media and political campaigns to the end of securing new exclusionary state policies on citizenship and asylum, while classed, deracialized discourses pitted representations of 'good migrant students' against their 'bad working-class Irish' classmates (Lentin 2004; Devine 2005; Kitching 2010a). Thus in contemporary Ireland as much as any other setting, intersectional ideas call on us to directly target the radical contingency and everyday effects of 'where', 'when' and 'how' privileged and excluded subjects of education are historically made and contemporarily remade. I turn next towards an account of critically researching identity, place and the centring and decentring of 'race', class and gender through the changing politics and processes partially characterising one Dublin school.

APPROACHING SCHOOL ETHNOGRAPHY USING POSTSTRUCTURAL, INTERSECTIONAL LENSES

The following three interview fragments were generated during a year-long ethnographic study in one mixed-sex second-level school in Dublin, given the pseudonym 'Dromray'. The study took place as the Celtic Tiger took its last gasps, in the 2007–2008 school year, prior to any real indication of the economic and social turmoil to come. Access to the school was initially granted as part of a planned study of ordinary, 'good' schools in the area, including Dromray and one of its linked, feeder primary schools. Of Ireland's population, 12.6 per cent self-classified in a category other than 'White-Irish' in 2006, but the region surrounding Dromray School became home to almost double the number of 'non-Irish' immigrants, according to census figures. The largest groups of 'non-Irish' residents in the region were Nigerian, Polish, Lithuanian and British, these groups ranging between two thousand and one thousand people approximately. I spoke at a staff meeting in April of the previous school year in Dromray School and the aforementioned primary school, and gained the initial consent of both school staffs to conduct the project. As the ethnography unfolded, I prioritised spending between one and two days per week in the postprimary school instead of the primary, particularly with third-year (usually 15-year-old) students, focusing on the more 'high-stakes' nature of secondary schooling at this particular age. I observed lessons and chatted with staff and students in the staffroom, on the corridor, on the yard and while going for lunch. Interviews were also recorded with students and staff, and records were taken of third-year student achievement on school-set tests. Access to classrooms and participant experiences and views was an ongoing, negotiated process. However, I was always frustrated with my accounts of the research when questioned by those who asked, or read the consent information I distributed, as my ethnographic and conceptual foci invariably developed and my view of my role changed. The overarching constant was that I was interested in participants' views and their practices in a time of major social change, and the social and educational experiences of minority students in particular. As the research on this school—which was highly respected by the community—progressed, I found myself increasingly drawn to the classed, racialized and gendered politics of peer groups and student subcultures (as demonstrated in the first and third data excerpts) and similarly to classroom and staff constructions of Otherness (as demonstrated in the second). My approach to generating and partially analysing these difficult themes here is discussed next.

Methodological, Ethical and Analytical Possibilities with Ethnographic 'Moments'

The forthcoming analyses are drawn from my doctoral work (Kitching 2010b), which uses many of the insightful ideas put forward and applied by my supervisor Deborah Youdell (see Youdell 2006). The data presented below are considered cogenerated between the participants and myself. There are a few issues with this view of interviews as cogenerated—and the subsequent use of discourse analysis—that require specific attention here. The first is that who 'I' am, or am perceived to be in different places and at different times, is implicated in the data generated in ethnographic exchanges: Teachers sometimes identified with me as a former (primary) teacher; this former self was sometimes implicit in the generation of talk with them, as ethnographic school research is extremely rare and my long-term presence was sometimes out of place. Certainly, my position as White-Irish, middle class, ethnographer and former teacher has an impact both on how I elicited participants' understandings (e.g., through questions about groups of students in the school), and their trajectories: that is, how they are taken up by various new migrant students, White-Irish students and the (entirely White, mostly Irish) staff. The second is that as subjects, the replaying or refutation of multiple discourses, identities and positions in the ethnographic process may not be under the full or sometimes even conscious/intentional control of the research participants or myself. For example, a range of discourses was deployed in discussions about 'girls' with some of the teenage boys I researched that allowed the assumption and positioning of me as 'experienced hetero-male', while at the same time, I could never be entirely sure that my part in ethnographic exchanges (e.g., my questions, position as White-Irish ethnographic 'friend', former teacher, etc.) did not incite students to resist, or stay silent because of the singular ways in which my project might require them to 'be an immigrant'. Some (all White-Irish) students appeared to test me with racist/foreigner jokes as they got to know me. Others approached me occasionally for a casual chat, whereas others maintained their distance, perhaps indicating they did not wish to be a part of my work.

Thus both the positive and troubling aspects of the three data fragments analysed below should not be viewed as cumulative 'evidence' of a good/ bad school or good/bad people. Analytically speaking, after Britzman (2000), 'I try to hold tightly to the ethic of not producing these subjects as persons of blame or as heroes of resistance. Instead my concern [is] one of questioning how the categories of blame and resistance are discursively produced and lived' (Britzman 2000, 32). Consistent with the view of identity as a social practice, I saw the construction of 'race' (e.g., white-ness) as an ongoing interactional achievement, and not the sole property of individuals: 'in other words, people don't have race in the conventional sense but are actively raced as they are drawn into the complex processes of economic, cultural and political racialization' (Best 2003, 897). Without analytical vigilance to shared achievements and contestations of 'race', we may expect, for example, the White woman to invoke a style of 'whiteness', or to perform aspects of 'womanhood' in a predetermined manner (Nayak 2006). I deliberately present the achievement of researcher-researched iden-tities below using binary citational chains (e.g., White-Irish, working class, Black-male-Nigerian, etc.). These chains preface the interview fragments in order to remind us of their intersectional, dynamic interplay and to remain vigilant to the central role of 'race', class, gender 'and so on' (Butler 1990) in making subjectivities and constructions of Self and Other possible and meaningful. The categories cited in these chains, whereas in no way are suggested as cumulatively or essentially 'making up' persons, are key tropes of identity performance: Again, as the subjects of discourse, individuals constantly deploy, refute, rework, notice and leave unnoticed the terms of their subjectivation.

The deep interpretive focus on brief 'moments' in the ethnography is deliberate: Interviews with different people on different topics (subculture, households, families, friends, classmates) are juxtaposed and unpicked as a means of demonstrating the need to confront how 'race', class and gender dynamically infuse the everyday. Certainly, the analysis presented here is 'an effect of contest of discourses, even if the ethnographer has the power to suggest what is at stake when identities are at stake' (Britzman 2000, 37). But as texts, the analyses of the potential workings of discourse below must be considered never entirely authoritative, interpretively speaking. While wary of the possibility of ever finitely representing White-Irish and new migrant students' voices, my position is that critical, provisional learning can be fostered first through the analysis of anxieties, defences, and certainties around 'race' and class, and second through the positive disruption of traditional school discourses available in the analysis of new migrant subjectivities (e.g., Theo and Franklin, below).

CLASS ANXIETY, 'RACE' CERTAINTY: AVOIDING 'SCUMBAG' AND CONSTRUCTING RACIAL CATEGORIES THROUGH PLACE AND YOUTH CULTURE

The first fragment of interview data was generated with Beth and Adrienne, two fifteen-year-old White-Irish girls. These students were sometimes as vocal as their other lower 'band' classmates, but they were also recognisable as somewhat different in terms of classed, subcultural markers of identity in this setting—perhaps even quasi-bohemian. During the interview, the girls referred to various peer groups such as 'rockers, scumbags, weirdos and swots'. When asked if they categorised themselves, Beth suggested a lot of people call them hippies, which they both seemed to embrace and be happy with. Their tone often inflected upward at the end of sentences, and their accents were relatively distinctive in the school, in that they could be categorised—depending on the categorizer—as metropolitan Dublin and/ or transatlantic teen girls.[1] A key part of the interview focuses on Beth's report that a former primary-school friend is now 'faking being a scumbag' in their second-level school. This supposed affectation, which apparently involves socialising with students from undesirable areas around the school, is even rendered bourgeois and pretentious. But the manner in which class mutability appears as the central issue perhaps is an artefact of the embedded contestation of *White-Irish peer group and* subcultural forms (e.g., rocker, scumbag, hippie) in the school. As anxiously and contradictorily as class is articulated, the ease with which variously 'positive' and 'negative'— and ultimately immutable—constructions of the new racial Other is produced through talk about peers, place and youth cultures provides a useful insights into everyday inequality reconfiguration processes in Dromray.

Generating data below:

Adrienne: 15-year-old White-French-Irish middle-class female student
Beth: 15-year-old White-Irish middle-class female student
KK: 28-year-old White-Irish middle-class male researcher

Beth: A scumbag is like, they walk round like this [swaggers and bobs in the seat] and all, like, they have a really common accent, like I know [our area of Dublin] is kinda common, but it's not, like as bad as a lot of places like. But I think half of them put on the accents. Just to make them sound tougher. Like I know scumbags and weirdos from town and everything and they have proper common accents and that's just like where they grew up and everything. But people around here like, they put it on and then people just take after them and everything like. I know a few girls that are like, they went to my primary school 'cause a lot of people in our year went to my primary school [St. Fiachra's] and em, there's a girl and she, in primary school, she was really girly and like, real sweet and everything and real nice. But since she came into secondary school and she had a really posh accent like, she was from St. Fiachra's Park, when she came into secondary school, and she started meeting people from like Ravensfield [beside Brookfield] and like St. Enda's and everything like that, she suddenly just developed a big scumbag accent and starting doing that stupid walk [both laugh].

KK: You [Adrienne] live in Brookfield don't you?

Adrienne: Yeah, I don't know anyone in my road and I won't go out with them

KK: Why?

Adrienne: Cause [inaudible as Beth speaks over her] | BETH: Cause she's afraid of them!

KK: What does your mum say?

Adrienne: She doesn't say anything, she doesn't really bother about it because she's not there until like, she'd be there in the morning and she comes back at 6 o'clock and goes back out so it's just like, she doesn't really live there? My sister has friends around the road so it's grand. And I just go to Cherry Meadow.

KK: You mentioned the Filipino kids?

Adrienne: There's nothing like, they all just hang out in the same bunch and they all—

KK: What I'm interested in is you didn't mention other people [i.e., other minority ethnic and/or migrant groups].

Adrienne: Oh, well em, there's no other cultures that bunch together like that. Like, black people, they don't like, they hang around with different groups and everything like. They hang around but they don't all hang around together.

KK: Who would they be, would they be mixed in with the groups you *already mentioned [Swots, Filipinos, Weirdos, Scumbags].*

Beth: Yeah.

KK: Which ones?

Beth: Mainly the scumbags.

Adrienne: Yeah, or the ones—

KK: Why is that?

Adrienne: Or the pimps. Seriously! [laughs].

Beth: It's cause like, you know the way if you're from a different country, and you come over and you start in another school, like, what's the group you'd mainly go for? The group who's like the loudest and seems to have the most friends and everything, or the weirdos who everybody seems to not like? You go for like, the scumbags because they have the most people and like, a lot of people are like, wouldn't really stand up to them and stuff?

KK: Yeah. So you think scumbag is the biggest group?

Beth: Yeah there's a lot of them.

While the interview above was conducted in a 'good school' in a class-ambiguous location (see the next interview with the principal), the neighbourhoods referred to by the girls in the interview are Cherry Meadow (desirable, where they both hang out); St. Fiachra's Park (desirable, close to where Beth lives); Brookfield (undesirable, where Adrienne lives); and St. Enda's (undesirable, very near the school). The above fragment is fraught with concerns about how tacit indicators of class are spatially mapped and should be naturalised. Housing, styles of movement, accents, leisure interests and friendship are idealized above as 'belonging' to discretely working-class/middle-class areas and mind-sets, but such binaries are not realizable in practice. Beth notes the authenticity of the 'real scumbags' and 'weirdos' of Dublin's inner city. Their right to be angry at living in difficult circumstances is represented above as being stolen by these 'suburban' scumbags (for whom life is not as difficult), and worse still, by teens who overtly 'pretend' to be scumbags. 'Scumbag' affectations are caricatured above as a common accent and a stupid walk. At the same time, the wider White working-class Other is overtly suggested as a threat to the security of bodies and homes: Beth suggests Adrienne is afraid of her neighbours. But 'their' presence in Dromray is also a tacit threat to the occupation of desirable subjectivity on an ontological plane, produced as it might be through notions of a stable, discretely classed neighbourhoods and classrooms. The sympathy expressed towards 'real, hard scumbags' might not be underpinned by moral outrage, but a tacit anxiety at the constant escaping of a desired, safe working-class/middle-class, inner-city/suburb chain of dichotomies. Adrienne is iteratively returned to certain markers of undesirable life when she goes home. She lives with her mother and sister in what she suggests is an unacceptable area with unacceptable people. Her mother 'doesn't even live there', which could be interpreted in numerous ways: for example, a representation of disgust with the area, or the multiple requirements of a one-parent family? Beth's family, while living in a unique and almost farm-like space near the suburban sprawl, might not necessarily be safely intelligible as 'middle-class, respectable' student either, for example, as her father is a construction labourer, and she is placed in a 'B' Band in school. As teenage subjects, Adrienne and Beth iteratively constitute and defend their identities as happy-respectable-fun-loving (White girls): They almost playfully refute undesirable places and dis-identify with Others. A mind/body split is devised and managed, as the girls can dwell in spiritual homes instead of undesirable places they officially belong to (e.g., Adrienne's house, the school). Adrienne attempts to produce herself really belonging in different locations (e.g., Cherry Meadow, shopping for less-tacky clothes).

But while class may appear somewhat precariously mutable to the girls, discourses of racial immutability, articulated through transnational and local imaginings of the now 'visible', 'racial' difference in everyday places, have the simultaneous effect of maintaining the 'purity' of White-Irish identity above. Much racializing work is done in characterising Filipino bodies *as clustered*: 'They hang around together and all . . . there's no other cultures that bunch together like that.' The representation of 'Filipino clustering' and 'Black mixing' appears tacitly underpinned by gendered imaginings of problematic racial Otherness: private, unintegrated Asianness and loud, uninhibited blackness (Archer and Francis 2007). Black kids are rendered innately promiscuous in gendered ways: they 'are' essentially louder and can deal with those who are uncouth, or they are uncouth already. The meaning of Black youth here takes a form that can often be simultaneously loved and hated by young White music buyers internationally (Yousman 2003): often aggressively sexualized and misogynist 'pimps'.

The articulation of identity in this shifting terrain necessitates the management of glaring contradictions about mixing with Others. Given who Adrienne's and Beth's classmates are, it is necessary to be sociable and to mix—even with 'scumbags'—in order to maintain a successful subcultural identity at school: but not outside of it. What appears to need explaining about Black kids is that they are different in their bodily distribution—they can mix with 'scumbag Whites' inasmuch as Beth and Adrienne can. By using a racialized mind/body split, it is possible for Adrienne and Beth to rationalize the idea that 'we can mix with Other, but we are not the Other' (e.g., Black, scumbag, Filipino). The girls can rework the meaning of being somewhere else, either by going to places they 'really belong', or by dis-identifying with this place: Filipino and Black African students, in this representation, cannot, or do not. Indeed, neither the particular Filipino or Black African (mostly Nigerian and Congolese) kids in this school are viewed as also drawing on complex racialized and classed processes in order to maintain a sense of viable identity.

The next analysis considers further the ways in which subjects choreograph and are choreographed by the un/certain, changing matrices of identity (Self/Other) and place (schools and households/neighbourhoods). Below, I demonstrate how the very tacit, classed and religioned defence of an Irish school as a neutral/good place facing the 'problem' of certain households might maintain barriers to critically examining emergent, congealing culturalism and racialization. As the fragment below suggests, classed and 'familied' discourses were traditionally worked to displace conflict into the social and out of the 'good' school. This meritocratic placing now works to frame not only good/bad working class and certain families, but also good/bad 'newcomers'. It is important to reiterate that these hegemonic dis/continuities emerge despite the genuine care ethic that is articulated in the interview below. Dromray, like other schools, is operating without much state support to help students and teachers understand migration and racisms, and resource new migrants' education (Devine 2005).

RE-PRESENTING SCHOOL/HOME: CLASSED DEFENCE AND RATIONALISING CULTURE CLASH

Generating data below:

P: Principal (50s White-Irish female)
KK: Interviewer (28-year-old White-Irish male)

P: Well when I started to live here [over two decades] ago, it was a nicely settled area and em, this school was built in [the early seventies]. The children coming here would come from a grand settled background . . . [Parents] would be very involved in their children's education. We still have a lot of children of that nature here. Em, but the area has aged. The demographics changed . . . So, eh, we are now taking our children from a broader catchment area. That catchment area would be more working-class, to some degree, there would still be children whose parents would send them here because they think it is the best education for their children . . . Then there would be more children who would come from single parent families as well and homes that would be em, in the more socially deprived areas—but still not a huge percentage of that. In fact, what we would have is children whose parents want them to come here because they don't want them to go to their catchment schools . . .

KK: Mmm. So the school itself would be consistently seen in the wider . . . area as maybe a cut above?

P: Yeah. Ah yeah. It would be. Em, then there are the overseas children coming in now. Which at this stage would be 12 to 15 per cent. Now, they wouldn't necessarily be deprived at all. A lot of them would be over here working. The eastern Europeans would be here to work and they would be ambitious people as well. The only thing is that both parents would be working . . . very hard and the children seem to be left alone quite a bit, evenings, night times, so supervision isn't there.

KK: Right.

P: That could be a problem. Then there could be a problem that they just wouldn't have an awful lot of money, they would have to come over to get jobs so that they would need support, financial support. The only financial support we could give them would be free books. And behaviour problems there might be a bit problematic. But then you get overseas children whose parents would be professionals themselves. They would be in the medical profession down in [the local] hospital: doctors, nurses, social workers, things like that. And they would be very ambitious for their children. And very steady backgrounds.

KK: Right. In terms of behaviour, you mentioned behaviour patterns there?

P: Mmm.

KK: Could you expand on that?

P: Well again, it depends. Some of the African children would be well-behaved. But there would be a tendency for some Nigerian boys to have a very different standard of what's right and wrong maybe. Some of them, em, tend to be very dramatic sometimes. To be loud sometimes. And em, I would also be nervous about bringing in parents for wrongdoing. Normally, our policy would be you contact parents, you get them on board and they work with you to remediate whatever the problem is. But there are times when I would definitely hesitate before I would—especially if I have had experience of the parents once . . . so we would try to deal with them another way.

KK: What strategies have you, have the school adopted if that's the case?

P: We would, well first of all, just talk to them. Get them to explain what's right and wrong. Then give them some punishment work within the school like cleaning the canteen or going on detention or something like that. And not get the parents involved if we think that wouldn't be wise.

This subjectivated/subjectivating depiction of homes by official education discourses is always multiplicitous and incomplete. Explanations of family participation in schooling can change, or can be reconstituted in different ways at different times. Above, a convergence of discourses of risk and pastoral care allow a definite 'cultural clash' ontology and familiar racialized meanings to be produced. These discourses divert attention away from already classed discourses of schools as bounded, good institutions. The framing of 'at risk' students cites modern epidemiological discourses: the public (school)/private (home) distinction perhaps is the very mode through which child 'risk' can be discussed (Harden et al. 2000), and tacit potential 'profiling' can take place. It is significant that the principal does not risk her identity in the discourses that are drawn upon to reiterate school/

home distinctions. Indeed, her performance acceptably reenacts the Irish constitution's positioning of teachers as being *in loco parentis*. The remarks are also entirely meaningful through another professionally acceptable discourse in Irish education: the deprived family, framed in Christian terms. Vaguely religious or pastoral terms (right and wrong, etc.) about 'overseas' students can be cited quite legitimately, and these discourses afford almost natural stability to the terms of school participation.

The above discourses afford rationality to popular and political ideas about defending boundaries while capitalising on the Other, particularly those which suggest migrants to Ireland are welcome as they can help support national economic, service and welfare needs. The requirements of 'Fortress Europe' and 'Fortress Ireland' often equate White immigrant with legitimate worker status, and Black immigrant as illegal/asylum seekers (Devine 2005; Lentin and McVeigh 2006). This has already been argued to influence Irish teachers' views of their students in recent years (Devine 2005). The thin erasure of 'race', nation and ethnicity from student acceptability is achieved by referencing family, stability, social class and, where appropriate, religion. Acceptable, desirable Other families are produced in this context through neo-Orientalist certainties which silence class relations and ignore the politics of migrant status. Many Asian families work in the professional medical sector in the locality: the families the principal is referring to are more likely to be those of Filipino, Indian, and Pakistani backgrounds. Many of the students in the school from these countries have one or two parents working in the large local hospital, or work in health care in other parts of the city. With particular reference to Filipino students in the school, an implicit cultural congruence is regularly drawn with normative conditions of Irish schooling (postcolonial, Catholic, diasporic, middle-class students). In this way, congruent cultures are made obvious, rather than historically conceived and given meaning through the subjective 'evidence' of everyday life.

Cultural congruence/clash ontologies position the school as 'fortunate' with some families, while having their hands tied with other, more problematic ones. Ideas about cultural clash suggest there is a very 'different standard' of right and wrong amongst newer communities which needs to be addressed within this school. Of course, this locates the perceived clash firmly within the student and *his* background which, again in this case, is based on citing a skin-nation-gender chain (Black-Nigerian-male), and ignores differences cross-sectioning this chain. Such meanings are not purely of the 'culturist' type, if such a purity exists: Colonial notions of the difficulty with educating the biologically inferior male, recognisable by his physiognomy, haunt the above excerpt. There is clear potential within these designations for institutional bias and selectivity, in terms of home-school contact. Whereas the school would appear to welcome contact with certain (hardworking, respectable) families, there is tacit suggestion that others require institutional distancing because of their perceived potential for abusive behaviour. The above practices may align contemporary, well-intentioned liberal educational orthodoxy of meeting 'individual' needs of students with pastoral care and support (by protecting certain students from harm at home). This co-articulation of discourses may unexpectedly elide sustained and patterned discriminatory treatment against the wider group that only certain individuals may be recognised as being 'part' of (Gillborn and Youdell 2000).

But as 'the local' fuses old and new discourses of class and 'race', shifting discourses and reclassifications are also taken up and deployed by new migrants. In the final fragment, a short analysis briefly unravels the leaving and remaking of home and school by Theo and Franklin, two boys who have come to Dromray in the previous two years from dialectically and geographically different parts of the Philippines.

MEMORIES OF HOME: DISRUPTING RACIALIZED AND CLASSED SCHOOL/HOME CONFIGURATIONS?

Theo and Franklin both live in a relatively new and somewhat upmarket development of apartments, duplexes and townhouses near the local hospital, and became close friends. Franklin's father is a nurse, while his mother is a medical-sales rep. Theo's mother is a nurse and his father is a mechanical engineer. Theo and Franklin always appeared very happy in the school. They considered living in Ireland, meeting new people, and so on, as 'great'. They stated they had friends of lots of different nationalities and loved playing basketball at lunchtime. Theo and Franklin reported accounts of occasionally overt racism from other (usually White-Irish-male) students, including one incident where a senior cycle student physically harmed Theo. The school, as always, quickly moved to deal with this occurrence and suspended the student.

Yet as the review earlier suggests, liberal antiracist, promigrant discourses often do not provide space to consider the complexity of inclusion and exclusion that may be somewhat beyond the growing, singular certainties about 'race' and ethnicity in this setting. This analysis focuses specifically on the boys' experiences as students in Ireland and the Philippines. Having got to know the boys throughout the year, I noticed how they often did not speak in front of the class during their (lower band) lessons. Having also met repeated characterizations of 'Asian' or 'Filipino' docility in teacher interviews, I was interested to incite the boys to speak about participation in school and class. The first question, 'How do you act?' itself invites the boys to speak truth directly to (racialized) identities, that is, to narrowly self-report and self-reflect on their relation to themselves. But the data generated allow us to partially open up the simultaneously classed and gendered terms through which they might become intelligible as 'good students'.

Generating data in this interview:

Franklin: 15-year-old Filipino male student
KK: 28-year-old White-Irish male researcher
Theo: 16-year-old Filipino male student

KK: How would you say you act in class?

Franklin: Me? Quiet. Sometimes a little giddy, get hyper!

KK: Would you be that way in the Philippines or in a different school do you think?

Franklin: In the Philippines? [laughs] Oh my God—I'm like crazy! [laughs] Yeah, like I'd be sent to the principal twice a week I think.

KK: You get into trouble all the time? Why doesn't that happen here?

Theo: It's a different country.

Franklin: People change.

KK: You've changed?

Theo: Yeah.

KK: Yeah. So why did you change, or what happened?

Franklin: It's just, I don't know. At first, I'm not that good in English. I don't talk, like.

KK: Did you find it difficult with English at first?

Franklin: Yeah, at first. Then I got good. Now I'm [OK].

KK: Yeah. What about you [Theo]? How would you say you act in class?

Franklin: Me? Same as him as well, I don't really speak that much more English. In the Philippines I was the same as him as well, really noisy in class, keep messin'. But when I came here, same as him as well, don't really speak that much more English. What do you call it, just find it quiet.

KK: Do you find it comfortable to talk in front of people in the class, like if the teacher asked you a question or whatever?

Theo: Sometimes, it's like. I'm always shy in class. That's why I'm doing Transition year, to build up more confidence in myself.

KK: Are you doing Transition year [Franklin]?

Franklin: Yeah, I think so. I need to work!

KK: How do you mean?

Theo: Cause you get working experience.

Franklin: I don't want to be like, askin' your parents for money

KK: OK, you want some independence?

Franklin: Yeah.

The reasons for the differences in the boys' experiences of school in Ireland (i.e., not being punished so often) are put down to moving to a different country, to people changing and to feeling shy about using English. But we can also theorize that when the boys cross the borders of the Philippines and shift from doing 'indigenous' to 'migrant', new student subject locations are choreographed for and by them. On a larger scale than Adrienne and Beth earlier, they must manage identity as they physically cross borders into very new contexts of emergence: Ireland, greater Dublin and Dromray. In this particular school, Filipinos were largely regarded positively in the academic and behavioural sense, and certain teachers viewed Asians more generally as 'good examples' for 'certain' White-Irish (usually working-class) students. It might not be surprising, then, that the boys articulate the need to maintain and use the advantages gained in the reputation that was often bestowed. In a second interview later in the year, Theo and Franklin talk more about norms: particularly the norms through which they often are recognised as students:

Franklin: Do you know the—some of the Irish think that Filipinos respect, respect others. Like you know, my dad told me that I have to be like, less talking and participate in class. So that our, what you call like, they like our kind like, Filipinos.

Theo: A lot of people respect us.

Franklin: [echoing] A lot of people respect us.

KK: Mmm.

Franklin: 'Cause we have a good (inaudible on recording)

KK: Yeah. So you need to—are you saying to me that you need to maintain or keep?

Franklin: Yeah, maintain.

KK: Do you ever feel like not doing that?

Theo: Well, at first, but we're used to it now!

KK: And what about your friends from the Philippines would they say the same thing?

Franklin: Some are like, real messers!

Theo: Yeah, they smoke, but we don't smoke. We just mess in class but we don't do really bad stuff like takin' drugs, smokin'. Mitchin'.

KK: Who smokes?

Theo: Some of our friends.

KK: Like who?

Theo: Filipinos.

Franklin: But we usually don't hang around with bad people and all, bad influence people. Students. We hang around with those good people, group of students.

The necessary contradictions in managing a respectable 'Filipino' identity and 'Dromray studenthood' are interesting here: Gendered, classed and subcultural discourses are deployed which elide 'race' as part of one's schools memories in the Philippines and reinforce its fixity in Dromray. Could Franklin and Theo be said to be 'doing Filipino' when they regularly got into trouble in school back in the Philippines? Were they 'doing boy', or something else, and what does it mean for them to 'do boy' here? In one instance, the boys quite overtly draw upon ethno-racial terminology to describe how well respected their 'kind' are by 'the Irish'. Yet in another, there are possibilities that there are 'bad' people who are Filipino, and that they themselves behaved badly back home. In other words, it is not that there is an essential Filipino (or boy) set of attributes, educational or otherwise, despite the boys' initial claim. Specific class, gender and subculture discourses work to shape their terms of 'Filipino-ness' internally, both with reference to school memories and Other Filipino teens in Dublin. The borders around being Filipino in Dromray are not fixed, but variously *worked*: Indeed, Theo appears to suggest that he has become 'used to' (naturalizing?) a certain 'version' in school.

The interplay of 'race', class and gender here is important to note when juxtaposed with the articulation of Filipino-ness and Asianness as an embodied, variously benign, and/or model minority culture in the previous ethnographic exchanges. Whereas the boys use the language of good/bad Filipino to maintain their position as acceptable students, their memories of school in the Philippines disrupt any externally imposed notion of good/bad migrant student suggested by the previous two analyses. The fragment above raises questions about how social class and subcultural divisions are decentred and hidden in the 'positive-negative' tying of 'Filipino-ness' to their bodies and behaviours (Archer and Francis 2007). While Theo and Franklin's words suggest their attempts to frame this new place via the prevailing 'positive' culturalism around Asian families (Archer and Francis 2007), analysis of their subjective migrations and memories also provide further ways of challenging the racialization of new migrant students' educational aspirations and participation.

CONCLUSION: THE IMPORTANCE OF DECENTRED SUBJECTIVITY TO COMPLEX ANTIRACISMS

The three analyses of places and identities above suggest 'race', class and gender power relations are iteratively defended, deployed and elided in ongoing performances of Self and constructions of places and Others (bodies, households). Privileged and excluded subjectivities are made available through everyday processes of recognition, disruption and, indeed, recuperation to further inclusions and exclusions (Youdell 2006; Kitching forthcoming). In the above data analysis, the coherent and contradictory defence, dismissal and change of certain identities and places provide examples of issues that could complicate antiracisms in educational praxis. For example, Beth and Adrienne's descriptions of perfunctory socialising with ('Black, Filipino, scumbag') Others in school does much 'rational' racializing and classed work, ironically, complementing intercultural policy in Dromray: *integrate, be sociable*. Positive policies which recommend mixing on the yard 'to be intercultural' without challenging the dynamic ways in which 'race' is constructed can fail to challenge White-Irish constructions of, for example, 'unsociable Asianness' and 'too sociable blackness'. By assuming that racism is challenged simply through 'appropriate mixing' and not by analysing wider production of meanings (e.g., social class, colonisation, migration, skin, gender-sexuality, family), the school compulsion to 'be intercultural' can become part of the congealing certainty of how 'race' works in this setting. The analysis of the second interview fragment suggests that destabilising the 'clear' articulation of decidedly unclear, shifting constructions of school as 'neutral' place and certain homes as 'problematic' can also help challenge the maintenance and emergence of classed, culturalist and racialized norms.

While representing the voices of new migrant students is a crucial factor in antiracist research, the approach adopted here is wary of creating either targets for blame (e.g., some of the White-Irish participants above) or heroes of resistance (e.g., Franklin, Theo, or even myself; Britzman 2000). Rather than deploying a singular approach to analysing the exchange with Theo and Franklin, I attempted to show how open interrogation of their identity constructions in two different places—memories of home and experiences of Dromray—can disrupt the congealing interplay of 'race', class and gender inequalities which position them as passively 'model' students. Intersectional analyses of place and identity help expose the fragility of maintained divisions and representations, whether in terms of housing, neighbourhoods, 'clustered' or 'promiscuous' bodies, imagined cultural clashes and congruencies, and renderings of neutral/conflictual places. But in particular, the analysis of how we dynamically, unauthoritatively and mundanely choreograph and *are choreographed* by 'stable' and changing constructions of identities and places—in other words, the analysis of subjectivation—is where possibility for interrupting racisms and redrawing inclusion endlessly lies.

NOTES

1. Both of the girls augment their uniform by wearing lots of bangles, subtle makeup (i.e., not fake tan) with heavy eye shadow: They might be yuppie-hippies? They don't get, however, how some people see them as being between a hippie and a rocker. Adrienne also had occasional traces of a French-speaking accent: Her father is French and has returned to France after he and Adrienne's mother separated

REFERENCES

Ahmed, Sara. 2004. Declarations of whiteness: The non-performativity of anti-racism. *Borderlands e-journal* 3, http://www.borderlands.net.au/vol3no2_2004/ahmed_declarations.htm

Ali, Suki. 2003. *Mixed race, post-race: Gender, new ethnicities and cultural practices.* Oxford: Berg.

Archer, Louise, and Becky Francis. 2007. *Understanding minority ethnic achievement: Race, gender, class and 'success'.* London: Routledge.

Ball, Stephen. J. 2003. *Class strategies and the education market.* London: RoutledgeFalmer.

Best, Amy L. 2003. Doing race in the context of feminist interviewing: Constructing whiteness through talk. *Qualitative Inquiry* 9: 895–914.

Brah, Avtar, and Ann Phoenix. 2004. Ain't I a woman? Revisiting intersectionality. *Journal of International Women's Studies* 5: 75–86.

Britzman, Deborah. 2000. 'The question of belief': Writing poststructural ethnography. In *Working the ruins: Feminist poststructural theory and methods in education*, eds. Elizabeth St. Pierre and Wanda S. Pillow, 27–40. New York: Routledge.

Bryan, Audrey. 2008. The co-articulation of national identity and interculturalism in the Irish curriculum: Educating for democratic citizenship? *London Review of Education* 6: 47–58.

———. 2010. Corporate multiculturalism, diversity management, and positive interculturalism: A vertical case study of the racialised dynamics of inclusion and exclusion in Irish schools and society. *Irish Educational Studies* 29: 213–229.

Butler, Judith. 1990. *Gender trouble: Feminism and the subversion of identity.* London: Routledge.

Crenshaw, Kimberlé. 1991. Mapping the margins: Intersectionality, identity politics, and violence against women of color. *Stanford Law Review* 43: 1241–1299.

Devine, Dympna. 2005. Welcome to the Celtic Tiger? Teacher responses to immigration and increasing ethnic diversity in Irish schools. *International Studies in Sociology of Education* 15: 49–70.

Devine, Dympna, and Mary Kelly. 2006. 'I just don't want to get picked on by anybody': Dynamics of inclusion and exclusion in a newly multi-ethnic Irish primary school. *Children and Society* 20: 128–139.

Fanon, Frantz. 2000. The Negro and psychopathology. In *Identity: A reader*, eds. Paul du Gay, Jessica Evans and Peter Redman, 202–221. London: Sage.

Gillborn, David. 1995. *Racism and antiracism in real schools: Theory, policy, practice.* Buckingham, UK: Open University Press.

———. 2008. *Racism and education: Coincidence or conspiracy?* London: Routledge.

Gillborn, David, and Deborah Youdell. 2000. *Rationing education: Policy, practice, reform and equity.* Buckingham, UK: Open University Press.

Harden, Jeni, Kathryn Backett-Milburn, Sue Scott and Stevi Jackson. 2000. Scary faces, scary places: Children's perceptions of risk and safety. *Health Education Journal* 59: 12–22.

Kenny, Colum. 2010. Finding a voice or fitting in? Migrants and the media in new Ireland. *Media Culture and Society* 32: 311–322.

Kitching, Karl. 2010a. An excavation of the racialised politics of viability underpinning education policy in Ireland. *Irish Educational Studies* 29: 213–229.

———. 2010b. Justifying school . . . and self: An ethnography on race, recognition and viability in education in Ireland. Unpublished PhD thesis, Institute of Education, University of London.

———. Forthcoming. Interrogating the changing inequalities constituting 'popular', 'deviant' and 'ordinary' subjects of school/subculture in Ireland: Moments of new migrant student recognition, resistance and recuperation. *Race Ethnicity and Education.*

Lentin, Ronit. 2004. Strangers and strollers: Feminist reflections on researching migrant m/others. *Women's Studies International Forum* 27: 301–314.

Lentin, Ronit, and Robbie McVeigh. 2006. *After optimism? Ireland, racism and globalisation*. Dublin: Metro Éireann Publications.

Leonardo, Zeus. 2007. *Imagining the urban: Race, class and the politics of schooling*. Paper presented at the American Educational Research Association Annual Conference, April 9–13, in Chicago, IL.

Nayak, Anoop. 1999. Pale warriors: Skinhead culture and the embodiment of white masculinities. In *Thinking identities: Ethnicity, racism and culture*, eds. Avtar Brah, Mary Hickman and Máirtín Mac an Ghaill, 71–99. Hampshire, UK: Palgrave.

———. 2003. *Race, place and globalization: Youth cultures in a changing world*. Oxford: Berg.

Rose, Nikolas. 2000. Identity, genealogy, history. In *Identity: A reader*, eds. Paul du Gay, Jessica Evans and Peter Redman, 311–324. London: Sage.

Skeggs, Beverley. 1997. *Formations of class and gender: Becoming respectable*. London: Sage.

Walkerdine, Valerie, Helen Lucey and June Melody. 2001. *Growing up girl: Psychosocial explorations of gender and class*. Hampshire, UK: Palgrave.

Youdell, Deborah. 2006. *Impossible bodies, impossible selves: Exclusions and student subjectivities*. Dordrecht, Netherlands: Springer.

Yousman, Bill. 2003. Blackophilia and blackophobia: White youth, the consumption of rap music, and white supremacy. *Communication Theory* 13: 366–391.

9 Beyond Culture

From Beyoncé's Dream, 'If You Thought I Would Wait for You, You Got It Wrong' (2008), to the Age of Michelle Obama

Namita Chakrabarty

ABSTRACT

A reading of the lyrics and video of Beyoncé Knowles's *If I Were a Boy* (2008), and its manipulation of race, gender and homoeroticism, positions this popular cultural text as a metaphor through which to view the actions of the struggle for equality, specifically in the age of Obama. Referring to the psychoanalytical theory of *The Uncanny* (Freud 2003 [1919]), and through critical-creative reflections on political events during 2009–10: Michelle Obama in London during the G20, and the election of a coalition government in the UK in 2010, the paper argues for the analysis of intersectionality combined with the activism of Critical Race Feminist Theory.

BACKGROUND—ON ACTION

This chapter seeks to explore, through cultural metaphor, the uncanny duality displayed in the dawning of the age of Obama: Obama would not have risen to power within the present system, a mixed-race man as the head of a Western country, without the work of others outside of the system. Without the struggle of the African National Congress (ANC) and the eventual success of Nelson Mandela against apartheid; without the binary legacies of Martin Luther King and Malcolm X in the US civil rights movement; and without the nonviolence of Gandhi and the global struggles against imperialism and towards self-determination; without this chain of actions Obama (Obama 2008, 27–30; Midday 2009) indirectly acknowledges the impossibility of his journey to becoming president in the White House. When I read back to myself the latter words I notice that the race for political equality appears gendered, even when raced: a male struggle for political minority representation. Yet women have also acted and continue to play their part in the struggle for civil rights, besides towards gendered political suffrage; this was shown in demonstrations in Riyadh as reported by Alsharif and Laessing via Reuters on 5 February 2011: 'Saudi women protest, web activists call for reform', the title reenacting the gendered clauses of political struggle within culture. Just as Obama's slogan of 'Yes, we can' (CNN 2008) heralded the rise of one man (and his wife and children), it has also ricocheted across the world on banners from UK students protesting tuition fees to the Middle Eastern demonstrations for democratic representation in the spring of 2011. However, the uncanny shadow slogan of 'Yes, we can' is 'only with others fighting for us who we will eventually leave behind'—an uncanny reversal of the original slogan revealing the intersections of the transgressive political moment. Intersectionality aids a deeper, more complex analysis through the traditional binaries of gender and race, or the traditional hierarchies of class and sexuality, as a means of exploring possibility. Critical Race Feminism (CRF), working within the paradigm of Critical Race Theory (CRT) but with a dual, not binary, focus, and whilst acknowledging the intersectionality of human experience, seeks via academic activism to explore the desires and also the aggression of the struggle for equality. This entails for the raced and gendered academic focusing her gaze on the uncanny other, beyond whiteness, and on power intersections.

OF *THE UNCANNY* AND OF RACE

'The uncanny . . . is in some way a species of the familiar.' (Freud 2003, 134)

Freud's strange, far-ranging and exploratory paper on *The Uncanny*, viewed within a CRT lens, in many ways aids a reading of race that produces the psychological experience of both being raced and of racing others. Freud's words, above, seek to frame what is unfamiliar inside the familiar, like race within and around the human body. The uncanny and its bearing on psychoanalysis and race, as inscribed in the title of Fanon's *Black Skin White Masks* (1986), is crucial to an understanding of political change and cultural development, seen through CRT. The symbolism of the uncanny is also a way of helping us understand sexism: The long-term battle for gendered equality is enshrined within the uncanny sameness of the human body but undermined by the precarious difference of gender characteristics. Judith Butler in her work on mourning and war wrote of the 'consideration of precarity as an existing and promising site for coalitional exchange' (2010, 28), foregrounding the intersectional moment of mourning where difference should be eroded but is not: the uncanny political differential of the treatment of dead bodies during war. Precarity is a key word for the intersectional gaze, focusing on the politics of limit, to explore the possibility of transgression within the intersectional moment.

POLITICAL CHANGE AND TRANSGRESSION

The uncanny duality of political change balances the signal of an extension of political possibility for minority groups such as those who are raced as minority, alongside the limiting of that possibility as encompassed in the cultural artefacts of the time as this chapter seeks to explore. The duality of cultural change is shown firstly in that political change towards equality may come through the democratic process if there is a convergence of interests with the status quo as shown by CRT (Bell 1995, 21–26). Secondly, that movement towards equality through the democratic process is catalysed through transgression, or actions outside of the state, to produce convergence in order to provoke change or, as the poststructuralists show, to at least 'awaken us . . . from immersion in our everyday ideological universe' (Zizek 2002, 9), to posit the seeds to future change.

Cultural continuity has been seen, by psychoanalytical theorists, as a result of the workings out of different forms of melancholic aggression (Klein and Riviere 1964, 5, 67–68). The theme of transgression, as a result of melancholic aggression, is central to discussion of the desire for political change and intercultural development. The transgressive moment is a key to examining how theories explore change. In this chapter two cultural artefacts are examined through these intersections of theory, firstly a popular music video of Beyoncé's *If I Were a Boy* (2008), and secondly video footage of Michele Obama speaking at a girls' school during the G20 talks in London (Elizabeth Garrett Anderson Language College 2009). These artefacts are posed as metaphors to explore the cultural context of current theoretical frameworks concerned with equality, specifically Critical Race Feminism (CRF) and intersectionality. The chapter concludes by indicating the relative lack of futurity of overt transgression as opposed to the futurity of transgression of annihilation of the other, whilst acknowledging the necessity of theory in excavating and recording this. The chapter is a critical-creative paper and thus uses CRT counternarrative in a literary psychoanalytical style, to echo the nature of the artefacts explored in the chapter. The chapter is divided by subheadings that indicate themes that emerge from the artefacts viewed through theory.

RACE/GENDER: CRITICAL RACE FEMINISM AND INTERSECTIONALITY

In this chapter it is acknowledged that CRF, with its foundations in the CRT analysis of the workings of law on race, and its use of counternarrative to give voice to the hitherto silenced, is fundamental in observing the intersectional workings of racial supremacy; CRF seeks to observe how hierarchies of oppression, of gender besides race and other forms of discrimination, are fixed in culture. As Crenshaw observes, 'Neither Black liberationist politics nor feminist theory can ignore the intersectional experiences of those whom the movements claim as their respective constituents' (2003, 31). The triangulation of intersectionality is a means to secure a reading of culture that draws on the interlinking constrictions against equality, of racism, sexism, homophobia and other aspects of cultural annihilation of the individual. Gilmore entitled the necessity of her coming to intersectionality and CRF as 'It is right to speak' (2003, 114–117). In the latter chapter Gilmore voiced her experience of how essentialist theories ignore fundamental aspects of individual experience of oppression, and thereby promote specific oppressions (ibid., 114), whereas intersectionality offered a means of negotiating the conflicting narratives of experience in shifting arenas (ibid., 115). CRF then enshrines the counternarrative as a method of data collection of intersectional narratives; these counterbalance the dominant cultural accounts within academic texts. A CRF counternarrative therefore accesses the voices beyond the White hetero-normative, fixing, in symbolic black words on white pages, the counterculture of struggle without which culture does not progress. CRF, like CRT, is politically activist in nature; it seeks to alter culture through focus on race and gender. CRF and CRT are uncanny academic theories: They use familiar academic discourse, but in centring the shadow texts of the silenced they are unfamiliar; like the automaton, the 'apparently animate doll' explored in *The Uncanny* (Freud 2003, 140), the reception of the shadow text in CRF, within academia, relates to the power of primal fear, of 'castration complex' (ibid.). In this paper the dual artefacts are gendered and raced; they are both uncanny in terms of the central characters' eventual presentation as automatons of the status quo.

I/You/Us–Counterstruggle

The terminology that we use to describe political counterstruggle is similar to those words that we use to delineate the counternarratives of sexual relationships: 'you'—those who do not understand us, the other, but who we desire to understand us; and 'us'—those with whom we are standing, inside an experience. The shadow terminology of both intimate and political relationships is the word 'honesty'—the communication of truth without which 'us' falls apart, and 'you' becomes severed from 'I'. In both the political and personal spheres, the word 'integrity' and the phrase 'acting with integrity' are about the actions of treating others as we would wish to be treated ourselves, and about abiding by principle. Integrity is fundamentally about the working out of how to construct and maintain a union of different parts, of othered desires. The metaphor of the intimate union therefore is paralleled by the political interaction that is explored through intersectionality.

CULTURAL ARTEFACTS AND TRANSGRESSION

The shared words, as discussed above, are clearly enunciated at the beginning of the Beyoncé music video, *If I Were a Boy* (2008). Cultural artefacts such as music videos on the Internet are uncanny in the way that they use the familiar, what is recognisable in a given cultural frame, to engrave the unfamiliar, what we do not know but want to try out. This familiar and unfamiliar intermingling gives credibility to what is unfamiliar; like dreams and nightmares it is the intermingling of this duality that produces the uncanny feeling (Freud 2003, 124).

The actions and interactions of the character played by Beyoncé in the music video (2008) are a useful metaphor to explore the uncanny of overt transgression and the intersectional politics of the political imagination, of how we imagine what we could do but then do not act out, from a stereotypical female-imagined male-gendered perspective.

A narrative written in the first person disrupts the cultural status quo of the third person academic paper / it's an act of transgression / an elision of cultural punctuation / we're supposed to wait but we won't / a disruption of narrative / a CRF counter-narrative begins . . .

At the first UK CRT conference in 2009, I was asked, just before I was about to present a paper on Beyoncé, whether I'd heard that Michael Jackson had died the night before. As it happened I had seen the news headline about his cardiac arrest but I had not heard that he had actually died. I decided to incorporate the news of Jackson's death into my CRF paper and I rewrote the first line of the paper. It then read, 'I'd like to dedicate this paper to Michael Jackson, who epitomised both the possibility of whiteness and the impossibility of transgression' (Chakrabarty 2009). Similarly for this paper I have thought for some time about Michael Jackson as a starting point for talking about intersectionality, a precursor to the possibility of the character played by Beyoncé in the 2008 video, but also as a metaphor for methodologies that may be used within higher education and in educational research for exploring the possibilities of political transgression.

I'm thinking to myself of how bell hooks writes and interacts with possibility (1994), that, in the spirit of Gandhi's words, it is only when we act on possibility that we may become part of the change that we envisage.

Beyoncé's *If I Were a Boy* (2008) imagines the possibility of power and the limitations of transgression just as Jackson expanded the transgressive range of popular culture heightened by the parallel ambiguous narrative in his personal physical transformation; however, his life and death demonstrate the limits of ambiguity in contemporary culture; if we have to change skin colour and gender to attain equality, then equality itself becomes an uncanny concept. If equality is about a performance of sameness, then it becomes a death of self, a kind of self-castration, reflecting the uncanny fear of action: The Beyoncé video explores imaginative transgressive action emerging from cultural desire for gendered equality in the first half of the video, the fantasy section, but in the return to reality ending it bluntly reflects the fantasy back on to the audience, a Brechtian alienation device, as if to say, Did you *really* think it would be possible for a woman to act like a man?

THE FUTURE OF GENDER AND RACE

So what happens in this magical uncanny moment where we hover almost, but not quite, where we can see what could be, if we acted? In Beyoncé's video *If I Were a Boy*, the female character wakes in the attitude of a cli-chéd man—she has an aggressive sexualised agency: she never thinks of affect on the other. She leaves her boyfriend at home and goes out to work as a police officer, with another male officer. He drives but the video is shot to show her power over others through her inhabitation of space and gaze. During the day she behaves aggressively: She's shown attacking people: Black males; the two colleagues are shown at a shooting range where she's in charge, her arms around the male, holding him and in control of the gun; the scene evokes her as a man in a gay porn anal sex shot. Then there's the locker room: as if she's a White gay man . . . but she's also a woman, about to fuck her colleague; and then she switches off her cell phone.

THE TRANSGRESSION TECHNOLOGY OF DESIRE

I'll pause here and reflect a moment on the technology of transgression—cell phones, as injured parties in infidelity cases know, are used against communication and allow the possibility of transgression but also evidence it (here in Beyoncé's case and multiplied a thousand time on the YouTube online comments of girls and boys who agree with Beyoncé's character's feelings in the video); and yet we also know that cell phones can be used to trigger bombs as happened in the Madrid and London bombings post-9/11. Over 9/11 there was shock at the ingenuity of the technology of transgression, and Damien Hirst's words (quickly taken back at the time because of the effect of capitalism on world art markets) expressed those of many about art and politics:

> In an interview, Hirst told BBC News Online: 'The thing about 9/11 is that it's kind of an artwork in its own right. It was wicked, but it was devised in this way for this kind of impact. It was devised visually.'
> Describing the image of the hijacked planes crashing into the twin towers as 'visually stunning', he added: 'You've got to hand it to them on some level because they've achieved something which nobody would ever have thought possible, especially to a country as big as America.' (Allison 2002)

Hirst's remarks underline the uncanny connection between the artist and the revolutionary—that to access the place beyond disempowerment involves ingenuity to take the step past the pivotal uncanny moment, past the affects of the intersectional moment, towards agency. In the video, Beyoncé sings that if she was not a girl she would be able to turn off her mobile phone; she wouldn't think about others, that she would abide by her own rules. The song transcribes the psychological structure of transgression as involving the aggressive negation of the other. This aggression Freud tells us under-pins culture and progress (2001, 122) and is crucial to the workings of the uncanny pivotal moment—this moment where we might overcome and take on the unfamiliar, or submit once more to the familiar. Beyoncé's video plays out the working against what we have known, whilst allowing a resurgence of aggression against the hitherto perceived restrictions to the desired state. In the area of gender and sexuality, Beyoncé's video role-plays a heterosexual woman behaving like a man towards other men, producing a transposition of gender and sexuality, beyond culture, beyond the culture of the age of Obama.

In the Beyoncé video, the pivotal moment is when she sees herself with the projected lover, as seen by the boyfriend, and she allows herself to feel the affect of the intersectional moment—at the point where she could move towards her desires—but instead, in her gaze in to his perceived reaction she loses her power, and the choice to act out her own desires. In the song she says that when a woman is in a man's position she feels the other's hurt and she listens to his feelings; she says a woman would be better at being a man. It is as though she's saying if a woman had the powers that a man has, the woman would use the power in a more ethical way.

Her knowledge, that is, the spectre of her inherited hurt, gives her gen-dered empathy but not the power to act with her other ghosts towards desire. Derrida positioned the ghost in between binaries in *Specters of Marx* (1994, xvii–xix); the ghosts converge within the intersectional moment towards the agency of futurity, but it appears to be agency that must be enacted within the psychological framework of authority, not of the spec-tral victim, but with the spectre of aggression. The ghost's sphere is in the agency of affect of the past in opposition to the status of present stability, the status quo, in the action of transgression. The uncanny moment in the Beyoncé video is her moment of recognition in between both spheres—the unfamiliar world of the future where she acts upon her desires and the familiar world of the past where she sees the affect on the other—the simul-taneity of the uncanny moment, the weight of her gendered past, does not empower her actions for futurity but returns her to the past. Her video and lyrics are both about gender, 'if I were a boy', but also about race, 'If I were White' (Chakrabarty 2009), and about sexuality, about power dynamics in same-sex relationships, about if I were the dominant one, the one with power. The metaphor glimpses the uncanny, the future, when we will all be equal, through the intersectional moment.

ABOUT POWER AND INTERSECTIONALITY

Beyoncé's 'if you thought I would wait for you, you got it wrong' (2008), echoes the familiar words of Malcolm X, but in the unfamiliar character of a woman, and yet the video's retrograde vision, a counterpoint to the lyrics, of what we do when we attain power, of wearing uniforms and acting on aggressive instincts, reenacts Freud's depiction of culture as being driven by the dual drives of sex and death (Freud 2001, 122). The message of the video and lyrics combined is against violence and a clichéd version of gender; it displays that duality in the closing shots, that militarism ends in death, not life, but the melancholic ending merges the familiar and unfamiliar, of what has come before in the video, the melancholic being a mourning for what has not yet arrived, the inclusivity that academic feminism, through intersectionality, and critical race feminism, seek to delineate, that the activism towards equality does not have to mean the annihilation of the other. Grabham, in her critique of elements of the theories of CRT, queer theory and intersectionality, cites Wendy Brown in *States of Injury* (1995) and her argument 'for a politics based on "I want this for us" rather than "I am" ' (2009, 186), demonstrating the intersection of theory against an emphasis on injustice and about the new age of Obama and 'Yes, we can' (CNN 2008). Obama's *The Audacity of Hope* (2008) acknowledges 'this new politics in its article of faith in the transgressive imagination of being, and leaving behind not being' (Chakrabarty 2009).

THE SEXUALITY OF TRANSGRESSION

In the Beyoncé video, transgression is seen as shaped in the stance of the oppressor; the work against transgression is shaped in the language of community cohesion; the result is shown to be division, the protection of authority, and a continuity of raced/gendered supremacy. An activist reading of the Beyoncé video is to read her play with the power of the other, its echo of the sadomasochist sexuality, and its use of the homoerotic framing, as denoting that transgression is sexualised (Freud 2001, 122), and that this is the energy that works on subverting traditional hierarchies. This is displayed in the homoerotic advertorial aesthetic of the Beyoncé video, the skewed imagery of transgression—the Levi/Calvin Klein style visuals of vest tops in sun, and in shadow, the prison bars of shadow, Black against White, the promise of the unleashing of restraint in the images of the locker room, the arse shots, the car in tunnel . . . the strange phallicism of female agency in the feminisation of the White male. When we are radical and revolutionary, turned, changed, we become elements of the music promo, the cinema advert, the cultural artefacts of persuasion, the uncanny duality of the familiar of culture and the unfamiliarity of the transgressive agent.

In the final frames of the video, when the 'real' boyfriend laughs at the woman's words, she is returned to reality from her imagining; she speaks to the viewer through her melancholic submissive stance, the message of not looking back: To succeed you must not see the once oppressor you've made a victim, because if you start to feel their hurt then you lose out and you're back at the bottom of the hierarchy. The metaphor indicates the necessity of affirmative action, and also of the need for monitoring and for critical educational practice, of the need to explore both affect and effect; in taking a CRF and intersectional perspective on this in terms of cultural and educational change, intersectionality is a key here to the balancing and rebalancing acts of change.

The YouTube online community comments to this video, used as a lens through which to view the role of struggle for equality, make us even more aware of the uncanny nature of political struggle. Online comments accuse Beyoncé of being racist and sexist; in other words, users of the site read the imagining as reality in their accusations, and it's a reality they don't like the look of. Many of the participants react in the effect the text has had on them as if in a personal interaction through the cultural artefact.

TRANSITIONAL CULTURAL ARTEFACTS

My thoughts turn beyond culture, to this place between binaries, at the point of the uncanny pivotal moment, when we are caught between two cultures, in transition. It's the 2nd of April 2009 and I watch Michelle Obama speaking in a video online during the events of the G20 in London. In this video, Michelle is at Elizabeth Garrett Anderson Language College (2009) in Islington; she sits on the stage watching a performance. It's a school I taught at some while ago, as a drama teacher; it's the stage that I worked on with the young people in the drama group. It's the school from whence Alex Burke emerged: a member of the drama group, and latterly the 2008 winner of the television talent competition *The X Factor*.

Michelle watches the girls sing whilst sitting at the side of the stage, girls who may one day become the future Beyoncés of the world—girls, in fact, like Alex Burke, who eventually sang with Beyoncé on *The X Factor*. Then Michelle Obama speaks. In her speech on 2nd of April 2009, she referred indirectly to the ghosts of the civil rights movement, against imperialism, colonisation and towards equality, by telling the girls that she liked getting A's in her homework, and being on time to school, sending the message from the spectres of the equality movement that we can all get somewhere by taking our education seriously and eventually getting to some kind of equality—she tells the girls that by behaving as though we're going to be treated equally, perhaps we will some day. And yet the familiar reality behind Michelle's speech is that she was speaking on an old rickety stage just off the Caledonian Road, Islington N1, not the global stage of the

Excell Centre at the G20, where her husband, President Obama, was standing at the same moment; the female speaks to young people of dreams and desires; the male speaks to world leaders of global actions. The other reality is the hetero-normativity of the event: Michelle is given a stage because of her relationship to her husband, not in terms of her own professional status. The reality of Michelle Obama's presence is interestingly contrasted by the number of videos on YouTube that show Michelle continuing to hug the multicultural schoolgirls whilst her White minders try to stop her, and fail; Michelle Obama's agency is in her uncanny proximity to power and her wording of the dream of equality, the potential for equality evoked in her continuing to hug the girls surrounded by the impotency of the minders. Michelle Obama's uncanny shadow here is the successful journey of Alex Burke to fame through the lottery of a talent contest. Their twin journeys underline the unfamiliar role of fate in cultural progression—where we are born, whom we meet, our social capital—balanced with the familiar: the gender of those in control, the husbands, world leaders, the hosts of talent shows. Intersectionality transcribes the interconnecting spheres of power and impotence; both intersectionality and CRF seek cultural change: unfamiliar characters transitioned into familiar roles.

OF EQUALITY AND TRANSGRESSION—FROM MY JOURNAL

What sticks in my mind from the evening of the 1st of April was walking through the streets of London. We had spent the evening at Cardboard Citizens Theatre Company—a discussion between Adrian Jackson, Cicely Berry and Julian Boal. Cicely Berry, the great voice coach of the Royal Shakespeare Company, talked of a precursor to Malcolm X, citing the words of Thomas Kidd in *The Spanish Tragedy*, 'that when words don't prevail, violence does', and reminded us that Shakespeare's words show 'the arc of human language' (2009); Jackson reminded us that Boal's work is of 'the stage of daily life' and that 'theatre rehearses transformation' (2009), a reminder of Beyoncé's video and Michelle's speech, both theatre of uncanny transformation, a rehearsal of gendered futurity in the intersectional moment.

After this inspiring talk of the power of political theatre, we walk home late that night deciding, on Adrian Jackson's suggestion, to walk past the great carnivalesque atmosphere at the G20 activist climate camp on Bishopsgate. In my mind there were memories of Greenham Common back in the eighties, of purple leggings and rainbow scarves, of singing peace songs, of the nonviolent direct action of the eighties feminist peace movement.

And then it happens. We turn the corner and we can't see the climate camp; it is dark but we can see lots of people milling around and the atmosphere is tense. We're all tightly packed and then I see why it's difficult to move; there's a band of riot police with shields and batons and they're rushing the crowd. Behind them are police dogs let loose on the protesters in their climate-change tents. We try to take photos but there's another surge and it gets very scary, people being beaten up and there's no transport; it's like the poll tax demo (of 31st March 1990) during the Thatcher years all over again. Peaceful political action doesn't change things and neither does violence. I'm at that pivotal intersectional moment again but this time I'm confused.

I think about Michelle in the video, and how just before her speech she shared a 'high five' with one girl as she finished performing; in the action there's an edge of militarism and aggression, the spectre of those others, without which we achieve nothing (Eliot 2009). It's there in Beyoncé's song too, in those words, 'if you thought I would wait for you, you got it wrong' (2008), that twenty-first-century echo of the words of Malcolm X, on education, and, on activism, at the Ford Auditorium in 1965, and those words that changed nations: 'to bring about the freedom of these people by any means necessary' (YouTube 2010), the spectre of 'our martyred dead', the words of *The Red Flag* (Connell 1889).

CONCLUSION: OF 2010 AND BEYOND THE AGE OF OBAMA

To talk of a time after Obama feels strange, and yet, if we do not voice what we desire, in the future there may never be another President Obama, or a President Michelle Obama, or someone gay or lesbian as a future head of state. Thinking forward to after Obama is about acknowledging, as we have found in the United Kingdom in 2010, that things have not progressed towards racial equality in areas such as education (Higher Education Funding Council for England 2010) under a changed administration voted in by minority groups, or indeed in other aspects of our lives (H M Government 2010). The latter reports spell out the slow progress towards equality through statistics; governments come and go and their use of report statistics is based on their own agenda. In the current UK political climate in 2010, the statistics over unemployment, educational opportunity, housing and welfare show that privilege still inherits the wealth of the state; the UK government has chosen to deal with the current economic crisis by targeting financially the other in terms of gender (House of Commons Library 2010). The experiences and events explored in this chapter, concerning the events of the years 2009–10, demonstrate that the singular, the election of a mixed-race president in the White House, would not produce equality but would at least herald a change of culture of what is possible and perhaps inspire change. Through the electorate choosing and voting for politicians who are intimate with othered experience, we hope to elect leaders who in turn produce governments who will act with integrity, and who will also voice with honesty the impact of their decisions. In 2009–11, across the globe the power of citizens' political demonstrations awakened the political order to an extent, but alongside this the impotency of activism without legislative power was seen.

The cultural artefacts explored in this chapter reflect the shifting and intersectional nature of power; power is seen to be produced by a manipulation of self, a transgressive performance of race, of gender and of sexuality, as shown in the metaphor of the Beyoncé video. Power relationships are shown to consciously manipulate difference by taking on the difference and performing it; for example, in political election campaigns we are used to seeing male politicians showing a feminised side of themselves by being affectionate to young children, whereas female politicians are shown being forceful and masculine in debate. The character of power performs a transitioning of race/gender/sexuality; thus, in ascent to power, character becomes the agency of transgression and performs the intersectional moment within self. The Beyoncé video displays thus how character mutates to inhabit power, harnessing agency via a performance of the other, a parallel with the merging of difference in love which the video projects into the future and back into the past, but does not portray. The Beyoncé video portrays power as singular not shared; the Michelle Obama video reflects the passive nature of the journey to equality under patriarchy in the uncanny performance of inheriting a reflected power via a sexual relationship with the authoritarian. Both videos in this way return power to spectres: In the Beyoncé video the boyfriend whom she resents for their lack of equality, and in the Michelle Obama video to those who came before in the civil rights movement whose work culminated in President Obama's ascent.

Intersectionality facilitates the excavation of the manoeuvrings and manipulations of those in power and the impact on othered experience; it also highlights how the struggle for equality might be shaped; CRF seeks to interrogate and also to act; in the spirit of the words of Beyoncé, 'If you thought I would wait for you, you got it wrong' (2008), to use knowledge as a tool of cultural change.

REFERENCES

Allison, Rebecca. 2002. 9/11 wicked but a work of art, says Damien Hirst. *The Guardian*, September 11, http://www.guardian.co.uk/uk/2002/sep/11/arts.september11.

Alsharif, Asma, and Ulf Laessing. 2011. Saudi women protest, web activists call for reform. *Reuters*, February 5, http://uk.reuters.com/article/2011/02/05/uk-saudi-protests-idUKTRE7141ZN20110205.

Bell, Derrick. 1995. *Brown V. Board of Education* and the interest convergence dilemma. In *Critical Race Theory: The key writings that formed the movement*, ed. Kimberlé Crenshaw, Neil Gotanda, Gary Peller and Thomas Kendall, 20–28. New York: The New Press.

Berry, Cicely, and Adrian Jackson. 2009. *Theatre in difficult times*. A discussion between Cicely Berry, Adrian Jackson and Julian Boal, presented by Cardboard Citizens Theatre Company, at Toynbee Studios, London, April 1.

Butler, Judith. 2010. *Frames of war: When is life grievable?* London and New York: Verso.

Chakrabarty, Namita. 2009. If I were white . . . From Beyoncé's imaginings to the age of Obama. Paper presented at Critical Race Theory in the UK conference, Institute of Education, London, June 26.

CNN. 2008. *Obama speech: 'Yes, we can change'*. Transcript of speech, January 27, http://edition.cnn.com/2008/POLITICS/01/26/obama.transcript/index.html.

Connell, Jim. 1889. *The red flag*. Lyrics of song, http://webpages.dcu.ie/~sheehanh/rf-lyrics.htm.

Crenshaw, Kimberlé Williams. 2003. Demarginalizing the intersection of race and sex: A black feminist critique of antidiscrimination doctrine, feminist theory, and anti-racist politics. In *Critical race feminism*, 2nd ed., ed. Adrien Katherine Wing, 23–33. New York: New York University Press.

Derrida, Jacques. 1994. *Specters of Marx*, trans. Peggy Kamuf. London: Routledge.

Elizabeth Garrett Anderson Language College. 2009. *Michelle Obama—Michele Obama visit*. Video of speech presented by Michelle Obama, at Elizabeth Garrett Anderson Language College, April 2, http://www.egaschool.co.uk/page.php?2.

Elliot, C. 2009. Glenn Burke: Inventor of the high-five. *Black Power*, http://www.blackpower.com/sports/homosexuals-in-pro-sports/.

Fanon, Frantz. 1986. *Black skin white masks*, trans. Charles Lam Markmann. London: Pluto.

Freud, Sigmund. 2001. Civilisation and its discontents (1930). In *The standard edition of the complete psychological works of Sigmund Freud*, vol. xxi, trans. James Strachey, 59–145. London: Vintage.

———. 2003. *The uncanny* (1919). Trans. David McLintock. London: Penguin.

Gilmore, Angela, D. 2003. It is better to speak. In *Critical race feminism*, 2nd ed., ed. Adrien Katherine Wing, 114–119. New York: New York University Press.

Grabham, Emily. 2009. Intersectionality: Traumatic impressions. In *Intersectionality and beyond*, ed. Emily Grabham, Davina Cooper, Jane Krishnadas and Didi Herman, 183–201. Abingdon: Routledge-Cavendish.

Higher Education Funding Council for England. 2010. *Student ethnicity: Profile and progression of entrants to full-time, first degree study*. May 2010/13 (Web only), http://www.hefce.ac.uk/pubs/hefce/2010/10_13/.

H M Government. 2010. *State of the nation report: Poverty, worklessness and welfare dependency in the UK*. Cabinet Office, http://www.marmotreview.org/AssetLibrary/resources/new%20external%20reports/cabinet%20office%20-%20state%20of%20the%20nation.pdf .

hooks, bell. 1994. *Outlaw culture*. London: Routledge.

House of Commons Library. 2010. *Budget gender audit*. Unpublished report, commissioned by Yvette Cooper MP, http://www.yvettecooper.com/women-bear-brunt-of-budget-cuts.

Klein, Melanie, and Joan Riviere. 1964. *Love, hate and reparation*. London: W.W. Norton.

Knowles, Beyoncé. 2008. *If I were a boy*. Music video, http://www.youtube.com/watch?v=eIkRiqxWcYU.

Midday. 2009. *Barack Obama dinner with Mahatma Gandhi.* TV interview, http://www.youtube.com/watch?v=kpDoYBpUn_o&feature=fvw.

Obama, Barack. 2008. *The audacity of hope.* Edinburgh: Canongate.

YouTube. 2010. *Malcolm X: By any means necessary.* Film of speech, http://www.youtube.com/watch?v=hhg6LxyTnY8.

Zizek, Slavoj. 2002. *Welcome to the desert of the real.* London: Verso.

10 Intelligibility, Agency and the Raced-Nationed-Religioned Subjects of Education

Deborah Youdell

ABSTRACT

Judith Butler is perhaps best known for her take-up of the debate between Derrida and Austin over the function of the performative and her subsequent suggestion that the subject be understood as performatively constituted. Another important but less often noted move within Butler's consideration of the processes through which the subject is constituted is her thinking between Althusser's notion of subjection and Foucault's notion of subjectivation. In this chapter, I explore Butler's understanding of processes of subjectivation; examine the relationship between subjectivation and the performative suggested in and by Butler's work; and consider how the performative is implicated in processes of subjectivation—in 'who' the subject is, or might be, subjectivated as. Finally, I examine the usefulness of understanding the subjectivating effects of discourse for education, in particular for educationalists concerned to make better sense of and interrupt educational inequalities. In doing this I offer a reading of an episode of ethnographic data generated in an Australian high School. I suggest that it is through subjectivating processes of the sort that Butler helps us to understand that some students are rendered subjects inside the educational endeavour, and others are rendered outside this endeavour or, indeed, outside student-hood.

INTRODUCTION

This chapter considers the usefulness for education of Judith Butler's thinking between Althusser's notion of subjection and Foucault's notion of subjectivation and the possibility for discursive agency and performative politics that this thinking opens up. While concerned with the broad utility of these conceptual tools, the chapter illustrates their usefulness by deploying them to analyse the processes of raced-nationed-religioned subjectivation at a 'Multicultural Day' event in a Sydney high school. In doing this, the chapter proceeds from a series of what might be termed 'left' or 'critical' concerns centred around the differentiating and exclusionary effects of schooling, and, with a focus here on the subjectivation of 'Arabic' students, on the operations of race, racism and whiteness.

These may seem unlikely points of departure for a chapter offered as a poststructural piece. But as Foucault's (1988a) discussion in *Critical Theory/Intellectual History* points out, 'left' thinkers have for some time been looking for tools for understanding and strategies for interrupting material inequality through an engagement with language; a decentred subject; and an unstable truth. Rather than asking what structures and institutions (economic, social or linguistic) produce material inequality, this move reconfigures this concern and asks how the self comes into being, what the costs of the self might be, and how the self might be made *again differently.*

A central project has been developing tools and strategies for interrogating the 'nature of the present' (Foucault 1988a, 36), an interrogation that seeks to expose the relationship between 'the subject, truth, and the constitution of experience' (1988b, 48). These efforts are wholly political in that they focus upon those aspects of the present that Foucault finds 'intolerable'. Foucault seeks to develop understandings of how the present is made, and so how it might be unmade, by 'following lines of fragility in the present', trajectories that might allow us to 'grasp why and how that-which-is might no longer be that-which-is.' (1988a, 37). Butler takes this further and posits a performative politics in which she imagines discourses taking on new meanings and circulating in contexts from which they have been barred or in which they have been rendered unintelligible, as performative subjects engage a deconstructive politics that intervenes and unsettles hegemonic meanings (Butler 1997a).

In exploring these conceptual tools and putting them to use, the chapter focuses on the subjectivation of a group of Lebanese and Turkish students. The analysis suggests a series of political, educational, popular and (sub-)cultural discourses that circulate in this school setting and beyond and which provide the discursive terrain on and through which these students are subjectivated. Specifically, the chapter explores how Lebanese and Turkish students (collectively called 'Arabic' in this setting) are subjectivated in ways that render apparently incommensurable constitutions of the good-Arabic-student-subject and the bad-Arabic-subject through the citation and inscription of an Orientalism (Said 2003) reinvigorated by post-9/11 anti-Islamic discourse (Lipman 2004). This, then, is the intolerable present I want to interrogate. The chapter also considers how these students render themselves through the possibilities for practices of self, or discursive agency, that subjectivation brings. This is a consideration that demonstrates the capacity of Butler's performative politics to maintain in view simultaneously a sense of the context of constraint in which these performatively constituted subjects are effected and the potential for these subjects to act and to act with intent.

METHODOLOGY

My experiences of 'Multicultural Day' in an Australian high school are situated in the conduct of a school ethnography during 2001. There has been significant debate about the implications, and even the possibility, of undertaking ethnography in a poststructural or Foucaultian frame. Critical, interpretive and feminist traditions in school (and other) ethnography have long emphasized the multiplicity of meanings and perspectives that exist within contexts; the complexities of and tensions within the roles and status of the researcher and the researched as well as relations between them; and the potential and limits of reflexivity (see, e.g., Carr and Kemmis 1986; Stanley and Wise 1993; Skeggs 1994; Delamont and Atkinson 1995; Hammersley and Atkinson 1995). These methodological insights have been usefully supplemented and, indeed, scrutinized in the light of poststructural ideas and adaptations of qualitative methodology informed by these ideas (see, e.g., Miller 1997; Prior 1997; Silverman 1997; Stronach and MacLure 1997; Britzman 2000; Lather 2000; McCoy 2000; St. Pierre 2000; Harwood 2001; Alvesson 2002; MacLure 2003).

In doing ethnography in school framed by a concern to interrogate the subjectivating effects of an intolerable present, I make use of the usual methods of interview, observation, collection of artefacts and texts. I am not, however, asking the researched to explicate their understanding of the context and relations within it. Rather, I am looking for moments in which subjects are constituted and in which constituted subjects act. I am looking for discourses and their subjectivating effects. I ask myself what discourses might be circulating inside and/or across school contexts, how these are being deployed, what their effects might be. Whereas at times it seems that discourses and their effects are clearly evident, more often it seems that these are subtle and oblique, needing to be teased out, to be deconstructed. Ultimately, I want to know whether thinking in terms of the subjectivating effects of discourse can help me to understand how students are made within particular constraints and how these constraints might be breached. This is not the collection of 'real' or 'actual' discourses but is wholly constrained by my own discursive repertoire—the discourse that I see and name—and my capacity to represent these. I am, then, absolutely entangled in the data I generate and the representations I produce.

These data are inevitably simulacra (Baudrillard 1994) of my own creation, copies without original that cannot reflect any 'real' moment in a field that is itself inaccessible without the mediating discursive frames that fill it with meaning. In this way the ethnographic data offered bear a heavy interpretive burden. I am not seeking to describe the nuances of the context and tease out what is happening within it. Rather, I am seeking to construct compelling representations of moments inside school in order to untangle the discursive frames that guide meaning and render subjects within it. My research process is unavoidably implicated in the very subjectivating processes about which it speaks. Yet these data are recognizable. They do not contain, expose or reflect any universal truth, but these *petite narratives* do resonate.

Given the focus on subjectivation in this chapter, the place of the subject deserves some further consideration here. Serious attention is increasingly being paid to the problematic relationship between the 'knowing' subjects implicit to empirical research and the 'troubled' subjects of poststructural writing (see once again Britzman, 2000; Lather 2000; and St. Pierre 2000). Yet there is no easy solution. Understanding the researching and researched subject to be perpetually but provisionally constituted through discourse means that research practice is wholly implicated in processes of ongoing subjectivation (of both the researcher and the researched) even as these subjectivities form the objects of study. Replacing sovereign agency with the notion of discursive agency (Butler 1997a)—which I will explore in some detail below—goes some way to illuminate and relieve these tensions, offering an ethnography that retains agency and intent in the context of discursive constraint without implicitly casting this subject a sovereign.

Understanding the subjects who inhabit schools and school ethnography in this way suggests that the discourses deployed by students and teachers (and researcher) may be both intentional and unintentional: discourses intentionally deployed may escape or exceed the intent of the subject who speaks or acts and/or the subject may unwittingly deploy discourses whose historicities and/or intersections assert unanticipated meanings. Indeed, discursive practices may entail the deployment of complex combinations of intentional and unintentional discourses and their discursive effects. Taking up Butler's notion of discursive agency, this analysis assumes multiple degrees of both intent and understanding amongst subjects in terms of the embedded meanings and effects of discourses. On the one hand, it suggests that subjects do not necessarily regurgitate discourse unwittingly. On the other hand, however, it suggests that discourses are not necessarily cited knowingly and that they are not necessarily known explicitly to the subject and/or audience. As such, subjects need not be self-consciously alert to the discourses deployed in order for their familiar and embedded meanings to be inscribed. Furthermore, the analysis suggests, again after Butler (1997a), that discourses do not need to be explicitly cited in order to be deployed. Rather, multiple discourses are referenced through the meanings, associations and omissions embedded in the historicity of apparently simple and benign utterances and bodily practices.

As I have explored elsewhere (Youdell 2005), these discussions render indeterminable the question of whether I should offer an account of myself as the researcher. The risk of slipping into an inadvertent essentialism tempts me to avoid such an account; however, the risk of assuming a disembodied authorial authority by not doing so seems much greater. Given the centrality of visual economies to prevailing discourses of gender and race (see Jacobson 1998; Seshadri-Crooks 2000), my own location within these discourses (woman, White) is undoubtedly 'visible' to and taken as immutable by the students involved in my research. Yet my social class, sexuality, subcultural and age locations are perhaps less singular or 'obvious' and, therefore, less tightly constrained. For instance, in the context of prevailing hetero-normative discourse, it is likely that students locate (constitute) me as heterosexual—the unspoken Same of the heterosexual/homosexual Same/Other binary—as long as an alternative sexuality is not asserted. And as a British ('English') woman doing school ethnography in Australia, nationality was an explicit axis of my subjectivation: Students who had speculated privately that I might be 'very posh' or 'from England' (but not both) were reassured by my Englishness (in ways that posh-ness may not have been reassuring in this low-income locale) and at the same time this Englishness was constitutive of my position as an outsider whose lack of knowledge of the context was acceptable and whose interest in it was comprehensible (or just about).

PERFORMATIVE SUBJECTS, SUBJECTIVATION, PERFORMATIVE POLITICS

As my discussion so far has indicated, this chapter is concerned with two interrelated threads—understanding (some of) the intolerable effects of education and the contribution that can be made to this by Judith Butler's work on the subject; the subject's potential to act wilfully; and politics. For me, it is in Butler's return to Althusser via Foucault that an understanding of subjection/subjectivation, agency and the political is most usefully developed (Butler 1997a, 1997b, 2004).

Judith Butler begins by adopting Foucault's notion of discourse as productive and uses this alongside the notion of the performative to consider the production of sexed and gendered subjects (Butler 1990, 1993). This is not the performativity, after Lyotard, of the marketised and corporatised education workplace that Stephen Ball (2003) writes about. Rather, this performative is borrowed from a debate between Derrida (1988) and Austin (1962) concerning the nature of language and its relationship to the world in which a performative is: 'that discursive practice that enacts or produces that which it names' (Butler 1993, 13). Butler suggests that

> Discursive performativity appears to produce that which it names, to enact its own referent, to name and to do, to name and to make. . . . [g]enerally speaking, a performative functions to produce that which it declares. (Butler 1993, 107)

Butler argues that the subject must be performatively constituted in order to make sense *as* a subject. Whereas these subjects appear, at least at the level of the everyday or common sense, to precede their designation, this apparently preexisting subject is an artefact of its performative constitution. A key contribution made to debates concerning the function of the performative is Derrida's (1988) assertion that any performative is open to misfire and so might fail or do something unintended or unexpected. And Foucault's (1990a) account of discourse insists that no discourse is guaranteed—whereas particular discourses prevail in some contexts and endure over time, the potential for the meanings of these to shift and/or for subordinate discourses to unsettle these remains.

Developing this notion of the performatively constituted subject, Butler (1997a, 1997b, 2004) takes up Althusser's notion of subjection and Foucault's notion of subjectivation to elaborate a nuanced understanding of production and constraint.

For Althusser (1971), 'subjection' is achieved through the action of 'ideological State apparatuses' (p. 136). These *ideological* state apparatuses are understood as representations of ideas, outlooks and beliefs that are imaginary or 'distortions' of a scientifically accessible 'real' (p. 153) (in Althusser's terms, the 'real' conditions of production and consumption). As these ideas are translated into actions and social practices and come to be embedded in social ritual, ideology is given a material existence that is at once a distortion and implicated in the production of this distortion. These ideological state apparatuses are both at stake in and the site of struggle, with the school identified as a key site.

For Althusser, ideology, and ideological state apparatuses, are inextricably linked with the subject (Althusser 1971). The subject, Althusser argues, is constituted by ideology which constitutes the individual as a subject. The subject is hailed as an individual, even as s/he is constituted a subject. This transformation of the individual into a subject, and the 'obviousness' of subjecthood, are key functions of ideology.

Recognition is central to these processes. The subject recognizes her/himself as s/he is hailed. Furthermore, s/he recognizes her/himself reflected in/by the subject—Althusser's 'Subject *par excellence*' (p. 167, original emphasis) who occupies the centre of ideology—by whom/on whose behalf the subject is hailed. This is Althusser's 'mirror-recognition' (p. 168). It is through this recognition that the subject is 'recruited'—subjecthood is freely taken and subjection is freely accepted by the good subject. In Althusser's neo-Marxist science, this recognition is, in fact, a misrecognition—the subject is not a reflection of the subject but *subject to* the subject: '*There are no subjects except by and for their subjection*' (1971, 169; original emphasis).

This recognition of the hail and transformation of the individual into a subject is simultaneous and inseparable. In Althusser's account there is no 'before' subjection when the subject was an individual—as Althusser asserts, 'individuals are always-already subjects' (p. 164). Nevertheless, just as ideology suggests real knowledge free from distortion, the individual/subject binary does seem to retain an implicit sense of an individual free from subjection. Freedom, albeit constrained, is suggested again by the idea that the subjecthood is freely taken up, even as this is a freedom taken *inside* subjection. Althusser argues the intrinsic ambiguity of the subject:

> In the ordinary use of the term, subject in fact means: (1) a free subjectivity, a centre of initiatives, author of and responsible for its actions; (2) a subjected being, who submits to a higher authority, and is therefore stripped of all freedom except that of freely accepting his [*sic*] submission. This last note gives us the meaning of this ambiguity, which is merely a reflection of the effect which produces it: the individual *is interpellated as a (free) subject in order that he shall submit freely to the commandments of the Subject, i.e. in order that he shall (freely) accept his subjection*, i.e. in order that he shall make the gestures and actions of his subjection 'all by himself'. (1971, 169; original emphasis)

A foreshadowing of Foucault's notion of the individual constituted in discourses and through the technologies of disciplinary power (1990a and 1991) or through practices of the self (1990b and 1992) is evident in Althusser's account of ideology and subjection. I am provoked to wonder, much as Judith Butler has, what would 'happen' if I were to think of ideologies (as well as the 'undistorted truth'), and ideological state apparatuses, and the subjection that ideological state apparatuses effect, as discursive, as performative.

According to Foucault, the person is subjectivated—s/he is at once rendered a subject and subjected to relations of power through discourse. That is, productive power constitutes and constrains, but does not determine, the subjects with whom it is concerned. Yet whereas Foucault indicates a concern with the subject at the centre of his work, he says relatively little directly about the notions of subjection and subjectivation.

Foucault says of the relation between productive power and the subject, and the subject's location in productive power:

> This form of power applies itself to immediate everyday life which categorizes the individual, marks him [*sic*] by his own individuality, attaches him to his own identity, imposes a law of truth on him which he must recognize and which others have to recognize in him. It is a form of power which makes individuals subjects. There are two meanings of the word subject: subject to someone else by control and dependence, and tied to his own identity by a conscious self-knowledge. Both meanings suggest a form of power which subjugates and makes subject to. (Foucault 1982, 212)

In a similar vein, in *Critical Theory/Intellectual History*, Foucault suggests that 'If I tell the truth about myself, as I am doing now, it is in part that I am constituted as a subject across a number of power relations which are exerted over me and which I exert over others' (1988a, 39). Here the echoes of Althusser's model of subjection resonates through Foucault's thinking about the subject, despite the very clear divergence of these thinkers in relation to the status of science, knowledge, truth and so on.

In Foucault's final interview he offers a direct account of his understanding of subjectiv(iz)ation. He says:

> I will call subjectivization the procedure by which one obtains the constitution of a subject, or more precisely, of a subjectivity which is of course only one of the given possibilities of organization of a self-consciousness.' (1988c, 253)

Whereas the operations and constraints of productive power remain evident, here power relations appear in the background, with the self, and the possibility of (contingent) self-knowledge and volition foregrounded. This is more clearly stated by Foucault in *An Aesthetic of Existence* when he says of the subject:

> The subject is constituted through practices of subjection, or, in a more autonomous way, through practices of liberation, or liberty, as in Antiquity, on the basis, of course, of a number of rules, styles, inventions to be found in the cultural environment. (1988b, 51)

Here, the self-conscious practices of the subject, and her/his involvement in her/his own constitution, are indicated as (potentially) 'practices of liberation' *at the same time as* the constrained context in which this subject acts is indicated by 'practices of subjection'. The subject acts, but s/he acts within/at the limits of subjection.

Perhaps more significantly, processes of subjection/subjectivation are demonstrated through Foucault's specific contextual studies in which the subject is a key field of concern at the same time as the subject *as* a field of concern is interrogated. In particular, *Discipline and Punish* (Foucault 1991) and *History of Sexuality Volume 1* (Foucault 1990a) show how the subject is subjected to relations of power as s/he is individualised, categorized, classified, hierarchised, normalized, surveilled and provoked to self-surveillance. These are technologies of subjection brought into play within institutions. This is not because such institutions are ideological state apparatuses as in Althusser's account. But because institutions improvise, cite and circulate discursive frames and coterminous technologies that render subjects in relations of power. As Althusser notes the simultaneity of subjection and the making of a 'free' subject, so Foucault notes the nonnecessary effects of discourse and the disciplinary technologies it makes meaningful and the persistence possibility of resistance intrinsic to productive power (Foucault 1990a). It is to the potentialities of being otherwise or, to adapt a construction of Foucault's, that-which-is-not, that Foucault's *Uses of*

Pleasure (1992) and *Care of the Self* (1990b) turn. Here the aesthetics, self-care, the technologies of self, allude to the possibilities of being otherwise not through lessons of/from resistance but from the self-conscious practices of subjects, even if these subjects come into being through the condition of subjection, or subjectivation.

Considering these Althusserian and Foucaultian accounts of subjection together, Butler asserts that

> 'subjectivation' . . . denotes both the becoming of the subject and the process of subjection—one inhabits the figure of autonomy only by becoming subjected to a power, a subjection which implies a radical dependency. . . . Subjection is, literally, the *making* of a subject, the principle of regulation according to which a subject is formulated or produced. Such subjection is a kind of power that not only unilaterally *acts on* a given individual as a form of domination, but also *activates* or forms the subject. Hence, subjection is neither simply the domination of a subject nor its production, but designates a certain kind of restriction *in* production. (Butler 1997b, 83–84; original emphasis)

Likewise:

> It is important to remember at least two caveats on subjection and regulation derived from Foucaultian scholarship: (1) regulatory power not only acts upon a preexisting subject but also shapes and forms that subject; moreover, every juridical form of power has its productive effect; and (2) to become subject to a regulation is also to be brought into being as a subject precisely through being regulated. (Butler 2004, 41).

Butler develops these ideas to detail how subjectivation as an effect of discourse and, more specifically, the performative offers political potential. She engages with Althusser's understanding of interpellation (Althusser 1971)—the turn to the hail of authority—to think about how the hail might be understood as a performative and how the performatively constituted subjects might engage in the sorts of insurrectionary acts that Foucault speaks of. She suggests that whereas the subject needs to be named in ways that make sense in discourse in order to be *'recognizable'* (Butler 1997a, 5; original emphasis), by being subjectivated the subject can subjectivate another. Butler writes:

> The one who names, who works within language to find a name for another, is presumed to be already named, positioned within language as one who is already subject to the founding or inaugurating address. This suggests that such a subject in language is positioned as

both addressed and addressing, and that the very possibility of naming another requires that one first be named. The subject of speech who is named becomes, potentially, one who might well name another in time. (Butler 1997a, 29)

Butler calls the capacity to name and so constitute that results from subjectivation 'discursive agency' (Butler 1997a, 127). By thinking of agency as discursive—as being the product of being inaugurated in and by discourse and so able to join its citational chains—Butler moves past an understanding of intent and agency that is the property of an a priori, rational, self-knowing subject but *retains* a subject who can act with intent. Discourse and its effects ultimately exceed the intent or free will of an agent, but, like Foucault's practices of self, the performatively constituted subject can still deploy discursive performatives that have the potential to be constitutive.

Butler suggests that as a politics these practices involve

decontextualizing and recontextualizing . . . terms through radical acts of public misappropriation such that the conventional relation between [interpellation and meaning] might become tenuous and even broken over time. (Butler 1997a, 100).

This 'performative politics' (Butler 1997a, 127) offers significant promise for a poststructural politics of change. Through such practices, Butler insists, the sedimented meanings of enduring and prevailing discourses might be unsettled and reinscribed; subordinate, disavowed, or silenced discourses might be deployed in, and made meaningful in, contexts from which they have been barred; and challenges to prevailing constitutions of subjects might be deployed self-consciously through the discursive practices of subjects who are themselves subjectivated. Butler sets out, then, a possible method for Foucault's struggles against subjection.[1]

These ideas have massive implications for education. With this understanding of subjectivation, the school student is so because he/she is designated as such. Indeed, whereas these designations appear to describe preexisting subjects, understanding these designations as performative reveals that *it is the very act of designation that constitutes these subjects* as if they were already students. Simultaneously, the practices of these discursive agents amount to a politics that insists that nobody is necessarily anything and what it means to be a teacher, a student, a learner might be opened up to radical rethinking. The political challenge, then, is to intercept these subjectivating processes in order to constitute students *again differently*. Butler's performative politics offer tools for thinking how this might be done. These are understandings that I put to work in the analysis of school data that follows.

SUBJECTIVATING PRACTICES AT 'MULTICULTURAL DAY'

Data

Multicultural Day, Plains High, Sydney, Australia, December 2001

It is an extremely hot, sticky day—even for Sydney's outer-west at the top of summer. Set up around Plains High's outside spaces there are stalls, dance and drama events, sports activities, and a ducking pool (offering up the male PE teachers for a dunking). Students and their family and guests mill around, visiting stalls, socializing and watching performances.

The deputy principal and a team of four male teachers, all White Australians aged around forty, patrol the school grounds, communicating with each other on walkie-talkies. I—a White Englishwoman invited to experience an 'Australian Multicultural Day' by some of the students who have been participating in my research—watch the deputy principal and his team watching the students and their guests as I wander around the school grounds from one event site to another.

As well as being a multicultural 'celebration', this is also a school fundraiser and a key part of this is the stalls provided by students, parents, family and friends. These stalls are set up under a covered walkway that surrounds three sides of the school's main quad. These have handwritten A3-size signs: 'International Hotdogs'; 'International Food'; 'Italian Food'; 'Hair Braiding' and 'Hair braiding started in Africa but is now popular around the world'; 'Flower Lais'; 'Make your own beads'; 'Philipino Food'; 'German Cafe'; 'Arabic Food' and 'Kebabs'.

White chalk on the fascia board above the Arabic-food stall reads, 'Lebanon' and 'Lebs Rule'. 'Lebs Rule' has been crossed out, but not erased, and 'Turks Rule' chalked next to it. A half moon has also been drawn there.

The Arabic food stall is constantly surrounded by a press of students, as well as guests and teachers, who wait for kebab rolls or chat with friends. The stall staff—a group of fourteen- and fifteen-year-old students and a small number of slightly older young men and women—work hard to keep up with demand. The atmosphere around the stall is buzzing, and it continues to trade long after the other stalls have sold out.

The deputy principal, or a member of his walkie-talkie team, regularly stands in the quad in front of the Arabic food stall watching.

Around the middle of the afternoon I see the deputy principal standing with two Arabic boys (aged roughly 16 to 18) who have been hanging out at the Arabic food stall on a BMX bike. The deputy principal tells the boys to 'leave the school premises immediately'. One motions towards a student on the stall and replies, 'You told him to invite his family and friends, well I'm his friend so I can be here'. The deputy principal responds, 'No, we say who can be here, now please leave'.

A while later, the deputy principal ejects another Arabic boy, also on a BMX, who has spent the afternoon at the stall. The deputy principal says to him, 'You were going to light up on the premises—now leave.' The boy cups an unlit cigarette in his hand. One of the students from the stall asks: 'Sir, what if I personally vouch for him?' The deputy principal does not respond to this offer and directs the boy away. The deputy principal watches me watching.

Later in the afternoon I walk past the car park behind the quad and see a police van parked there. The deputy principal stands nearby with one of his walkie-talkie team and says to him, 'The thing they have to realize is that we decide who comes onto the premises.' His colleague replies, 'They don't realize that.' (Fieldnotes)

Critical multiculturalism, critical antiracism and, more recently, Critical Race Theory (CRT) in education offer significant criticisms of the sort of pluralist multiculturalism that appears to frame Multicultural Day at Plains High. These critical accounts argue that pluralist (as opposed to political or critical) multiculturalism presents cultural difference as naturally occurring and neutral, and race/ethnic harmony (tolerance) as following on from a recognition and celebration of these differences. This version of multiculturalism is criticised for ignoring the persistent (discursive) constitution of race/ethnicity as axes for differentiation and stratification, erasing historical and contemporary exploitations and subjugations, and failing to note, let alone challenge, the enduring supremacy of the majority race/ethnicity. There is not scope within this chapter to explore these criticisms as fully as might be justified, but see Gilroy 1986; Gillborn 2004; Ladson-Billings 2004; McCoy 2000; Rizvi 1997 for excellent accounts.

Work in these areas has also extended significantly our understandings of race and racism. In particular, critical analyses of whiteness and the mechanisms whereby White supremacy (Gillborn 2005) or White hegemony (Youdell 2003) are secured; White noise becomes overwhelming (McCoy 2000); and whiteness is reproduced as at once normative and invisible (Leonardo 2004), offer extremely fruitful tools for interrogating the discourses that circulate in school settings and the subjectivating effects that these discourses might have. Also particularly useful for the analysis offered here are Lipman's (2004) account of how anti-Islamic discourses are pervading educational discourse and settings 'post- 9/11' and McCoy's (2000) reminder of the sense of 'epidemic' and being 'out-of-control' that infuses official and popular discourses (including pluralist multiculturalism) and so frames the terms in which difference might be intelligible.

The data that I produce and analyze here offer a series of moments from 'Multicultural Day' at Plains High. These readings are tentative and inevitably incomplete. They are also contentious and unsettling. The 'tokenism' of one-day-only ethnic food and craft stalls, wearing of traditional dress and ethnic music and dance that form the focus of many such days of 'celebration' is evident (Solomos and Back 1996). And the inclusion of the traditional 'Aussie' dunking pool and cricket match underscores the refusal of whiteness and its cultural forms to be shifted from the centre for even this token day. This, then, seems to be a very typical example of a (pluralist) 'Multicultural Day'. Also evident, and the focus of this analysis, is struggles over the place and meaning of the 'Lebanese', 'Turkish' and 'Arabic' subject within this contemporary Australian high school.

Edward Said's works *Orientalism* (2003) and *Representing Islam* (1992) usefully identify the peculiarity of the 'Orient' and the 'Oriental', and later Islam, in the Western imagination. For Said, the problematic is the gap between how the Orient, the Oriental, Islam, and the 'Arab' actually are, and how these are envisioned and represented in Western ideas and media. Whereas Said's work stresses heterogeneity and change, what is at stake for him is the distance between the real and the imagined. Taking a Foucaultian approach to these ideas, in particular approaching them through Butler's conceptions of performativity and subjectivation, radically unsettles this real/imagined divide. It does this by underscoring the discursive construction of this real and, therefore, exposing Orientalism(s) as constitutive of subjects, as performative, as subjectivating. Thinking about Orientalism as discourses steeped in historicity and sedimented meaning helps to expose how the scientific rationale of colonial north Africa; the religious rationale of Crusades in the near and Middle East; and the empire's deployment of these in the construction of the Orient as the Occident's exotic Other and the Oriental/Arab as in the proper service of his [*sic*] colonial master all suffuse contemporary Western discourses of the Orient and of Islam. The 'Savage Arab' once in need of taming and Christianizing comes, in contemporary discourse, to be in need of Westernizing, 'democratizing'. And these are needs heightened to epidemic levels in post- 9/11 discourses of 'terror'. As Butler (1997a) notes in *Excitable Speech*, such discourses do not need to be made explicit or spoken to be cited and to have performative force. On the contrary, discourses that go unspoken, that are silent or silenced, remain constitutive. Furthermore, Butler suggests that the subjectivated subject acts her/his place in the discourses through which s/he has been rendered intelligible, through which subjecthood, albeit subjectivated and subjugated, is effected. In a discursive frame in which whiteness (synonymous with Western-ness) is normative and these enduring (but mobile) discourses of the Orient/Islam continue to be cited, the White/Anglo/Aussie and the Arab act their respective place in discourse (but not necessarily always). And in a discursive frame of school authority in which a teacher/ student binary is a fundamental subjectivating divide, the teacher and the student act their respective place in discourse (but, again, not always).

These conceptual tools, then, help us to identify these discourses as they are deployed, resisted, recuperated, and deployed again in the events of Multicultural Day. This is not an exhaustive account of the discourses that frame this setting (such an account is surely impossible). Further discourses are also clearly at play, intersecting the prevailing discourses of the Orient/

Arab that I have sketched above, for instance, adult and youth heterosexual-masculinities, street/youth subculture, national and religious pride. This partial account, then, is offered as fragments of a porous network of discourses that are particularly significant to the subjectivations I am exploring here.

In the school's acceptance of the Arabic students' donation of an Arabic food stall, the school constitutes 'Arabic' as a legitimate axis of minority cultural difference and subjectivates the Arabic subject as a good student. And in donating the stall and participating in Multicultural Day, this good-Arabic-student-subject takes up this subjecthood. In doing this, just as the school cedes the good-Arabic-student-subject, so this subject cedes the authority of the school institution by which s/he is subjectivated. And the students gain the rights of the student (to invite guests) but also subjection to teacher authority (to have their guests ejected).

The stall, the food it sells, and so the students and others who staff it, are named (by the students?) 'Arabic'. This collective performative interpellation is particularized by the further performative names 'Lebs' and 'Turks'. And nationalism meets competitive team sports (or in another discourse something more sinister) in the chalked proclamation (performative?) 'Lebs Rule' and 'Turks Rule'. The crossing out, without erasure, of 'Lebs Rule' (by the author of 'Turks Rule'?) does not lessen the constitutive effect of this textual practice. That the crossing out, the replacement of one 'ruling' nationality with another, is left for public display continues to cite the claim as well as the erasure and the overthrow that calls up. It seems that this is not a battle but a playful skirmish—Lebanese and Turkish students have organised and are staffing the 'Arabic food' stall together under that collective given and taken name 'Arab'. Indeed, there is a collectivity evident in these claims. Rather than erasing each other's self-constituting performatives, then, each claim in this apparent contest acts to render the other intelligible (Butler 2004), even if this is also a subjectivation.

In a discursive frame of normative whiteness, the claim that Lebs or Turks rule cannot have performative force. The subjectivating practices of the school render the Arabic subject (the Leb or the Turk), but s/he remains (reviled?) 'ethnic'[2] in this context—in the school and the wider social context of contemporary Australia, Lebs and Turks certainly do not rule. Yet this practice of self, made possible through the prior subjectivation of these raced-nationed-regionalized subjects, is simultaneously felicitous. That is, Lebs and Turks may not rule, but the statement is not empty. Instead, it silently calls up once again the threat of the savage Arab Other. What might be read as (invisibly) written on the fascia board is 'Arabs Rule'. And the crescent moon of Islam drawn alongside these claims interpellates collective regional identity in religious terms—these good-Arabic-student-subjects also silently constitute themselves Islamic. And the constitution 'Islamic' alongside a proclamation of ruling calls up that deepest of post-9/11 Western/White fantasies—that Islam aims to rule. And the spectre of

9/11, anti-Western 'terror' silently rises. In this discursive frame, the Lebs and Turks (Arabs and Islamist) do not rule, but they would. And so these once good-Arabic-student-subjects are potentially subjectivated (through the coalescence of performative practices as external as the US media and as intimate as their own) as Islamic-fundamentalist and even potential terrorist threats—and in urgent and absolute need of surveillance. And as the Arab/Islamist threatens to burst out of the confines of service and studenthood, this is not the surveillance of the panopticon, but a very immediate and visible coercive surveillance—the White, male, senior teacher stands in the quad in front of the stall, walkie-talkie in hand.

This, then, is a moment in which the 'Arabic' students in the school gain public recognition as legitimate, and this subjectivation opens up the opportunity for self-constitution. But, given the discursive terrain of this subjectivation and practices of self, this self-constitution is one that threatens to slide back into injury and the constraint of the savage Arab/Islamist threat.

It appears from this reading that it is the students' practices that have suggested confrontation, a possible risk or danger—the wider discourse of Arabic threat is implicit in the claim that Lebs/Turks rule. Yet it is likely that the discourse of Islamic/Arabic threat would permeate this context at this moment without these chalked claims, that it would be 'on the lips' of White teachers—it was already one of the discourses of the Other that effect whiteness and its normativity long before 9–11 happened. Again, Said's reading of the relation between the Occident and the Orient, inflected with a notion of discourse and the performative, is pertinent. These long-established discourses echo in contemporary contexts without ever being spoken. Indeed, perhaps the absence of the need to explicitly cite a discourse in order for it to be cited goes to its endurance and performative force. But the appearance that this discourse was deployed by the students and only *responded to* by the school renders 'legitimate' the teachers' apparent diagnosis of cultural discontent or threat and makes their move to police this threat not a raced and racist subjectivation but a necessary response. This is not to say that the squad of senior teachers armed with walkie-talkies is a response to this constitutive chalked claim—the establishment of this squad and the procurement of walkie-talkies to facilitate the best government of this population surely dates back to the students volunteering to mount the kebab stall, their arrival in the suburb, the school, the White Australia policy, the refusal of Orientals at nineteenth-century colonial ports.

Butler's theoretical tools, then, enable us to see how the teachers subjectivate these students as particular raced-nationed-religioned subjects, with the possibilities for discursive agency and the constraints of the discursive terms of subjection that this entails. Whereas the pronouncement 'Lebs/Turks Rule' might be a performative constitution of self as Arab not normally permitted in school, practicing these technologies of self simultaneously evokes the very discourses of epidemic difference and threat through which a school and wider society infused by whiteness subjectivates the Arab Other. As Butler's work suggests they will, these students act their place in this web of discourses. And the school subjectivates these (no longer good) students in these terms and 'responds' accordingly—by keeping vigilant watch at the Multicultural Days' most popular stall (and no doubt biggest fund raiser) and by ejecting from the premises any Leb/Turk/Arab youth who fails to fulfil the school's requirements of the 'good ethnic'. Indeed, the Arab as a good-student-subject might be outside prevailing intelligibility after all.

The notion of subjectivation also allows us to see how these teachers (and potentially their colleagues inside and beyond this school) are constituted by prevailing discourses of education, professionalism, the teacher and teacher authority (perhaps no longer the good teacher) as well as wider discourses—particularly pressing here hetero-masculinity and whiteness. And, within this discursive frame, they are also constituted by their own practices of self: White supremacy-masculine authority/entitlement is inscribed through their surveillant practices even as it also subjectivates these men racist and vulnerable (and so perhaps not masculine at all). The cost of being made subject here is not borne by the Lebanese/Turkish/Arabic subject alone. Indeed, by understanding these discursive practices as subjectivating we can begin to consider how these constitutions and their framing discourses might effect other students and subjects more broadly.

A series of tensions seem to endure through these subjectivations. First, the students are good students who contribute (very well) to the school's fund-raising effort. They are also good 'ethnic' students who participate in Multicultural Day by displaying their 'difference'. But at the same time they are 'bad' students, or bad subjects: Their ethnic(ized) subcultural display—Islamic crescents, Lebs/Turks Rule proclamations and BMX bikes—are all well outside the good student-subject. Second, this ethnic(ized) subculture is entangled with a further axis of tension in the subjectivation of these students—the discourse of the Islamic threat presses here and overwhelms the possibility of the good student—in this discursive frame the Arab/Islamist is a bad subject. Finally, multicultural pluralism (as enacted by Multicultural Day) also sits in tension with the Islamist threat and the policing of this. And yet, in post-9/11 Western contexts, perhaps this pluralism and policing are reconciled in the subjectivation of the good teacher and good citizen who celebrates diversity as long as it remains minoritized, marginalized and willing to be (impossibly) Westernized.

PERFORMATIVE POLITICS, OR POLITICS IN SUBJECTIVATION

Butler uses the notion of the performative, the notion of discourse, and the notion of subjectivation to think about the constitution, constraint and political possibility of the subject. This chapter has demonstrated the deployment of these notions for understanding practices inside schools and begun to show how performative politics might begin to destabilise both the explicit and silent discursive ties between biographies and studenthood, ties that make possible, and normal, the continued subjectivation of differentiated student-subjects.

Yet the relationships between the performative, discourse and subjectivation and the significance of these relationships for thinking about a poststructural politics merit further consideration.

The performative, Butler tells us, enacts what it names; it names and makes. In this sense, all categorical names and claims to action are potentially performatively constitutive of the subjects to whom they refer. But it is not only utterances that have the potential to act performatively. Butler (1997a, 1997b) also notes the possibility of bodily practices being performative and examines this possibility through her consideration of Bourdieu's (1991) bodily *habitus*. I have not pursued this here, but if we reflect on the bodies of the teachers and students in the episode above, we can begin to see how, for instance, the *particular way* that the boy sat on his BMX bike, unlit cigarette cupped in his hand, and the *particular way* that the deputy principal stood legs apart, shoulders square, walkie-talkie in hand, are bodily practices that simultaneously enact particular sorts of subjects.

In the move from the performativity of names to wider utterances, and from utterances to practices, the performative can be seen as a function within discourse. Indeed, it might be helpful to think of the performative as a particular element of discourse *and* as a nuance within the discursive processes through which discourses come to have productive effects. Discourse itself might be as performative. This suggests that the performative might be understood very specifically, after Butler's earlier engagements with the idea, and that the specific performative *and* the wider discursive field in which it is located can be understood as discursively constitutive.

Subjectivation understands the constitutive effect of discourses in this way, but the notion of subjectivation underscores how this constitution *is simultaneously and unavoidably entangled in the production of discursive relations of power*. Constitution within constraint is always present within the notions of the performative and discursive constitution, but when we take up a notion of subjectivation this simultaneous constitution within constraint—made subject *and* subjected to/by—becomes wholly explicit. Indeed, that discursive relations of power are integral to being a recognizable subject is central to the notion of subjectivation.

Subjectivation is effected through discursive practices, and understanding the performative is an important tool for understanding the constitutive effects of these discursive practices. But it is the more explicit sense of the way that power is implicated in subjectivation that I find particularly helpful. And this has led me to think, alongside Butler's (1997a) notions of performative politics and politics of hegemony, about a *politics* in *subjectivation* in which discursively constituted and constrained subjects deploy discursive agency and act within and at the borders of the constraint of their subjectivation. By interrogating and rendering visible the subjectivating practices that constitute particular sorts of students tied to particular subjectivities and, by extension, particular educational (and wider) trajectories, we begin to uncover the potential of Butler's performative politics or a politics in subjectivation. Whether challenging the effects of, for instance, discourses of poverty, heredity, intelligence, hetero-normativity, or, like here, racism and whiteness, understanding these processes helps us to see where discursive interventions might enable new discourses to be rendered intelligible or enduring discourse to be unsettled within school contexts.

In mapping the subjectivating practices of a school and its teachers, and the practices of self of teachers and students, the chapter demonstrates the importance of engaging these ideas for making sense of the practices and effects of schooling. The particular analysis offered here adds another layer of understanding to existing analyses of enduring patterns of raced educational inequality and exclusion. Yet it is not a pessimistic analysis—these theoretical tools insist that the potential to act with intent and, therefore, shift meaning is inherent to the contingent nature of discourse and the discursive agency inherent to subjectivating processes. The teachers' and students' practices that I have interrogated here are performative politics that both reinscribe and unsettle hegemonic meaning. These teachers are involved in practices of whiteness that subjectivate raced-nationed-religioned students and these students are involved in practices of insurrection as they are subjectivated. The teachers' performative politics constitute themselves and Arabic students in their respective places in enduring discourse. The students' performative politics are the skirmishes that these subjectivated subjects engage in when their discursive agency is worked against the prevailing discourses through which they are subjectivated. Or when these subjects deploy subjugated discourses through their practices of self, even if these discourses, and the subjectivities they constitute, are rapidly recuperated. Performative politics does not entreat us to identify the subjectivation and then move on to design a corresponding performative insurrection (although at the level of collective action activists/academics might want to do this). Rather, these are *politics* in *subjectivation*, enacted at any (every?) moment of constitution.

NOTES

1. In *The Subject and Power* (1982), Foucault suggests that we might recognize three forms of struggle that exist in 'complex and circular relations' (p. 213): struggles against domination; against exploitation; and against subjection. These struggles against subjection, for Foucault, are increasingly significant both to the subjects who struggle against their own subjection and to the enquirer into the present. At the centre of Foucault's work, then, is a concern with struggles for change. This is not a struggle for the liberation, or self-determination, of the subject but struggles played out through the persistent

potential for resistances in the circulation of counter and subjugated discourses (Vol. 1) and the freedom suggested by the possibility of transformation (1988a).
2. In this setting, like many in multiethnic, urban Sydney, 'ethnic' is commonly used on its own to name minority ethnic individuals and communities. Indeed, it has become the object of ironic recuperation.

REFERENCES

Alvesson, Mats. 2002. *Postmodernism and social research.* Buckingham, UK: Open University Press.
Althusser, Louis. 1971. Ideology and ideological state apparatuses. In *Lenin and philosophy,* trans. Ben Brewster, 170–186. London: Monthly Review Press.
Austin, John L. 1962. *How to do things with words.* Oxford: Clarendon Press.
Ball, Stephen J. 2003. 'The teachers' soul and the terrors of performativity. *Journal of Education Policy* 18 (2): 215–228.
Baudrillard, Jean. 1994. *Simulacra and simulation.* Ann Arbor: University of Michigan Press.
Bourdieu, Pierre. 1991. *Language and symbolic power.* Cambridge, MA: Harvard University Press.
Britzman, Deborah. 2000. "The question of belief": Writing poststructural ethnography. In *Working the ruins: Feminist poststructural theory and methods in education,* ed. Elizabeth St. Pierre and Wanda S. Pillow, 27–40. London: Routledge.
Butler, Judith. 1990. *Gender trouble: Feminism and the subversion of identity.* London: Routledge.
———. 1993. *Bodies that matter: On the discursive limits of "sex".* London: Routledge.
———. 1997a. *Excitable speech: A politics of the performative.* London: Routledge.
———. 1997b. *The psychic life of power: Theories in subjection.* Stanford, CA: Stanford University Press.
———. 2004. *Undoing gender.* London: Routledge.
Carr, William, and Stephen Kemmis. 1986. *Becoming critical: Education knowledge and action research.* London: Falmer.
Delamont, Sara, and Paul Atkinson. 1995. *Fighting familiarity: Essays on education and ethnography.* Cressuill, NJ: Hampton Press.
Derrida, Jacques. 1988. Signature event context. In *Limited Inc.* 1–23, Jacques Derrida. Elvanston, IL: Northwestern University Press.
Foucault, Michel. 1982. The subject and power. In *Michel Foucault: Beyond hermeneutics and structuralism,* eds. Hubert L. Dreyfus and Paul Rabinow, 208–226. Brighton, Sussex: Harvester.
———. 1988a. Critical theory/intellectual history. In *Michel Foucault—politics, philosophy, culture: Interviews and other writings 1977–1984,* ed. Lawrence Kritzman, 17–46. London: Routledge.
———. 1988b. An aesthetics of existence. In *Michel Foucault—politics, philosophy, culture: Interviews and other writings 1977–1984,* ed. Lawrence Kritzman, 47–56. London: Routledge.
———. 1988c. The return of morality. In *Michel Foucault—politics, philosophy, culture: Interviews and other writings 1977–1984,* ed. Lawrence Kritzman, 242–254. London: Routledge.

———. 1990a. *The history of sexuality volume 1: An introduction.* London: Penguin.

———. 1990b. *The care of the self: The history of sexuality volume 3.* London: Penguin.

———. 1991. *Discipline and punish: The birth of the prison.* London: Penguin.

———. 1992. *The uses of pleasure: The history of sexuality volume 2.* London: Penguin.

Gillborn, David. 2004. Anti-racism: From policy to praxis. In *The Routledge-Falmer reader in multicultural education: Critical perspectives on race, racism and education,* eds. Gloria Ladson-Billings and David Gillborn, 35–48. London: RoutledgeFalmer.

———. 2005. Education policy as an act of white supremacy. *Journal of Education Policy* 20 (4): 485–505.

Gilroy, Paul. 1986. *There ain't no black in the Union Jack.* London: Routledge.

Hammersley, Martyn, and Paul Atkinson. 1995. *Ethnography: Principles in practice,* 2nd ed. London: Tavistock Publications.

Harwood, Valerie. 2001. Foucault, narrative and the subjugated subject: Doing research with a grid of sensibility. *Australian Educational Researcher* 28 (3): 141–166.

Jacobson, Matthew F. 1998. *Whiteness of a different color: European immigrants and the alchemy of race.* Cambridge MA: Harvard University Press.

Ladson-Billings, Gloria. 2004. Just what is critical race theory and what's it doing in a *nice* field like education? In *The RoutledgeFalmer reader in multicultural education: Critical perspectives on race, racism and education,* eds. Gloria Ladson-Billings and David Gillborn, 49–68. London: RoutledgeFalmer.

Lather, Patti. 2000. Drawing the line at angels: Working the ruins of feminist methodology. In *Working the ruins: Feminist poststructural theory and methods in education,* eds. Elizabeth St. Pierre and Wanda S. Pillow, 258–312. London: Routledge.

Leonardo, Z. 2004. The souls of white folk: Critical pedagogy, whiteness studies, and globalization discourse. In *The RoutledgeFalmer reader in multicultural education: Critical perspectives on race, racism and education,* eds. Gloria Ladson-Billings and David Gillborn, 117–136. London: RoutledgeFalmer.

Lipman, Pauline. 2004. *Education accountability and repression of democracy post 9/11.* Paper presented at American Educational Research Association Annual Conference, April 2004, San Diego.

MacLure, Maggie. 2003. *Discourse in educational and social research.* Buckingham, UK: Open University Press.

McCoy, Kate. 2000. White noise—the sound of epidemic: Reading/writing a climate of intelligibility around a "crisis" of difference. In *Working the ruins: Feminist poststructural theory and methods in education,* eds. Elizabeth. St. Pierre and Wanda S. Pillow, 237–257. London: Routledge.

Miller, Gale. 1997. Building bridges: The possibility of analytic dialogue between ethnography, conversation analysis and Foucault. In *Qualitative research: Theory, method and practice,* ed. David Silverman, 24–44. London: Sage.

Prior, Lindsay. 1997. Following in Foucault's footsteps: Text and content in qualitative research. In *Qualitative research: Theory, method and practice,* ed. David Silverman, 63–79. London: Sage.

Rizvi, Fazal. 1997. Educational leadership and the politics of difference. *Melbourne Studies in Education* 38 (1): 90–102.

Said, Edward. 1992. *Representing Islam.* London: Penguin.

———. 2003. *Orientalism.* London: Penguin.

Seshadri-Crooks, Kalpana. 2000. *Desiring whiteness: A Lacanian analysis of whiteness.* London: Routledge.

Silverman, David. 1997. Towards an aesthetics of research. In *Qualitative research: Theory, method and practice,* ed. David Silverman, 239–253. London: Sage.

Skeggs, Beverley. 1994. Situating the production of feminist ethnography. In *Researching women's lives from a feminist perspective*, eds. Mary Maynard and June Purvis. London: Taylor & Francis.

Solomos, John, and Les Back. 1996. *Racism and society.* Basingstoke, UK: Macmillan.

Stanley, Liz, and Sue Wise. 1993. *Breaking out again: Feminist ontology and epistemology.* London: Routledge.

St. Pierre, Elizabeth. 2000. Nomadic enquiry in the smooth spaces of the field: A preface. In *Working the ruins: Feminist poststructural theory and methods in education*, eds. Elizabeth St. Pierre and Wanda S. Pillow, 258–283. London: Routledge.

Stronach, Ian, and Maggie MacLure. 1997. *Educational research undone: The postmodern embrace.* Buckingham, UK: Open University Press.

Youdell, Deborah. 2003. Identity traps, or how black students fail: The interactions between biographical, sub-cultural, and learner identities. *British Journal of Sociology of Education* 24 (1): 3–20.

———. 2005. Sex-gender-sexuality: How sex, gender and sexuality constellations are constituted in secondary school. *Gender and Education* 17 (3): 247–270.

Conclusion
Intersectional Theories and 'Race': From Toolkit to 'Mash-Up'

John Preston and Kalwant Bhopal

INTRODUCTION

In this concluding chapter we consider the potential for intersectional analysis with regard to 'race' in the light of the preceding chapters. Firstly, we discuss whether focusing on 'race' (as a key of personhood, positioning or abjectification) is productive. In doing so we warn against the adoption of intersectional approaches to 'race' which seek to submerge its status as a social relation. We use the work of Fanon (1986) to argue for the merits of focusing on the *singularity* of 'race' albeit amongst other social characteristics. Although the chapters in this book (and we as editors) have argued for an intersectional approach throughout, we maintain, alongside many of the authors, an appreciation of the uniqueness of racial oppression. Secondly, we argue that rather than being applications of existent theories, intersectional approaches, such as the ones contained in this volume, encourage the creation of new theoretical entities and border theorising. Specifically, intersectional theories are constructions that work apart from, but are influenced by, the theoretical orbit of existing theories. They are 'mash-ups' rather than being constructions from a theoretical 'toolkit'.

INTERSECTIONALITY AND 'RACE' ANALYSIS

In each of the chapters, intersectionality around 'race' has primarily been based around its correspondence with 'class' and 'gender', although some of the chapters have pointed towards wider conceptions, in particular around sexuality (Kitching, Chakrabarty), disability (Rampersad) and faith (Dewan, Shain). This is important as the 'matrix of oppressions' (Hill-Collins, 1999) in which racialized/raced subjects find themselves in (or position others in) are not only about the dynamics of oppression but also about the ways in which categorisations are arranged within that matrix. According to Hill-Collins (1999), any particular matrix of domination has ' . . . a particular arrangement of intersecting systems of oppression e.g. race, social class, gender, sexuality, citizenship status, ethnicity and age' and 'a particular arrangement of its domains of power e.g. structural, disciplinary, hegemonic and interpersonal' (300). In Brah and Phoenix's terms, this can involve an analysis of how ' . . . multiple axis of differentiation—economic, political, cultural, psychic, subjective and experiential—intersect in historically specific contexts' (2004, 76). Hence attentiveness to all oppressions within a system of domination is important and we note that, aside from the chapters in this book, there are attempts elsewhere to examine 'race' and intersectionality in terms of cis/transgender (Renn 2010; although Chakrabarty's analysis of Beyoncé in this book could be applied to this topic) and in terms of critical theories of disability, most notably crip theory (James and Wu 2006). Although there are some parts of personhood, or aspects of oppression, that may have been missed in analysis, the centrality of 'race' in analysis of intersectionality should not be occluded. Fanon's strong concession that in centring on 'race' that 'The analysis is above all, regressive' (Fanon 1986, 15) should always be read alongside the statement 'There is a fact: White men consider themselves superior to black men' (Fanon, 1986, 12). Whilst understanding the *limits* of foregrounding 'race' within an analysis of intersectionality, there are also *possibilities* in doing this. In particular, through the way in which it might extend our thinking about 'race' and so subvert the ways in which, whilst it has usually been intersected with other relations (in theorising this is particularly class, often gender, rarely sexuality), it is sometimes productive to consider it as a substantive category of its own. A casual observation that we have made about the academy is that whilst thinking about class in itself or gender in itself is still (despite intersectionality) perceived to be a relatively respectable position, to think about 'race' as a primary social relation is considered to be a project which is at best essentialist and at worst nationalist, even *racist* (in the bizarre constructions of those who consider that reverse racism may exist). Intersectionality, in thinking about the relations between aspects of personhood (or abjectification, Alcoff 1998) is admittedly difficult work in terms of always coming back and returning to what constitutes the subject. Like Lieutenant Columbo (in the television series), who always returns to the suspect to ask 'one more thing', the productivity, but also the obsessive nature, of intersectionality is that this return is always made. When speaking about 'race' in education, many of us have been faced with the question 'What about class/gender/sexuality/disability/faith?' whereas rarely are speakers on these topics asked, 'What about "race"?' A focus on 'race' in analysis is indicative, for some academics, as a sign of pathology or suspicion. Indeed, even Fanon is readily criticized for his supposed ignorance of gender and sexuality:

'When identifications are their most insistent they are also their most suspect, as a survey of the dominant discourses on the subject reveals. What then does the theorist otherize in intervention? Diana Fuss . . . (1994) . . . in the chapter of *Identification Papers* entitled 'Interior Colonies: Frantz Fanon and the Politics of Identification', delineates the different direction taken by Fanon, the difference between identification made metaphor for much of the dominant ideology as opposed to that which those who are colonized view with diffidence and disdain For those who are denied subjectivity as well as otherness, identification is not a requisite component of psychical existence. Fuss relates that Fanon's own 'resolutely masculine self-identifications, articulated through the abjectification of femininity and homosexuality, take shape over and against colonialism's castrating representations of male sexuality'. She argues that Fanon's thesis is contained by the discourse of colonial subjectivity, that Fanon 'does not think beyond the presuppositions of colonial discourse to examine how colonial domination itself works partially through the social institutionalisation of misogyny and homophobia,' and she suggests that Fanon's 'otherwise powerful critique of the scene of colonial representation does not fundamentally question the many sexualized determinations of that scene'. Fuss refers in some focus to the work of Gilles Deleuze and Félix Guattari, whose *Anti-Oedipus* demonstrates the 'historical emergence of both colonization and oedipalization [which] participate in a double ideological operation where each serves effectively to conceal the political function and purpose of the other'. (Schiff 2007: http://www.janushead.org/4-2/schiff.cfm).

'When identifications are most *insistent* they are at their most *suspect*' (our italics). This is not necessarily true; the subtle and the playful in analysis can also be suspect but this is often hidden by the rhetoric of the 'knowing theorist' steeped in irony. To accuse Fanon of not thinking beyond his historical and cultural context (whereas Deleuze and Guattari are wonderfully ideologically free of theirs, able to see through both colonisation and oedipalisation) is to accuse Fanon's analysis of being stuck in a singular consciousness, focused on 'race'. Bell's (1992) rules of racial standing whereby Black speakers are not taken seriously in terms of the value of what they are saying about 'race' applies here. In this case, what Fanon is saying is judged not only to be misogynist, but also as special pleading. Schiff is implying that Fanon must be taken back to each scene of the 'racial' crime to pick up on the 'other thing' being gender relations (and another thing ... what about disability?). In writing this conclusion, then, we are wary that for some 'race' always calls out for the type of intersectional analysis which obscures it. Intersectional analysis does not mean that we cannot 'speak' to 'race' alone, and we should address its primacy when necessary.

This is not to say that intersectionality between 'race' and other social characteristics can't be complex. It can be depicted as multiple intersections in terms of constellations (categorical identities might be conceived of and interrogated as shifting, nonnecessary constellations of categorisations, constellations that are themselves shifting and nonnecessary ... (Youdell 2006, 29) or nonlinear and often ambiguous sidewinders (Johnson 2003, 9) between 'race' and other aspects of personhood). However, these analyses should not (and in the case of the named authors do not) obscure the centrality of 'racism' as a system of oppression. This is not a scalar concept in that some individuals are classed to be 'more' human than others, but a categorical one in that 'race' can represents the dividing line between those individuals who are classified (in policy, in social relations, in everyday discourse) as worthy of agency. For few other categories of personhood other than 'race' have humans been *systematically* enslaved and murdered. It also pervades every institution (in terms of institutional and systematic racism) in terms of White supremacy. So-called White people (Ignatiev 1996, 11) are privileged and this does not arise from accident but due to a global system of political economy (White supremacy) which all so-called White people participate in (Allen 2001; Leonardo 2005; Gillborn 2005, 2006; Chakrabarty 2006). This is even when (especially when?) they take moral actions to critique White supremacy whilst leaving its institutional and systemic structures intact. In short, despite an emphasis on intersectionality, we must be aware that intersectionality itself, by exploding oppressions into multiplicities, does not become (paradoxically) an example of ' . . . the technologies that conceal the intersectionality of dominant structures of difference' (Mirza 2008, 7). We would therefore signal that the chapters in the book are testament to the centrality of 'race' in understanding oppression, and not of its marginalization in social theory.

INTERSECTIONAL THEORY: TOOLKIT OR MASH-UP?

All of the authors contained in the book would testify to the importance of the analysis, if not the primacy, of 'race', racism and racial oppression. As the chapters show, intersectionality and 'race' are currently being approached through multiple theoretical perspectives in education and that it is possible to identify poststructural, queer, psychoanalytic, Marxist, class-culturalist, feminist and Critical Race Theory (CRT) strands in analysing 'race' intersections. This theoretical pluralism means that it is not possible to speak of an independent 'intersectional approach' and that, as might be expected, many approaches arise from what might be called established, even classical, sociological and cultural theories. What is most productive about the intersectional analyses contained in this book, aside from their empirical novelty, is the innovative, even playful, ways in which they approach theory and construct their arguments. The Foucaultian metaphor of the 'toolkit', from which researchers are bringing a set of concepts (perhaps from one, usually from many theories) to bear on the problem of intersectionality, is a powerful one here. Within this metaphor is the idea that theories are used partially, discarding conceptual apparatus as required. Additionally, there is the move away from preciousness in terms of absolute adherence, or coherence, to theories which are used as ' . . . heuristics or tools towards solving local problems' (Sawicki 2005, 380). Although seductive in terms of its implication of construction of new theory, the toolkit metaphor is perhaps overtly linear, perhaps even mechanistic. Taking parts from theories, even in a theoretical bricolage, implies a purposive, even technicist, construction. In examining these chapters, and in thinking about future directions in intersectionality and 'race', the toolkit metaphor needs to be stretched further towards examining intersectional theory as not even assemblage but perhaps hodgepodge (Deleuze and Guattari 2004, 7). That is ' . . . the ability to rearrange fragments in new and different patterns or configurations; and as a consequence, an indifference towards the act of production and the product, towards the overall instruments to be used and toward the over-all result to be achieved'. We consider that the ways in which intersectional theory is being performed does not fit easily into established models of the development of educational theory, even by metaphors of the 'toolbox' of theory. Rather, it requires elements of theoretical bootstrapping (using metaphor or artifice to create a self-sustaining theory) and retrofitting (adding new theoretical elements to existing theories). The theories that emerge, rather than being (necessarily) consistent social theories, can be best thought of 'mash-ups' (a term that has previously been applied to the development of music or software). We consider that 'mash-up' social theories are a productive way to consider the development of intersectional theorising by not only examining what might be called the crossroads of personhood but also in terms of new theoretical integrations (or disintegrations). The metaphor of the 'mash-up' can show how specific incidences of Marxism/CRT, feminism/poststructuralism and class-cultural/ethnic pluralist theories in tension can be useful for future theorising. The implications for educational theorising extend beyond the scope of 'race' and intersectionality in education and suggest a space for theory that is playful and idiosyncratic. In terms of Web applications, for example, the purpose of what is known as a 'reflexive mash-up' is to ' . . . subvert applications to do what they could not do otherwise by themselves' (Navas 2010, 169). These reflexive mash-ups are shown in the book where 'grand narrative' social theories, which often tend to collapse intersectional approaches into a single explanatory framework, drawing perhaps from the same toolkit (sometimes even to the extent that intersections are collapsed into a single element of social existence such as the collapsing of 'race' into an epiphenomenon of 'class' in Marxist theories of racialization), are used to reapply the theoretical apparatus to an alternative domain (e.g., applying Critical Race Theory to an analysis of class inequality or applying Marxism to an analysis of racial oppression). For example, the work of recent Marxist scholars on racialization has developed some of the intricacies of 'race' with regard to marginality in whiteness and forms of xeno-racialization within an orthodox Marxist framework (Cole 2009a, 2009b, 2009c, 2009d; Cole and Maisuria 2007). Similarly, as shown by Zeus Leonardo and David Gillborn's chapters, Critical Race Theory is used to demonstrate the mechanisms of class oppression. For David Gillborn, the concept of interest convergence is used to illustrate how class inequalities are reproduced through the positioning of the White working class as a 'buffer' between competing 'race'/class interests. For Zeus Leonardo, an even more radical integration of 'race'/class is proposed with an integration between the 'objective' status of class with the 'subjective' elements of 'race'. For critical race theorists, as opposed to Marxists, the extension of theory to include multiple oppressions is perhaps not such a large move as critical 'race' theorists have always been aware of the positioning of 'race' within other elements of personhood (Crenshaw 2002). The intersections between these theories can also lead to new forms of oppression which are not accounted for in one or the other theoretical perspectives. To take the theory discussed by Maisuria, Marx's analysis of capitalism can be extended to explore racialization as related to the mode of production. However, racial projects in capitalism could be interpreted at a deeper level of abstraction than at the level of concrete (racialized) labour. Projects that aim to integrate CRT and the Marxist critique of capitalism, such as the ones suggested in this book, could place 'race' not only at the 'base' of capitalist production but as a first principle at a high level of abstraction, linking it to the Marxist concept of value and the commodity as the 'cell form' of capitalism (Preston 2010). Leonardo's chapter, in particular, points towards a reflexive 'mashing up' of CRT and Marxism.

More extensively than the 'reflexive mash-up' where new meanings are obtained through the playing out of theory where it (perhaps) should not be made to go (the incursion of CRT into class or Marxism into 'race') are those interpretations where theory itself may be described as poststructural, recoiling from grand narratives and reflexive in understandings of power in the construction of 'class' and 'race'. Youdell's chapter, for example, deliberately sets out to think Althusser and Foucault through Butler and examines the subjection/subjectivation nexus. Through this reading of Althusser through Butler, she writes: 'I am provoked to wonder, much as Judith Butler has, what would "happen" if I were to think of ideologies (as well as the "undistorted truth"), and ideological state apparatuses, and the subjection that ideological state apparatuses effect, as discursive, as performative.' We would argue that in doing this, Youdell is not using a 'toolkit' approach (taking components from each theory to integrate Althusser, Butler and Foucault) but engaging in a reading-through of Butler, a 'mash-up' of voice that does not make claims to independence of critical position. Similarly, in Karl Kitching's chapter the decentring of 'race' and 'class' discourses is played out on various levels which incorporate global and local tensions where the meanings of such terms are both decentred and recontextualised from situation to situation. This is also indicated in the chapters by Ravi Rampersad, Indra Dewan, Andrew Morrison and Namita Chakrabarty, where a range of theoretical perspectives are brought to bear on empirical contexts. Here the use of theory is eclectic and experimental but brought to bear on differences in experience that can not necessarily be explained by a single theoretical perspective. For example, Rampersad and Dewan both experiment with existing theories (Critical

Race Theory and racialization) and interestingly apply them to areas where the lack of binary relations would appear to be a problem for such theories (pigmentocracy and dual heritage). Chakrabarty goes further and draws on an elaborated palate of theories including Critical Race Theory, feminism, psychoanalytic theory and Marxism. Such theoretical alternatives can not be described as bricolage but are the creation of 'new' theoretical entities—in short, 'mash-up' theories.

In conclusion, the study of 'race' and intersectionality is one where the production of new theory, to meet the complex worlds of the empirical, is constantly called for. These theories have arisen from spaces where there was no previous theory to explain objective and subjective conditions: in particular from Black feminism (Bhopal 1997; Hill-Collins 1999; Brah and Phoenix 2004; Mirza 2008). As new theories are created, 'mashing up' traditional conceptions of 'race' and intersectionality, we should remember that theory in this area arose as a direct challenge to White patriarchal structures in the academy and in wider society. We hope that future thinking on 'race' and intersectionality remains critical, experimental but most of all aware of the continuity of these structures and the necessity for continuous opposition to them.

REFERENCES

Alcoff, Linda. 1998. What should white people do? *Hypatia: A Journal of Feminist Philosophy* 13 (3): 6–27.

Allen, Ricky Lee. 2001. The globalization of white supremacy: Towards a critical discourse on the racialization of the world. *Educational Theory* 51: 467–486.

Bell, Derek. 1992. *Faces at the bottom of the well: The permanence of racism*. New York: Basic Books.

Bhopal, Kalwant. 1997. *Gender, race and patriarchy: A study of South Asian women*. London: Ashgate.

Brah, Avtar, and Ann Phoenix. 2004. Ain't I a woman? Revisiting intersectionality. *Journal of International Women's Studies* 5 (3): 75–86.

Chakrabarty, Namita. 2006. *On not becoming white: The impossibility of multiculturalism while 'race' is fixed/fucked*. Performance/paper at Clandestino festival, 8 June 2006.

———. 2009a. The color line and the class struggle: A Marxist response to Critical Race Theory as it arrives in the UK. *Power and Education* 1 (1): 111–124.

———. 2009b. *Critical Race Theory and education: A Marxist response*. London: Palgrave.

———. 2009c. Critical Race Theory comes to the UK: A Marxist critique. *Ethnicities* 9 (2): 246–269.

———. 2009d. On 'white supremacy' and caricaturing Marx and Marxism: A response to David Gillborn's 'Who's afraid of critical race theory in education?' *Journal for Critical Education Policy Studies* 7 (1).

Cole, Mike, and Alpesh Maisuria. 2007. 'Shut the f*** up', 'You have no rights here': Critical race theory and racialisation in post-7/7 racist Britain. *Journal for Critical Education Policy Studies* 5 (1).

Crenshaw, Kimberlé. 2002. The first decade: Critical reflections, or "a foot in the closing door". *UCLA Law Review* 49: 1343–1372.

Deleuze, Gilles, and Félix Guattari. 2004. *Anti-Oedipus*. London: Continuum.

Fanon, Frantz. 1986. *Black skin, white masks*. London: Pluto Press.

Fuss, Diana. 1994. Interior colonies: Frantz Fanon and the politics of identification. *Diacritics* 24 (2–3): 19–42.

Gillborn, David. 2005. Education policy as an act of white supremacy: Whiteness, critical race theory and education reform. *Journal of Education Policy* 20: 485–505.

———. 2006. Rethinking white supremacy: Who counts in 'whiteworld'. *Ethnicities* (6): 318–340.

Harris, Cheryl. 1993. Whiteness as property. *Harvard Law Review* 106 (8): 1709–1795.

Hill-Collins, P. 1999. *Black feminist thought: Knowledge, consciousness and the politics of empowerment*. London: Routledge.

Ignatiev, Noel. 1996. Abolish the white 'race' by any means necessary. In *Race traitor*, ed Noel Ignatiev and John Garvey. London: Routledge.

James, Jennifer, and Cynthia Wu. 2006. Race, ethnicity, disability and literature: Intersections and interventions. *Society for Multi-Ethnic Literature of the United States* 31 (3): 3–13.

Johnson, E. Patrick. 2003. *Appropriating blackness: Performance and the politics of authenticity*. Durham, NC: Duke University Press.

Leonardo, Zeus. 2005. The color of supremacy: Beyond the discourse of 'white privilege'. In *Critical pedagogy and race*, ed. Zeus Leonardo, 37–52. Oxford: Blackwell.

Mirza, Heidi. 2008. *Race, gender and educational desire*. London: Routledge.

Navas, Eduardo. 2010. Reflexive and regressive mash-ups in sampling culture. In *Mashup cultures*, ed. Steffan Sonvilla-Weiss. Dordrecht, Netherlands: Springer.

Preston, John. 2010. Concrete and abstract racial domination. *Power and Education* 2 (2): 115–125.

Renn, K. 2010. LBGT research in higher education: The state and status of the field. *Educational Researcher* 39 (2): 139–141.

Sawicki, Jana. 2005. Queering Foucault and the subject of feminism. In *The Cambridge companion to Foucault*, ed. Gary Gutting. Cambridge: Cambridge University Press.

Schiff, M. 2001. Histories and theories of nationalism: A semiotic reproach. *Janus Head* (4): 2, http://www.janushead.org/4–2/schiff.cfm.

Youdell, Deborah. 2006. *Impossible bodies, impossible selves: Exclusions and student subjectivities*. Dordrecht, Netherlands: Springer.

Contributors

Kalwant Bhopal is Reader in Education and Director of the Social Justice and Inclusive Education Research Centre at the University of Southampton (School of Education). She has published widely on the educational experiences of minority ethnic groups. She is the author of *Asian Women in Higher Education: Shared Communities* (2010: Trentham) and is currently carrying out research on the educational experiences of Black and minority ethnic academics in higher education.

John Preston is Professor of Education at the University of East London. His research interests are in critical whiteness studies, Critical Race Theory, disaster education and inequalities in lifelong learning. He uses interdisciplinary research methods drawing on political economy, sociology, cultural studies and security studies. A collection of his work, *Whiteness and Class in Education*, was published by Springer in 2007 and he has published widely on whiteness and its relation to class and masculinity. John's current research involves looking at 'whiteness' and inequalities in disaster education. He was principal investigator on an ESRC (Economic and Social Research Council) funded research project ('Preparedness Pedagogies and "Race" ').

Alpesh Maisuria is a Senior Lecturer and Pathway Leader BA (Hons) Education and Childhood Studies at Anglia Ruskin University. Alpesh is affiliated to the Institute of Education University of London, UK; and Göteborg Uppsala Universities in Sweden. Alpesh engages with scholarship in issues of social justice and education, particularly the intersection of social class with 'race', and educational policy and neoliberalisation. Alpesh is an editorial member of the *Journal for Critical Education Policy Studies*. He also co-convenes the 'Marxism and Education: Renewing Dialogues' seminar series in London.

Farzana Shain is a Senior Lecturer in Education at Keele University. She has written widely on issues of professionalism and managerialism in further education but is more recently known for her work on identities and schooling. She is the author of *The Schooling and Identity of Asian Girls* (2003: Trentham) and *New Folk Devils: Muslim Boys and Education in England* (2011: Trentham).

Namita Chakrabarty is a Senior Lecturer at the University of East London. She has worked on both the creative and business sides of the cultural industries, and also in education. She uses recorded and live performance, and creative and critical writing, to explore themes of race and culture. She was co-investigator on the ESRC-funded project 'Preparedness Pedagogies, and Race: An Interdisciplinary Approach' (2009–10), using a creative performance response to preparedness education.

David Gillborn is Professor of Critical Race Studies in Education at the Institute of Education, London. His work focuses on the production of social inequality in education. His previous studies include the books *Rationing Education* (2000, with Deborah Youdell) and *Racism and Education: Coincidence or Conspiracy?* (2008), both of which won first prize in the annual book awards by the Society for Educational Studies (SES). David is active in antiracist politics and is also founding editor of the international journal *Race Ethnicity & Education*.

Ravi Rampersad did his PhD at the Institute of Education (IOE), University of London, where he worked with Professor Heidi Safia Mirza. His PhD thesis was entitled '*Routes to Achievement': The Intersections of Race, Class, Gender and Colour and the Underachievement of Afro-Trinidadian Boys.* He was also given the opportunity to work with Professor Mirza as lead researcher on the IOE's project with the International Alliance of Leading Educational Institutes (IALEI) in examining multiculturalism and education in the UK. He is currently in negotiations with COSTAATT to return to Trinidad as a lecturer and to initiate a research centre into masculinities in Trinidad.

Andrew Morrison is a lecturer in Education Studies at University of Wales Institute Cardiff, where he specialises in the sociology of postcompulsory education. Prior to this, he taught in further education for a number of years. His publications and research interests lie in the area of young people's educational and occupational decision making, and of how these processes are mediated through lived experiences of 'race', class and gender.

Karl Kitching is a lecturer in the School of Education, University College Cork. Formerly a primary-school teacher in an area of rapid immigration in Dublin, Ireland, his research interests have been shaped by the manner in which identities are performed and denied in such settings. He is currently piloting research with children who are/are not making their first holy communion in Ireland's largely denominational school system, focusing on their lifeworlds and on the manner in which the media proliferates racist and class-based discourses about certain children and families.

Zeus Leonardo is Associate Professor of Education and Affiliated Faculty of the Critical Theory Designated Emphasis at the University of California, Berkeley. Professor Leonardo has published several dozen articles and book chapters on critical educational theory. He is the author of *Ideology, Discourse, and School Reform* (Praeger), editor of *Critical Pedagogy and Race* (Blackwell), and co-editor (with Tejeda and Martinez) of *Charting New Terrains of Chicano(a)/Latino(a) Education* (Hampton). His articles have appeared in *Educational Researcher*; *Race Ethnicity & Education*; and *Educational Philosophy and Theory*. His recent (2009) books are *Race, Whiteness and Education* (Routledge) and the *Handbook of Cultural Politics and Education* (SensePublishers), and he is working on *Critical Frameworks on Race and Education* (Teachers College Press) and *Education and Racism* (Routledge).

Deborah Youdell is Professor of Education at the Institute of Education, University of London. Her work is located in the sociology of education and is concerned with educational inequalities in relation to race, gender, sexuality, religion, social class, ability and disability and the way these are connected to student subjectivities and everyday life in schools. Deborah is coauthor of the award-winning *Rationing Education: Policy, Practice, Reform and Equity* and author of both *Impossible Bodies, Impossible Selves: Exclusions and Student Subjectivities* and *School Trouble: Identity, Power and Politics in Education*. She is regional editor of the *International Journal of Qualitative Studies in Education* and is on the editorial boards of the British *Journal of Sociology of Education*; *Race Ethnicity Education*; and *Critical Studies in Education*.

Indra Dewan's research interests focus on the construction of social identities within education contexts, and centralise the interplay between race, ethnicity, class and gender. Drawing on research with people of mixed heritage in particular, she considers the links between narrative, academic theory, public discourse and education policy. Her extensive work in education and community settings in the UK and Germany informs her current interest in developing participatory and critical approaches to pedagogy and research with young people. Indra presently teaches at the University of East London and in London comprehensive schools.

Index